Good

Good

Aesthetic Politics 2

Seán Cubitt

Goldsmiths Press

Copyright © 2025 Goldsmiths Press
First published in 2025 by Goldsmiths Press
Goldsmiths, University of London, New Cross
London SE14 6NW

Distribution by the MIT Press
Cambridge, Massachusetts, USA and London, England

Text copyright © 2025 Seán Cubitt
The right of Seán Cubitt to be identified as the author of this work has been asserted by him in accordance with sections 77 and 78 in the Copyright, Designs and Patents Act 1988.

Every effort has been made to trace copyright holders and to obtain their permission for the use of copyright material. The publisher apologizes for any errors or omissions and would be grateful if notified of any corrections that should be incorporated in future reprints or editions of this book.

All Rights Reserved. No part of this publication may be reproduced, distributed or transmitted in any form or by any means whatsoever without prior written permission of the publisher, except in the case of brief quotations in critical articles and review and certain non-commercial uses permitted by copyright law.

A CIP record for this book is available from the British Library

ISBN 978-1-915983-30-5 (hbk)
ISBN 978-1-915983-31-2 (ebk)

www.gold.ac.uk/goldsmiths-press

152017994

Contents

0	Demands	1
1	Wealth	11
	1.1 Posthumous	43
2	Love	63
	2.1 Apathy	106
3	Cosmopolis	131
4	Imagination	183
5	Coda: Commons	237

Analytic Contents

		Acknowledgements	ix
0		**Demands**	1
1		**Wealth**	11
		The Tragedy of 'The Tragedy of the Commons'	11
		Mont Pèlerin, 1947	20
		Who Owns the World?	30
	1.1	**Posthumous**	43
		After the End: The Divje Babe Flute	43
		The Waste Land and Other Non-Cochlear Sonic Objects	48
		Voyager	55
		Preclusion	58
2		**Love**	63
		The Liar's Paradox	63
		The Intercostal Clavicle	78
		Zero Plus	87
		Connecticut	94
	2.1	**Apathy**	106

3	**Cosmopolis**	131
	Legal Persons	131
	Declarations	137
	Jackson Pollock, 1949	143
	Alter-Cosmopolis	145
	The Calculus of Freedom	153
	The Mass Unconscious	162
	Theology and QR Codes	172
4	**Imagination**	183
	General Cognition	183
	Gods and Ancestors	191
	Control Systems	201
	Tandoori Chicken Barbecue	207
	Against Nostalgia: Archive Politics	220
5	**Coda: Commons**	237
	Manifesto	245
	References	247
	Index	281

Acknowledgements

I acknowledge the Bunwurrong people of the Kulin Nation, the traditional custodians of the unceded land where most of this book was written, and pay tribute to their elders past, present and emerging.

This book is dedicated to the memory of my dear sister, Paddy Parnaby.

With gratitude to friends and colleagues who have provided help and advice throughout, including Marie-Luise Angerer, Marco Bellano, Jonathan Beller, Jody Berland, Simon Biggs, Ryan Bishop, Peter Bloom, Roger Burrows, Valentino Catricalà, Ivan Cerecina, Wendy Hui Kyong Chun, Justin Clemens, Will Davies, Michael Dieter, Cristobal Escobar, Giovanna Fossati, Emile Frankel, Myria Giorgiou, Ben Gook, Linda D. Henderson, Erkki Huhtamo, Alessandro Ludovico, Celia Lury, Alberto Lusoli, Laura Marks, Scott McQuire, Nicholas Mirzoeff, Salma Monani, Cynde Moya, Paula Muraca, Sam Nightingale, Nikos Papastergiadis, Jussi Parikka, Parichay Patra, Stephen Rust, Arron Santry, Zia Sardar, Melanie Swalwell, Paul Thomas, Nathaniel Tkacz, Pasi Valiaho and Annie van den Oever.

Many thanks to the anonymous reviewers of this manuscript for their insights and support. For reviews and reactions to drafts and fragments published from the materials making up this book I am grateful to the editors of the *International Journal of Cultural Studies* ('Turning Disaster into Crisis'), *The Routledge Handbook of Ecomedia Studies* ('Posthumous Ecomedia'), *Critical Muslim* ('Apathy' with Ben Gook) and *Cultural Politics* ('Posthumous Sound and the General

Imagination' with Ben Gook), and to John Potts ('Anthropocene Archival Ethics'). My thanks likewise to organisers and audiences at the Indian Institute of Technology Jodhpur; the Digital Democracies Institute at Simon Fraser University, Vancouver; the University of Toronto; Università degli Studi di Padova; Ca' Foscari University of Venice; the Environmental Media and Aesthetics program of Aarhus Universitet; the 'Distance and Proximity' seminar at the University of California, Los Angeles; and the Archiving Australian Media Arts conference 'Born Digital Cultural Heritage 3' at the Australian Centre for the Moving Image, Melbourne. Research for this book was supported by two Australia Research Council grants: DP200102781 Digital Photography: Mediation, Memory and Visual Communication; and LE220100057 The Australian Emulation Network: Born Digital Cultural Collections Access.

0
Demands

Le réel, c'est l'impossible

Jacques Lacan

Soyons réalistes! Demandons l'impossible!

Situationist slogan, May 1968

What is good? Raindrops on roses and whiskers on kittens are good, but no list is ever exhaustive. There is an equally interminable and probably self-contradictory list of types of good – pleasurable, instructive, quotidian, exotic, comforting, disturbing... To avoid listing everything that you enjoy (and that maybe I do not), philosophers have tended to ask the singular question: what is the good? Ancient Greek philosopher Aristotle divided his ethics (what is good for me?) from his politics (what is good for us?) and included some chapters on friendship at the hinge point between the two. Ecocritique tells us that the good is not limited to individual, interpersonal or social domains of human interests. Taking Aristotle ecologically means opening politics back towards the ethics of me and you, and forward towards planet and universe, expanding to include non-human worlds, from micromolecular to cosmic. Aesthetic politics cannot avoid the question of the good because, politically and ecologically, not even the isolated 'I' can have a good life on its own (it cannot live at all without a supporting world), while ecocritical aesthetics commits to taking account of senses that humans do not have: the sensory experiences of mined lands, flooded forests and polluted oceans. Ideally, ecocritique would make it impossible to consider the look and feel of good things, natural or artificial, without considering what they are made of, who or what can experience them, where those feelings and meanings come from and go to, and what is the ultimate destination of the materials they depend on. This is hard, not just because it is so complicated, but because it implies resolving another task ecocritique sets itself.

Ideally, ecocritique would also stitch together the physical metabolism that meshes the living and their world with the historical fact of human estrangement from technologies and ecologies. 'I' is a crossroads where gut flora and oceans interact with cameras and gardening, generating a self of varying degrees of coherence and instability. 'I' is also a crossroads in time, reliant on ancient practices of language and cookery, and evolving new grammars and recipes for future generations. The living self is constantly under construction, looking simultaneously up and down and forward and back, consulting what will gradually appear as protagonists of aesthetic politics, gods and ancestors. What 'I' wants – individually, interpersonally or politically – is unclear. Good only becomes murkier when we try to take responsibility for those who will come after and those who died before. The question of 'what is good?' does not have a singular answer, and its many answers change over time. The scales of the good – individual, interpersonal, social and cosmic – are processes with different speeds and durations, sometimes in harmony, sometimes at odds, sometimes going forward together, sometimes turning back at seemingly random points along the way. We cannot just ask what is good; we have to ask about where and when it is good.

Demands 3

Aesthetic questions concern whether the good can be spoken or written, pictured, told, sounded – more generally, whether it can be represented other than as an endless list of bright copper kettles and warm woollen mittens. Can the good be sensed? Or is goodness just an abstraction from all the nice things we enjoy and our feelings when we enjoy them? Does it escape human senses entirely? Is it something we can only intuit? Aesthetics can only describe a good that exists, because of its roots in the senses. Politics wants to coax a non-existent good into existence in some nearer or further future. Aesthetic politics has somehow to work through this incompatible pair: the present good you can experience and a future good you imagine and wish for, but which otherwise does not exist. An aesthetic politics cannot escape time, braiding together yearning for the good old days, desire for something good right now and hope for the good to come.

It is possible that once upon a time we could describe goodness but no longer can because the good (singular) no longer exists, and perhaps never did. That could imply that everyone must pursue their own good – an impossibility if the environment that supports life collapses. Or it could mean that the good is yet to arrive. Perhaps people used to be able to describe goodness because they believed in its imminent arrival. That faith, if it persists, is no longer faith but hope. You can only avoid narcissistic wish fulfilment and fantasies of domination through hope – of the kind that first emerges in love and imagination. True, hopes can be played on, love can be betrayed and imagination can be exploited. Advertising campaigns and populist politicians (despite their angry rhetoric) typically promise future harmony and resolution: pie in the sky when you die. An aesthetic politics of imagination does not. It embraces conflicts, in the psyche, in the world and in their relations. Expanding the pursuit of the good to the more-than-human commons means negotiating, as love does, between incompatible times and scales, 'now' and 'forever' in love, the deep past and the far future in the ecological commons.

The absence of political good in the present is terrible evidence that the worst has already happened. Hope is no longer enough, not unless it ascends beyond the benevolent desire that everything should be for the best in the best of all possible worlds. The United Nations' COP Climate Change Conferences are a case in point; the assembled corporations and governments combine to announce their inability to change, and their readiness to hope for the best. Cultural economist Joseph Vogel opens his 2017 book *The Ascendancy of Finance* with the maxim 'Economic crises are opportunities for making the politically impossible politically inevitable'. The opposite is true of ecological catastrophe, which, at time of writing, appears to have made the inevitable abandonment of fossil fuels politically impossible. A telling example of hoping for the best (in public) while actively supporting the worst (behind closed doors) is described in the International Institute for Sustainable Development (Laan et al. 2023) report that the G20 nations had invested at least USD 1 trillion in subsidies to fossil industries despite pledges at COP conferences and in defiance of their electorates. Politicians lure their citizens in with the kind of false hope that is untrue and neither good nor beautiful. Yet without hope, there would be no voice raised to demand anything different. The one thing that a political system cannot tolerate is demands. The status quo resists as long as it can, on the basis that it is 'unthinkable' to open politics to slaves, and then women, and now migrants. But no political system can withstand articulate demands forever, so that political philosophers Jacques Rancière (1999) and Chantal Mouffe (2005) define politics as the process of change brought about by new demands. Neither pious nor patient, hope is the engine of demands. Politically, hope can never be reduced to wishing that everything should come out right in the end. Hope drives action for change, or it is not hope.

It became apparent as I came to the end of my previous book that any claim to say something true about the world necessarily interrupts truth in process (later I discovered the philosopher Jean-Luc Nancy [1998: 12–15] had beaten me to it). Truth-statements only exist as facts (*facta*: words, numbers or pictures that have been made after the event they describe). From the point of view of statements of fact, reality is ephemeral, but from the world's perspective, it is not reality but statements that bob into the light and sink away again. The everyday political status quo relies on this steady simmer never reaching boiling point. Hope is the extra flame under the pot. It defies the facts that constitute the steady state, not with 'alternative facts' designed to benefit some faction hunting a bigger slice of the same old pie but, recognising that systemic facts are more ephemeral than the world they pretend to define, by creating new hopes and new demands. Politics as the art of the impossible. Like any truth-statement, political facts do not have to be true or permanent to have effects. It is possible that hope is the last virtue, but that even hope is vulnerable unless it has a powerful admixture of imagination. Driven by imagination and hope for a future that by definition does not (yet) exist, demands have consequences. Even if it lacks the presence and solidity of present suffering, we would be fools to give up hope.

A word on terminology. Mediation refers to the underpinning flows that permeate everything and everyone, characterised by continuity. Communication, on the other, hand refers to actual historical and social conditions of life, characterised by discontinuity and division. Mediation describes the fundamental continuity of bodies and energies regardless of whether they appear to us as human, machinic or natural. 'Appear' might suggest that there is something false about the distinctions we make between social, technical and ecological domains, which would be incorrect: those distinctions are our historically existing conditions with real effects on how we perceive, feel, think and act. Technology is the domain of ancestors. The idea comes from Marx's insight that machines embody the skills and knowledge of 'dead labour' (Marx 1973: 459–461). Ecology is the domain of gods: other-than-human forces operating throughout the physical world, including living creatures, places, heavenly bodies, matter and energy. Society is the essential quality of humans. Individuality comes logically and historically after the commons of language and shared spaces. The relationship between ancestors, gods and societies changes, over time and depending on whether they appear through mediation or communication. Broadly, human society mediates (or communicates) between ancestral technologies (including languages) and ecologies, while technologies communicate (or mediate) between societies and ecologies. As mediation, ecology embraces the other domains, for example, delivering the consequences of fossil-fuel technologies to suffering human bodies; but, seen as communication, it is excluded from both. Aristotle believed that 'if all communities aim at some good, the state or political community, which is the highest of all, and which embraces all the rest, aims at good in a greater degree than any other, and at the highest good' (Aristotle 1995: 4265). Aesthetic politics is bound to go beyond the human, where Aristotle drew the boundary of politics. Promoting the good for all, not just humans, needs a different insight from another ancient Greek philosopher, Plato (1892: 284), who uses the term *pankalon*, 'all-good', in the *Euthyphro* to describe 'that fair work which the gods do'. The present enquiry into the good takes these concepts as staring points. It would be unusual if it did not change them as it develops. The three-body problem of social–technical–natural has no closed-form solution and does not repeat. Nonetheless, it seemed at least respectful to shape the book around four claimants to the crown of goodness – wealth, love, freedom and imagination – and to round them off with a more twenty-first-century and expansive candidate, the commons.

The enquiry into the good had to start with the bad: wealth. The problem is not wealth as such – we need enough to live well, and to share. The problem came when wealth, as in common wealth, became profit. Wealth was always a relation; with profit, it became a relation of deprivation. Worse, profit does not enjoy wealth; it stores it, but in a way that makes accumulated wealth and the owner who gathers it together disappear into their own singularity like a black hole. This first chapter asks whether the good can be had now and how come good things disappear. So the chapter on wealth and inheritance is irresistibly followed by a digression on the posthumous condition, the afterlife where demands go to die.

Chapter 2 strikes a trail through the midnight woods of love, not forgetting to look at love for the woods and for the stories told about them as well as the amazement of lovers. Emerging from the privations of private property, the chapter tracks love's obligations, the risks it demands and the harrowing possibility that love can too easily become abusive, proprietary and violent. Affection – feelings of sympathy and empathy – is an affect: an emotional and cultural human response to the circulation of energies through bodies and things. It is about how people strive to make the good arrive by promising to be and do good for someone or something else. Against sympathy and empathy, apathy, the theme of the digression that follows, deals with affectlessness. The opposite of love is not hatred, which it combines with all too readily. The opposite of love is to feel nothing. Love is wonderful but it is also intensely local. It belongs to the living, and life is fleeting. The aim is to make clearer how love belongs with and generates hope by demonstrating that opposing hope with despair is a theological hangover: today, hope's opposite is numbness and inaction.

The third chapter exchanges interpersonal love for a cosmopolitan politics which has pinned its hopes on how certain aesthetic-political virtues make it possible to imagine a good future. Chapter 3 moves into politics proper, in its human dimensions. It begins by contesting equality, the legal discourse of rights and specifically how rights are traded away every day. Freedom to buy and sell only reveals the right to be bought and sold. At a time when code is at least as significant as any older media of connection and debate, the unconscious that used to be structured like a language is structured like code. Populists' adored 'freedom' is always missing, mislaid in a glorious past that populism promises to restore, or stolen by some villainous 'they'. 'They', in the language of fascism, are cosmopolitans: intellectuals, ethnic others, those who move freely between states. Ironically, populist freedom depends on neo-liberal globalisation, a perversion of the very cosmopolis they blame for stealing their freedom. Even the most virtuous plans impose a present image of virtue onto the future. Plans pre-empt any really new future that might emerge. Politics is not about freedom and rights but about obligations extending not only to posterity but to ancestors. The chapter works through ideas of mass unconscious and general cognition in pursuit of an alter-cosmopolis grounded in the new technological conditions for an emergent collective unconscious.

The fourth chapter, on imagination, reverses the imposition of the present onto the future and expands beyond the human. It seeks out ways that future goods can impose themselves on the present and how they might act on the lost past.

The figure of imagination knots together the threads of wealth, love and freedom as varieties of the good in the ambit of ecologies, local and planetary. In the face of extinction, we can no longer uphold 'nature' as a good in itself – not if its survival requires the elimination of the human species. Challenging systems thinking while developing new understandings of demand beyond the merely human, the chapter advances the idea of a general imagination shared by societies, technologies and ecologies. Reconfiguring imagination makes it possible, indeed necessary, to reimagine hope, reversing philosopher Ernst Bloch's (1988: 16) adage 'Hope would not be hope if it could not be disappointed' to assert instead that 'Hope isn't hope if it can't be realised'.

The previous book in this trilogy of *Aesthetic Politics*, *Truth*, set out to find out what the world demands of us; this one searches for ways to evaluate the demands we and our others make of ourselves and the world (a planned third volume, *Beauty*, will address how demand works). In *Truth*, I tried to set up some basic concepts that reappear in *Good*, including the virtue of consideration, the idea that truth is worthless if it does not care for the full complexity of situations and the consequences of saying or doing something about them. Even when it celebrates imagination, *Good* returns to consideration, care not only for futures and pasts but for the living, including the other beyond and the other in me. The Coda thinks towards the domain of the good as commons – neither dominant nor alienated but integral; not a fact but a demand. Humanity is only a phase that technics and nature go through, but one whose responsibilities, another name for love, place it as a crucial mediator between them. A theory of the good adequate to the Anthropocene must include the good of (and for) the commons, grounded in the transformation of hopeful demands and demanding hopes into a common imagination.

By way of a method, I have coloured the twists of argument with anecdotes drawn from wherever intuition, memory and imagination have found inspiration: in films, tools, poems, archaeological finds, finance markets, paintings, declarations, songs, organisations, recipes, computer programmes and ideas, which are also anecdotes – crossings of ancestral traditions and emerging potentials. For reasons explored throughout the book, no one theory could cover every aspect of goodness and its opposites. Each anecdote raises its own objections and its own avenues renewing thinking. The Western tradition set up the initial questions, but at every step alternative ways of sensing, making, thinking and doing called out for new navigations. If this method needs a name, call it eclectic, a term too often used to demean a drive to go beyond the familiar, essential to any aesthetics or politics for these times. Neither the one who thinks nor the thing they think about is singular or static. There is an overriding theme guiding the writing. Ecocritique acknowledges that no one and no species, least of all human, is alone. In genre terms, *Good* is an essay; it tries out ideas, testing them in encounters where, if the ideas cast light, it is almost always scattered in unexpected rainbows, not always in visible wavelengths. An essay is made of words. This one is full of the names of writers and encounters, often emerging from decolonial, feminist and intersectional histories I am a stranger to, that challenge every assumption it started from. Aesthetic politics, this oxymoron, demands no less.

1
Wealth

This is the only sort of universality that there is: when from a specific enclosure, the deepest voice calls out.
Édouard Glissant, *Poetics of Relation*, 74

The Tragedy of 'The Tragedy of the Commons'

When the poet William Blake wrote in his *Proverbs of Hell* 'The road of excess leads to the palace of wisdom' (Blake 1988: 35), he was not talking about money. Blake pitched life – the physical capacity for enjoyment – against a puritanical ethic of self-control and diminution. The last thing on his mind was accumulating. For Blake, spending – which still carried its older connotation of orgasm – was the path to pleasure and enlightenment, not piling up and stashing cash. Humans need affluence only so we can spend it. Accumulation, we could speculate, started with the creation of private property on the ruins of common wealth. Private property is founded on privation: the power to deprive others. What I accumulate, I deny to you. My pleasure depends on excluding you from it. My anxiety is that you might steal it, or that an undefined 'they' may devalue it. Those anxieties encourage me to acquire more and to stash it away. To ensure I amass more, I deny first your pleasures and then my own (the misery of misers). In the olden days, the miserable built castles with their accumulated wealth to defend the wealth they spent building them from the people they took it from. Today the same miserable class defend their wealth by buying space capsules so they can escape the planetary fate that they are in great part responsible for. At time of writing, '252 men have more wealth than all 1 billion women and girls in Africa and Latin America and the Caribbean, combined' (Oxfam 2022: 7). What we call wealth, this accumulation of private property, has not been collected for enjoyment's sake, but the absolute contrary: its purpose is to exclude the vast majority of the world, human and non-human, from enjoyment.

There is nothing wrong with wealth as basic subsistence. Article 25 of the Universal Declaration of Human Rights (United Nations 1948) says as much, reading in part, 'Everyone has the right to a standard of living adequate for the health and well-being of himself and of his family.' Gender presumption aside, all other aspirations depend on this: that no one be condemned to ignore every other dream or desire because they lack food and shelter. Prosperity is good when it secures enough for everyone to be able to aspire, not just survive. The sad fact is that even that has become an economic and political problem. The philosopher Theodor Adorno was right when he wrote 'There is tenderness only in the coarsest demand: that no one shall go hungry any more' (Adorno 1974: 156). When wealth acts against this fundamental need, it is evil.

Economic textbooks tell us that money is a measure of value, a means of storage and a medium of exchange. As measure, it tells us what something would be worth if we exchanged it. As a store, it coagulates the value that would accrue if we exchanged it. So value and storage are secondary: both derive from exchange. If we do not exchange, money ceases to be a store or a measure, accumulating and solidifying instead into 'wealth': static money. It is intriguing that two significant works about money, almost a hundred years apart, focus not on storage but on exchange. Emile Zola's novel *L'Argent* of 1891, updated on film by Marcel L'Herbier in 1928, revolves around fraudulent shares. Robert Bresson's last film, *L'Argent*, a 1983 update of a 1911 novella by Tolstoy, concerns counterfeit bills. In the two novels and films, the circulation of money is the thread that draws a complex cast of characters into moral labyrinths that consume them. Citing both films, the philosopher Gilles Deleuze (1989: 77) argues, 'what defines industrial art is not mechanical reproduction but the internalized relation with money. The only rejoinder to the harsh law of cinema – a minute of image which costs a day of collective work – is Fellini's: "When there is no more money left, the film will be finished." Money is the obverse of all the images that the cinema shows and sets in place, so that films about money are already, if implicitly, films within the film or about the film.'

L'Herbier (1979: 149) described his obsession with 'filming at whatever price, even (paradoxically) at very great price, a fiery indictment of money'. Deleuze emphasises that, as investment, the artistic autonomy of a film is an end-point of money's life as exchange. Every film (an industrial art like recorded music, broadcasting, even modern publishing) is an expression of money: films that address money as a theme, even if they never mention filmmaking, are implicitly films-about-film. We should only add that, in their finished and to that extent autonomous form, films are themselves examples of wealth, money brought to a standstill, just as much as they are evidence that, as Paul Valéry (1933: 399) observed of poems, a film is never finished, only abandoned. Films can be treated as art because they are the trace of money at the moment of its vanishing.

More recent films from the age of digital money find it more difficult to picture money itself. Like many people, I have not been paid in cash for many years and, since the pandemic, rarely carry any. My cashflow is entirely invisible, intangible, soundless, anaesthetic. It appears onscreen on my banking app, which guides me with infantile icons ('Home' is a doll's house; 'Rewards' are flagged with a gold star). The finances displayed on my app are personal, and the economy they and my bank are embedded in does not show at all – as if we could get weather forecasts but never know about the climate. My money has no sensory presence beyond these symbols. Like the portolan charts preceding modern maps, banking apps tell me which direction I am travelling, but not about the ocean I have to cross. On the app, my money is reduced to a set of numbers, abstracted from going hungry or having enough to eat, and isolated from the vast economic machines – the bank and the market – that have swallowed it whole.

Money has vanished into circuits we no longer see or understand and which, judging by the 'cost of living' crisis that kicked off in 2022, are beyond the control even of those who claim to manage it. The economy might be described as an interconnected network of databases tracking money's digital ecology, leading to the thought that our models of economics and environments are suspiciously similar, both suspiciously kin to digital systems. In their *Cartographies of the Absolute*, cultural theorists Alberto Toscano and Jeff Kinkle (2015) place this anaesthetic vanishing in the context of cultural critic Fredric Jameson's aesthetic struggle for 'cognitive mapping' (Jameson 1991: 50-53). Jameson's point was that the present lacks maps for our condition: we have no cultural forms equivalent to epic poetry or nineteenth-century novels that pictured social relations as a whole. Toscano and Kinkle's argument is that even when we do have maps – in the shape of financial software, for example – they are not available for 'cognition'; they are not designed for humans, operating faster and at magnitudes greater than humans can sense or comprehend. Nonetheless, just like the maps with blank spaces that inspired European colonisers from Christopher Columbus to Captain Cook, these maps are 'performative' (Butler 1988), not just geographical descriptions but instruments of exploitation, not only describing but changing the world that they picture. Semi-autonomous finance software 'maps' amass funds in quantities beyond any human need or desire, and in the process abandon Blake's palace of wisdom in favour of numerical fortresses.

We are still prey to the idea that money equates to human good. Perhaps the most notorious statement of support for private property in ecological circles is Garret Hardin's 1968 essay 'The Tragedy of the Commons', which has become a talismanic reading for environmental humanities – and on neo-right websites – more than half a century after its first appearance. A tirade against what Paul Ehrlich (1968), only months later, would call the Population Bomb, Hardin set out his presumptions in the form of a parable about common pastoral land. Because 'each herdsman seeks to maximise his gain', 'Each man is locked into a system that compels him to increase his herd without limit – in a world that is limited' (1968: 1244). Betrayed by its gender bias, unsupported by any histories or anthropology of pastoral societies and artificially limited by focusing on pastoralism, unsupported by gardening or hunting, Hardin's parable has been accused of misremembering history (Cox 1985), of using parable and tragedy as literary genres to overcome the rationalism he otherwise touts (Nixon 2012) and of 'over simplified and deterministic' analysis (Feeny et al. 1990: 14). It also stands or falls on the foundational belief in the individual and the presumption that 'he' is motivated exclusively by desire for accumulation.

To his credit, Hardin understood that his herdsmen's goal of accruing as much as they can leads directly to deprivation. Increase without limit is not spending but accumulating; money as a store is a means to stop other herders expanding their herds. Hardin ignores care for and sharing the commons, practised for millennia, instead seeing common land as a feudal overlord or colonial master would: as a resource to plunder. From the moment it is reduced to exploitable resource, there is no longer a commons, only property (Milun 2011; Federici 2019). Meanwhile, when accumulating private property is the only motive governing action, the only sensory pleasure is avarice, the cold fetishism of gold itself. Money can be bequeathed to offspring for future enjoyment, but this closest pass to a different pleasure, a kind of self-contained generosity, depends on self-deprivation. Saving up to ensure your kids inherit feels so archaic because it evokes intensely physical, local wealth, like a castle or a chest full of coin, where digital money is as delocalised as it is dematerialised. The promise 'to pay the bearer' on old bank notes swore that there was real cash somewhere, even if you could never lay hands on it. Today, a century after the abandonment of the gold standard, 'real' cash is even more abstract: no longer a pile of metal, but a value guessed at in an interminable auction, at the whim of players, almost none of whom are human. Money is always elsewhere. Imagining it is your property is an illusion.

Even calling money a 'unit' is misleading when it is a medium of relationships lacking any final standard of reconciliation. As recently as the Great Depression of the 1930s, it was possible to believe that money was a matter of trust; as long as people believed paper had value, it had value. When that faith dissolved, it had none (disturbingly, the word credit means not 'I believe' or even 'you believe' but 'it believed'). Today value is no longer a matter of what people believe.

Fluctuating algorithmic predictions, operating beyond the velocity of thought or control, determine relations between currencies and commodities. 'It' has conquered. When I no longer have any control over my cache of loot, in what sense can I claim it is my property? Nonetheless, I act as if money was a store of units, each with some intrinsic value, the sad illusion underlying the moral outrage of customers denied access to 'their own' money by Lebanese banks at the latter end of 2022.

The Lebanese banking collapse was also a collapse of trust, whose vanishing popped up in Hardin's essay. When 'Each man is locked into a system that compels him to increase his herd without limit' (1968: 1244), the only possible means of communication is money, and that communication fails. We normally say, Hardin observed, that 'goods are incommensurable … but in real life incommensurables *are* commensurable' (1968: 1244) once a criterion is established and a means of weighting; he suggested survival as the natural criterion, and natural selection as its weighting mechanism. In Hardin this had two effects: humans act in imitation of natural selection, the blind workings of (a notoriously controversial) 'natural law'; and they are incapable of any other kind of connection. Outside a miser talking to his coins, money offers no pleasures of its own. As store, it offers only the *concept* of what it might buy, not the pleasures themselves. The problem of money's disappearance into its own concept was deftly caught by economist and philosopher Alfred Sohn-Rethel: 'The abstraction [money] belongs to the interrelationship of the exchanging agents and not to the agents themselves … We face a pure abstraction but it is a spatio-temporal reality which assumes separate representation in money … Money is an abstract thing, a paradox in itself – a thing that performs its socially synthetic function without any human understanding' (Sohn-Rethel 1978: 45).

The herdsman does not own his herd or its meadows; property is only relationship, the difference between accumulation and deprivation. Money measures and creates differences with real effects on relationships between people, and because it is abstract, money creates unequal societies without anyone perceiving it or knowing how it works. The paradox is that money not only has no intrinsic value, but that it has no meaning. That does not imply that money does not exist. Sohn-Rethel referred to it as a *real* abstraction because it has the power to make things happen, even though it does not signify anything. It is only in moments of crisis that the valueless, meaningless nature of money becomes visible, and with it the immense abstraction of capital as database, system and counter-ecology.

The more abstract it becomes, the more meaningless money is. Whether metal, paper or electrons, when we exchange money, we exchange symbols. This is why money is said to be a medium. In 1948, Claude E. Shannon published the first version of his mathematical theory of communication. As symbols exchanged through a medium, money obeys the rule set out in his second paragraph: 'The fundamental problem of communication is that of reproducing at one point either exactly or approximately a message selected at another point. Frequently the messages have meaning; that is they refer to or are correlated according to some system with certain physical or conceptual entities. These semantic aspects of communication are irrelevant to the engineering problem' (Shannon 1948: 379).

Shannon's first step is to assert that communication is comprised of messages, such as numbers symbolising a sum of money. Second, a message is selected from a bank of alternatives, all of which are, from the point of view of the system, entirely equivalent to one another, like units of currency. Third, the messages have to move from one place to another, which in money's case is the process of exchange. Last, meaning is irrelevant; it does not matter what commodity is being symbolised: 'incommensurables *are* commensurable' when we abandon the goods themselves and focus only on the symbolic measure of their exchangeability. The only thing that matters is that the numbers, the symbols representing money, arrive at their destination. Nobel Prize-winning economist Elinor Ostrom (2015) notes how 'The Tragedy of the Commons' similarly left out the role of meaning and values in the communal management of common resources.

Like Shannon's communications system, the money system does not discriminate between notes and coins, promises-to-pay and gold, cheques and digital signals, just as it does not discriminate between cabbages and computers. A commodity is a commodity, whether it takes the form of goods or services, and money is money whatever shape it takes, just so long as it is exchanged. Hardin could forget about every other form of survival – foraging, hunting, raising crops – in favour of the single activity of herding because the real activity does not matter, only the abstract principle of accumulation. Shannon's essay, written for Bell Telephone, may have been inspired by, or shared the same zeitgeist with, his contemporary Paul A. Samuelson's mathematising of economics. Samuelson hypothesised that markets are systems in equilibrium. Hardin's herdsman seeking 'to maximize his gain' (1968: 1244) transcribes Samuelson's belief that all agents active in markets are out to get as rich as possible. 'Even where there is no context for purposive maximizing behavior', Samuelson wrote, 'reduction to a maximization problem may be a convenient device for developing properties of the equilibrium, from which, however, no "teleological or normative welfare significance" is warranted' (Samuelson 1947: 52–53). Neither value ('welfare significance') nor meaning (the 'context for purposive maximising behaviour') are relevant to the functioning of the market that, from the godlike abstraction of mathematics, reduces all social interaction to calculation. Like Shannon, Samuelson is interested in managing a system, not the realities or meanings that it handles. The tragedy is that Hardin, like Shannon and Samuelson, abandoned the real, fragile Earth and replaced it with an abstraction.

Mont Pèlerin, 1947

Samuelson's and Shannon's writings appeared in the wake of massive strikes in the USA that culminated in 1947 with the Taft–Hartley Act, which has severely curtailed trades union activities ever since (Davis 1986: 82-93; Goldfield 1987; 2020). This was also the era of the Chinese Revolution and the Partition of India. The USSR alone among world powers emerged from two world wars and a revolution with its empire not only intact but at its greatest ever geographical extent, while Germany and Japan failed in their thirty-year attempt to join France and Britain as imperial nations, dragging the European empires down with them and opening the way for the rise of the USA as global hegemon. This was also the peak moment of the Welfare State among Western democracies, which it has been the task of conservative governments ever since to roll back. The highest political achievement of the period was perhaps the Universal Declaration of Human Rights promulgated by the United Nations in December 1948.

Hardin's attack on the Universal Declaration was not unique in its universalist rejection of universalism. Under the crosshead 'Conscience is Self-Eliminating' Hardin set up the pseudo-Darwinian argument that when people elect, from good conscience, not to have children, they are out-bred by those who go ahead and breed. In due course, conscience will be bred out of the population, regardless of whether conscience is genetic or a product of education. Disproving this eugenicist nonsense is simple: on the principle that gay men and lesbians have fewer offspring, why are there millions of homosexuals? The Southern Poverty Law Centre (n.d.; see also Nijhuis 2021) names Hardin as a white nationalist over his racist views on eugenics and immigration. Hardin explained the 'tragedy' of his title by citing vitalist philosopher Alfred North Whitehead (1948: 7): 'The essence of dramatic tragedy ... resides in the solemnity of the remorseless working of things', in Hardin's case of Malthusian 'laws' of population growth and 'natural selection'. 'If we love the truth', he writes, 'we must openly deny the validity of the Universal Declaration of Human Rights'. Coming from a very different intellectual tradition, ethicist Alasdair Macintyre contradicted what he believed to be the idea at the basis of the Universal Declaration: that there exist 'rights attaching to human beings simply *qua* human beings ... there are no such rights, and belief in them is one with belief in witches and in unicorns' (Macintyre 1981: 69). Speaking specifically of Article 15 of the Declaration, which describes the family as 'the natural and fundamental group unit of society' which is 'entitled to protection by society and the State', Hardin viscerally rejected a reading of it by then-Secretary General U Thant to the effect that 'any choice and decision with regard to the size of the family unit must irrevocably rest with the family itself', admitting – in a spooky pre-echo of Macintyre – that 'denying it, one feels as uncomfortable as a resident of Salem, Massachusetts, who denied the reality of witches in the 17th century' (1968: 1246).

Despite their and my criticisms, it is certainly the case that without the UN Declaration, things would have been even worse, and we can agree with historian of the Declaration Johannes Morsink (2009: 35) that 'the ideology of human rights can serve as an intellectual umbrella for people who do indeed have very different intellectual backgrounds' – even if (and perhaps because) it is only an ideology. One way of assessing that is by comparing the UN document with another produced in the same year which asserts equally metaphysical ideologies but without the good intentions. The Statement of Aims of the Mont Pèlerin Society became the credo of aggressive neo-liberal economics in Thatcherism and Reaganomics in the 1980s and the foundational economic policy of the 2020s. Two versions of the Aims exist, a draft dated 7 April (reprinted in Hartwell 1995: 49–50) and the final version dated 8 April, now a quasi-official part of the Mont Pèlerin Society's website (1947). As Dieter Plehwe explains in his introduction to an anthology devoted to the history of the Society, the first draft was already problematic:

even this relatively nonspecific and anodyne set of neoliberal ten commandments proved too contentious to gain the assent of the individualists gathered at Mont Pèlerin, and so the oxymoronic Committee of Individualists deputed a redraft to Lionel Robbins, who complied and produced the 'Statement of Aims' ... All those gathered on April 8, 1947, except one (the French economist and Nobel laureate Maurice Allais) fully accepted this rather less informative manifesto, which to this day remains the only 'official' statement of the MPS.

(Plehwe 2009: 4)

The instability of this founding statement is in some ways symptomatic of a movement without a core, but in others a formally correct expression of a group that could no longer share the theological certainties of the original 'ten commandments', or the Modernist manifesto-like assertions of the UN

Declaration (Hayek 1967). In many respects the Mont Pèlerin Statement is a direct negation of the Declaration. It is likely that it has had as much impact on the world as the UN.

Here are the opening lines of the adopted version:

> The central values of civilization are in danger. Over large stretches of the Earth's surface the essential conditions of human dignity and freedom have already disappeared. In others they are under constant menace from the development of current tendencies of policy. The position of the individual and the voluntary group are progressively undermined by extensions of arbitrary power. Even that most precious possession of Western Man, freedom of thought and expression, is threatened by the spread of creeds which, claiming the privilege of tolerance when in the position of a minority, seek only to establish a position of power in which they can suppress and obliterate all views but their own.
>
> (Mont Pèlerin Society 1947)

Like the UN Declaration's, the Mont Pèlerin Statement's emphasis on freedom is understandable in the context of the then-recent defeat of fascism and the imminent threat of the Cold War. That explains the territorial fear, but not the 'current tendencies of policy', very probably a reference to the founding of the British Welfare State and similar social policies elsewhere in the world. Like the Declaration, the Statement emphasises individuals, with a proviso for voluntary associations because this was the founding document of just such a group.

Hayek's opening address asserted that 'effective endeavours to elaborate the general principles of a liberal order are practicable only among a group of people who are in agreement on fundamentals, and among whom certain basic conceptions are not questioned at every step' (Hayek 1967: 149). Consensus in the MPS voluntary association, overriding individual opinion and debate, was also a political necessity: there could be no discussion of 'the central values of civilization'. Independent thought, supposedly the banner ideal of liberalism, does not seem to have survived even the Committee of Individualists who drafted the 7 April Statement of Aims. But even those values could be overridden. Economic historian Philip Mirowski cites an ally of Hayek's, the American economist Milton Friedman, giving an even more brutal statement of the neo-liberal position: 'Businessmen, who may be bankrupted if they refuse to face facts, are one of the few groups that develop the habit of doing so. That is why, I have discovered repeatedly, the successful businessman is more open to new ideas ... than the academic intellectual who prides himself on his alleged independence of thought' (Mirowski 2019: 7).

Hardin was more circumspect about facts, noting that 'the morality of an act cannot be derived from a photograph', specifying that 'the essence of an argument cannot be photographed: it must be presented rationally – in words' (1968: 1245). Even though at various points – including the reference to von Neumann and Morgenstern – he resorted to mathematical argument, systems thinking of the kind Hardin espoused has sound reasons for doubting that a photo is unambiguous evidence of anything; we need to know not just the event but the circumstances. But there is the risk, when ignoring historical evidence in favour of logic and mathematics, of missing the messy details, processes and connections that would counter the clarity and hygiene of pure logic. As long as there are only identically motivated individuals chasing a single goal, the math holds good, even if it is false anthropology. But when disparate people talk about multiple conflicting goals (mental and physical health, ethical and spiritual values, respect for land, custom and gods, animal and environmental welfare...), the 'photographic' anecdote comes into play: how do real people in real situations really do things? In context, Hardin's tragedy looks like an attempt to exonerate shameful acts by resorting to eugenic 'science', even more so because he assiduously avoids any non-economic communication between his individuals. The reduction of human intercourse to economic exchange unites 'The Tragedy of the Commons' with the founding documents of the Mont Pèlerin Society.

Hayek explained his resistance to questioning by asserting that 'the dangers which we are facing are the results of an intellectual movement' (1967: 150), further specified when he instructed the assembly, 'You will probably agree that the interpretation and teaching of history has during the past two generations been one of the main instruments through which essentially anti-liberal conceptions of human affairs have spread' (1967: 154), singling out emphasis on mass movements over individuals and material necessity over ideas. He went on to blame 'an aggressive rationalism which would recognise no values except those whose utility ... could be demonstrated by individual reason' – a rationalism that, since the French Revolution, had tainted even traditional liberals with 'an intellectual hubris', opposed to 'true liberalism that regards with reverence those spontaneous social forces through which the individual creates things greater than he knows' (1967: 155), that is, of which 'he' is entirely unconscious. Reason, which might have been presumed to be a 'central value of civilization', was sinful: it is a duty to know nothing. Hayek's speech identifies 'aggressive rationalism' in 'the twin movements of Positivism and Hegelianism'. The Romantic philosopher Georg Wilhelm Friedrich Hegel believed that history obeyed a pre-existing Law. Dismissing that belief removes at least one alternative source of rules, but also denies any role for pseudo-scientific 'laws' like Hardin's adored natural selection. On the other hand, positivism is a belief in the power of facts as opposed to any law-like reasons operating beyond or behind the world. Dismissing both Hegelian laws and the positivist facts that Friedman's businessman prized so highly leaves liberalism in the dark, a victim of truths and forces it must not understand but cannot help but obey. This is either submission to darkness or so elevated it sacrifices reality and principles to a world without either.

The paradoxes are not over yet. The adopted Statement announces that personal freedom is being eroded by 'arbitrary power', which the Statement wants to use to defend 'central values of civilization'. The same conflict between freedom and control is clear in the fifth aim of the 7 April Draft ('The preservation of an effective competitive order depends upon a proper legal and institutional framework'), and the third priority of the adopted Statement ('Methods of re-establishing the rule of law'): to establish and maintain the freedom of the market, law will be necessary. The Draft distinguished law from state, in the fifth aim arguing that 'The preservation of an effective competitive order depends upon a proper legal and institutional framework', but in the sixth tempering that with the proposal that 'As far as possible government activity should be limited by the rule of law'. The determination to reduce the role of the state parallels Hardin's aphorism that 'the social arrangements that produce responsibility are arrangements that create coercion' (1968: 1247) Again like Hardin, the Draft insisted on the rule of law. Hardin's example was property law, which he was forced to admit does not work all the time, for example, encouraging pollution of resources, such as rivers, that are not my property. He goes so far as to say that 'our legal system of private property plus inheritance is unjust – but we put up with it because we are not convinced, at the moment, that anyone has invented a better system. The alternative of the commons is too horrifying to contemplate. Injustice is preferable to total ruin' (1968: 1247).

For Hardin, Darwinian and Malthusian 'laws' force humans to be selfish; on the other hand, legal systems limit their selfishness and, in the case of inheritance laws, are nowhere near restrictive enough ('legal possession should be perfectly correlated with biological inheritance' [1968: 1247]). And yet Hardin feared alternatives, including the commons itself and the Welfare State, which he blamed for combining 'the concept of freedom to breed with the belief that everyone born has an equal right to the commons', which he describes as 'a tragic course of action', going on to argue of then-Secretary General U Thant's gloss on Article 16 that 'Unfortunately this is just the course of action that is being pursued by the United Nations' (1968: 1246).

In the Mont Pèlerin Society's founding Statement of Aims we find, among Hardin's 'social arrangements that produce responsibility', private property and the competitive market, both of which congeal around a word that filled Hardin with dread: freedom. The first two items in the Draft Statement produced by Hayek and the Committee of Individualists outline freedom as a spontaneous social force which, however, cannot survive on its own.

1. Individual freedom can be preserved only in a society in which an effective competitive market is the main agency for the direction of economic activity. Only the decentralization of control through private property in the means of production can prevent those concentrations of power which threaten individual freedom.
2. The freedom of the consumer in choosing what he shall buy, the freedom of the producer in choosing what he shall make, and the freedom of the worker in choosing his occupation and his place of employment, are essential not merely for the sake of freedom itself, but for efficiency in production.

(Hartwell 1995: 49)

For the nascent neo-liberal movement, the free market was social intelligence: no lone intellect could ever match its capacity to adjudicate human affairs. This explains the accusation of hubris aimed at rival schools of thought: puny humans can never think at the scales and speeds of the market – Sohn-Rethel's real abstraction. Hayek's twin attacks on law and facts prefigured postmodern assaults on European rationality, but with a very different aim, introducing another strange contradiction for a forum devoted to freedom: the idea that individual reason is hubris, and individualists should entrust themselves to the spontaneous operation of mysterious social forces deemed to be inherently and irrationally beneficial, but with no explanation about why they mean well to humanity.

There is another attempt to assert the beneficent operation of private property in the sixth aim, which claims, 'In general an automatic mechanism of adjustment, even when it functions imperfectly, is preferable to any which depends on "conscious" direction by government agencies.' Hayek's gesture towards the automatism of market forces is a quiet nod towards the emergent cybernetic theories of the late 1940s, only fully realised in algo-trading half a century later. According to economic historian E. Roy Weintraub, the question of automatic processes caused a split in mid-twentieth-century economics 'between those who would argue that mathematical rigor (and scientific knowledge) must develop not from axioms but from observations (about the economy) and (economic) data, so that the truth of a theory or model may be tested or confirmed by reality … and those who would claim that mathematical (economic) models are rigorous (and "true" in the only useful scientific sense of the word) if they are built on a cogent axiom base – like von Neumann and Morgenstern' (Weintraub 2002: 100). Weintraub is referring to the influential *Theory of Games and Economic Behavior* by pioneer cybernetician John von

Neumann and economist Oskar Morgenstern (1944, also cited approvingly by Hardin [1968: 1243]). An early review noted that 'The mathematically trained reader will find the reasoning stimulating and challenging. As to economics, a limited background is sufficient' (Copeland 1945: 498), indicating the impending triumph of mathematical reasoning over direct or historical observation (also queried by critics of Hardin's 'Tragedy'). The 'automatic mechanism' of the sixth aim ensures the model operates spontaneously. Buyers and sellers need only conform to it. In his concluding paragraph, Hardin quotes the expression 'Freedom is the recognition of necessity' without a source, probably because it comes from Marx's comrade Friedrich Engels (1947: 140), who says it comes from Hegel, though there is no equivalent expression in the paragraph Engels refers to. Engels concludes, 'Freedom does not consist in any dreamt-of independence from natural laws, but in the knowledge of these laws, and in the possibility this gives of systematically making them work towards definite ends', but Hardin has it that 'The only way we can preserve and nurture other and more precious freedoms is by relinquishing the freedom to breed'. For Engels, understanding the laws of history made revolutionary change possible. For Hardin, it only enforces prohibitions on women's bodies so that presumably masculine freedoms including property and the free market can persist. It is a sleight of hand that Stalin would have been proud of.

The Mont Pèlerin signatories did not imagine governments regulating themselves. The final aim of the adopted Statement speaks of creating 'an international order conducive to the safeguarding of peace and liberty and permitting the establishment of harmonious international economic relations'. Attempts through the United Nations to create an International Trade Organisation between 1945 and 1948 – the same time as the Mont Pèlerin meeting – foundered when the

US Congress declined to join in 1948, setting up the opportunity to convene an international body outside the UN system, the General Agreement on Tariffs and Trade (GATT), and its successor, the World Trade Organisation (WTO) (Hoekman and Kostecki 2009; Hoekman 2019). Part by design, part by accident (Van den Bossche 2021), world trade came under the aegis of a legal body outside what Mont Pèlerin and Hardin criticised as the Enlightenment project of the UN. Although the WTO has struggled to include environmental issues, the legal necessity to add 'and trade' to any non-trade-based matter in WTO disputes makes them permanently secondary to economics (Gomula 2010). As political scientist Tony McGrew (2011: 28) noted, intentions are not everything: 'the institutional design and functioning of the WTO gives primacy to the achievement of trade liberalisation even at the expense of other aspects of its original mandate, to protect the environment, advance living standards and promote full employment'. In a demonstration of the power of saying what the powerful want to hear, today's 'rules-based order' of global trade brings to fruition the Mont Pèlerin Society principle that wealth is the greatest good. That statement rests on legislating and policing private property and, an even more primal dogma, the deeply self-contradictory faith in freedom as condition and destiny. Without those pillars, it is hard to see how wealth can be owned, and how it can be both a law of nature and a source of freedom. Ownership and freedom both require a subject: one who is free and has property. Does such a subject exist?

Who Owns the World?

One of neo-liberalism's greatest achievements has been to reduce the UN Declaration's right of free speech to intellectual property. Mirowski (2002: 6-7) noted a move from the neo-classical definition of economics as 'The optimal allocation of scarce resources to given ends' to the new cybernetic economics after von Neumann, centred on 'The economic agent as a processor of information' (Wark's 2019 claim that capital is dead and has been replaced by information is only a slight overstatement of Mirowski's case that capital has become information). The idea of a marketplace of ideas arose as an alternative to free speech, powered by media industries profiting from it and organisations based on it, like GATT. When money is the measure, how much information an 'economic agent' can afford becomes critical. If information is rationed by price, is economic agency definitionally unequal? What kind of freedom can there be for a subject whose only function is information processing? When computers are far more efficient information processors than humans, are economic subjects bound to be human? Wealth only demands individuals in two residual roles: as the legal owners of property (a flexible usage, as a corporation or any legally constituted abstraction can be a 'legal person') and as agents who can get into debt. Anxiety, the experience of privation that debt causes, is constitutively individual. Selfishness is by definition a quality of a self. Collectives can be afraid or angry; they cannot be selfish or experience anxiety. The evils of selfish wealth and anxious debt are necessary outcomes of accumulating wealth (Graeber 2011). Thus the subject of economics – all those individuals whose mindless activity produces the wisdom of the market – is bipolar: selfish or anxious or unstably both. The evidence for instability is that economic activity as practised for the last several centuries has constantly had to rebuild individuality and remind it of its obligations. That is the job of financial advertising which, adopting the three moments outlined in Hyman Minsky's (1992) financial instability hypothesis, addresses in turn investors who can afford both the loan and the interest, those who can afford the interest but not the principal, and finally the 'Ponzi' investors who can afford neither the principal nor the interest (and plunge the system into crisis). Finance and financial advertising oscillate between conservative anxiety and liberal euphoria.

Owning and owing money involves arresting time. The owner accumulates wealth, but from the point of view of wealth itself, the owner is a mere receptacle, a gravity well that wealth flows towards, a point of rest with no further need to circulate – the opposite of Blake's 'energy'. For the debtor, all the money they will ever earn has already vanished, leaving an empty totality that can never be repaid. This second emptiness, again from the perspective of money itself, is the same as the totality and rest of accumulation. The harrowing truth of wealth as personal good thus staggers into view just at the moment of its disappearance; for wealth itself, owning and owing are simple effects of its one function: to disappear. From wealth's point of view, this rest-state is the eternity it seeks. But economic eternity is strapped to the present, a fiscal event horizon that is perpetually now because wealth exists, has being, possesses itself in its fullness, only now, in an eternal present. Past wealth is gone; future wealth does not exist yet (which is why debt appears as ravenous to debtors and as lucre to creditors). But when eternity is the eternal now, wealth tries to secure its stasis by suborning the law to its service in the form of inheritance. A succession of anonymous owners and debtors follow one another down the dusty avenues of time in service of immortalising wealth's presence to itself. The human is utterly marginal to this process. Because wealth is impersonal, it can never serve a personal good. We do not ultimately own it, nor in the end does it own us – it uses people as it uses any other resource.

In 1948, this disappearance took on domestic dimensions in a banal but for that reason fascinating film comedy,

Mr Blandings Builds His Dream Home, produced by Dory Schary, who, during the production of the film in 1947, signed the Waldorf Declaration in which studio bosses aligned themselves with Senator Joe McCarthy's House Un-American Activities Committee (HUAC). The story of the titular New York advertising executive (Cary Grant) bleeding money to build a home in rural Connecticut, the movie was shot by distinguished cinematographer James Wong Howe, who, despite living in the States for forty-two years, had only been granted citizenship on the expiry of the Chinese Exclusion Act in 1943, and whose marriage was only recognised after California finally abolished its anti-miscegenation laws in the year the film was made. For one of its most astute commentators Catherine Jurca (1998), *Mr Blandings* belongs to the era of HUAC, specifically for its anti-communist sentimentalisation of the then-current housing crisis, its parodic handling of 'radical' ideas ('Miss Stellwagon says advertising makes people who can't afford them buy things they don't want with money they haven't got') and its quiet embrace of advertising as integral to the American Way. Structured around the rural/urban divide, its main plot details how Jim Blandings' cash vanishes into a money pit (the title of the 1986 remake starring Tom Hanks in the Mr Blandings role). Its interest in our context is not only the disappearance of (meticulously detailed amounts of) money but how Grant's character is both producer and dupe of advertising copy, although neither term quite captures his role. The slogan that saves the family comes from the faithful Black maid, played by Louise Beavers, not Jim Blandings, and although he is sucked in by advertising copy for a rural retreat, the film's moral, that 'you *do* buy with your heart and not your head', promises satisfaction, so underwriting the emotive appeal of advertising.

Jurca cites a 1940 lecture by James Webb Young (1994), 'an executive at J. Walter Thompson and an important figure in the history of advertising. In a lecture delivered to the Business School at the University of Chicago, Young claimed that the way to form ideas was to let the unconscious (sleeping) mind do the work of synthesizing bits of information that had been gathered and contemplated in advance; once the idea was released, the conscious mind then polished and perfected it' (Jurca 1998: 27).

After witnessing Jim's struggle to waken, in a scene meant to show overcrowding in the Blandings' New York apartment, Jim and wife Muriel (Myrna Loy) compete for the bathroom mirror. When she asks why he does not get an electric razor, Jim responds, 'Because I prefer the clean sweep of the tempered steel as it glides,' before she interrupts with 'No advertising copy please.' The rhetoric of Madison Avenue has churned through his sleeping self until he speaks an alien language. This is the dream of advertising in the cybernetic age – to come from and speak to unconsciousness, just as Jim's money flows from his bosses into the stillness of his finished house.

Jim's unconscious participation in the vanishing of 'his' money is true to the spirit of 1948, since when the evanescence of money has accelerated, while unconsciousness has intensified. As information processors, economic agents, including humans, process code largely made up of logic and algorithms, and only to a diminishing extent of language. Language was always motivated by lack, pursuing, according to Lacan, the lost object of desire down endless lines of talk (Lacan 1977: 148–156). Code introduces a new condition, where that lack is itself lacking. In the old Symbolic order, desire took the form of a lack endlessly displaced along the chain of signifiers chasing an illusory future when it would finally achieve its object. Now that linguistic chain has become a digital network, and desire is suffused throughout the system. There is no longer a missing object. Humans presume it is present somewhere in the network, economists that it is equivalent to the sum total of all possible connections. As language users we inhabited signs, deferring satisfaction into the future; as information processors we produce data, condemning us to a futureless present. The unconscious is no longer exclusively structured like language (Lacan 1988: 20), but increasingly like code. From the perspective of the system, the remainder – non-numerical life – is only noise, experienced by data-processing economic agents as disorientation, disaffection, anxiety, alienation and mental illness (Panayotakis 2021). All this conforms to the cybernetic economism established at Mont Pèlerin. In a more recent turn towards profiting from contingency, even this noise becomes a source of profit.

In the order desired and to a degree established by Samuelson, Shannon and Hayek in the late 1940s and celebrated by Hardin in the 1960s, people consumed commodities in endless pursuit of a satisfaction they could never achieve. Always dissatisfied and therefore condemned to repetition, consuming was the final act in the cycle of production. In the twenty-first century, however, any act of consumption is also an act of production, producing more value in the shape of data. In the half-century following the cybernetic model's entry into the public domain, consumption was subsumed 'formally' under capital: we paid for what we needed. Now consuming is 'really' subsumed: as disciplined as factory labour. No longer the grave of production, consuming only produces more value. The unconscious recycling of copywriters' dreams by dreaming consumers is now supplemented when half-awake consumers' wishes and desires can be encoded from their choices and behaviours and recycled to new advertising copy for new products.

This real subsumption of consumption under capital was managed at first through regimes of control, planning and risk management. Around 2002–2004, in the wake of the dot-com crash late in 2000 (Kuo 2001), social media including Friendster, LinkedIn, 4chan, Orkut, Flickr and Facebook launched net-native business models that rapidly discovered their data-harvesting functions (van Dijk 2013). In the latest turn, dating from about the time of the Global Financial Crisis (GFC) of 2007, prediction is no longer profitable enough, and market-makers seek out contingencies and randomness as the privileged site of the differences where capital can derive profits (MacKenzie 2006; Ayache 2010; 2015; Appadurai 2016). In a book on the philosophy and practice of music, Jacques Attali (1985) proposed the idea that most arts, including film, are shaped by the ideologies of the time when they were made, but music predicts the future. From this perspective, for example, the discipline of the twelve-tone row imposed by the Second Vienna School (Schönberg, Berg and Webern, broadly 1921–1933) foretold the cybernetic obsession with system, while the use of chance by composers like Karlheinz Stockhausen and John Cage in the 1950s, guiding listeners to perceive musical form in random or at least improbable sounds, pointed towards our new financial obsession with contingencies. Cage and Stockhausen drew on cybernetics but they rejected its systemic thrust. Reacting against cybernetic control with experimental, participatory happenings, their works of the 1960s prophesied the assimilation of contingency into capital, even though they were convinced that they were tools for liberation. Similarly their mystical themes and methods, intended to subvert Western rationalism, mark the first aesthetic steps towards the vanishing of consciousness from the economic world and its substitution by the new code-shaped unconscious. The subject of digital-financial capital has always been excluded from wealth, treated as environmental resource and economic externality (the technical term for a resource used or abused by economic activity without having to be paid for). Today, however, that subject is no longer the perpetually lacking seeker of desire but a data cloud of dispersed, ephemeral and partial satisfactions. Like the code extrapolated and privatised from the general intellect, human information processors are increasingly formed in and as code, nodes in a network they are supposed to be unconscious of.

In 1948, cyberneticist Norbert Wiener declared that 'the present time is the age of communication and control' (1961: 39). In 'Postscript on the Societies of Control', written in 1990, the philosopher Gilles Deleuze extended the political history outlined by his friend Michel Foucault, who analysed 'disciplinary' societies regulated by institutions and internalised as discourses (organised ways of speaking and behaving). Deleuze believed discipline was giving way to control. Discipline had been verbal; control was numerical and algorithmic, a matter of code. In law, disciplinary societies kept their citizens in line through 'apparent acquittal' (as in Kafka's *The Trial*) where societies of control used 'limitless postponements'. Economically, 'discipline always referred back to minted money that locks gold in as numerical standard, while control relates to floating rates of exchange'. Sociologically, 'We no longer find ourselves dealing with the mass/individual pair. Individuals have become ... masses, samples, data, markets, or "banks" ' (Deleuze 1992: 5). The old, disciplined, industrial labour force has become the market, and individuals have become 'dividuals', unstill, networked clouds of data and desires, both tracked and managed by statistical sampling. Deleuze believed these changes began in the wake of World War II, the period of Shannon's mathematical theory of communications and the Mont Pèlerin beginnings of neo-liberalism. *Mr Blandings* gives us an insight into how those changes were experienced at the time. The 2022 film

Everything Everywhere All At Once speaks from a period when these trends accelerated in the aftermath of the GFC.

The framing story of the multiple-universe narrative in *Everything Everywhere All At Once* concerns a tax audit. The auditor Deirdre (Jamie Lee Curtis) introduces the theme of control when she tells Evelyn (Michelle Yeoh), 'with nothing but a stack of receipts, I can track the ups and downs of your life'. The film's structure and setting bear out this control scenario, its events at first seemingly random gradually forming a pattern rather than advancing to a conclusion. But unlike an earlier cycle of 'database narratives' in films like *The Usual Suspects* (1995) and *Lock, Stock and Two Smoking Barrels* (1998), *Everything Everywhere* adds in a plot device: in order to jump between universes to gather the skills needed to win each set-up, characters have to do something utterly unexpected – eat a chapstick, sing opera, declare their love for someone they hate and fear… Though the plotting is not entirely coherent, each world has a different Evelyn whose life has taken a distinctive turn as a result of some choice she made. So the film reiterates the ideology of free choice, but this time as an expression of the new role of contingency in the post-GFC world: each apparently random gag also serves the overarching order of the multiverse we see on various mapping devices.

However, as Evelyn confronts herself and her nemesis in a play on the old joke about the Buddha in a hamburger joint saying 'Make me one with everything', it becomes clear that these events have not changed their worlds but only Evelyn's life. *Everything Everywhere*'s homage to randomness seems at first to belong to the order of the event as philosopher Alain Badiou (2019: 81–2) sums it up: 'something that is locally produced in a world, and which cannot be deduced from the laws of this same world … the apparition of new possibilities for thought and action'. Each unpredictable act opens up the way to a wholly different world. Badiou's idea is not all that far from a thought of Enlightenment philosopher Immanuel Kant's to the effect that 'We must, then, assume a causality through which something [Badiou's 'event'] takes place, the cause of which is not itself determined … by another cause antecedent to it, that is to say an *absolute spontaneity*' whose effects, nonetheless, ripple out in conformity with the laws of nature that the spontaneous act broke free from (Kant 2003: 410–411; see Adorno 2000: 33–43). At first glance, the random acts forcing the new world to spring into existence seem to match both Kant's idea of spontaneous novelty that brings about a new constellation of possibilities and Badiou's theory of 'fidelity', loyally committing to the consequences that an event sets in motion. But seen from the audit frame-story, the film's events reduce to statistical improbabilities that ultimately maintain the system that at first they seemed to rebel against. The grand dénouement respects the initial brief Evelyn receives, 'to take us back to how it's supposed to be'. After touching on at least three of the four domains Badiou prioritises (maths, art and love), the film ends with a realist portrayal of a loving family in just one universe. The result – the 'happy ending' – is, in Badiou's terms, only satisfaction ('I am satisfied when I can be assured that I am well integrated with the world' [Badiou 2019: 88]). Evelyn's reward is to return to a well-ordered world where she pays her taxes. Control not only samples and tracks but, since the GFC, assimilates even the most ludicrous transgressions of expectable behaviour in the interests of systemic equilibrium.

At least in fiction. The historic effect Wiener described that brought control into systemic union with communication should have produced just such a consolidation, particularly of the collective good that sociologist Jürgen Habermas (1989) called the public sphere. Ironically, Habermas' ideal shared space of public debate has shattered in parallel with the dissolving individuals into Deleuze's dividual concatenations of data and behaviours. There is no longer a public sphere because it is not One anymore (Fraser 1990). The new media that emerged from the conjuncture of control and communication that once seemed to be the perfect global village, specifically the internet, has split between the public web and the dark net, and along linguistic, technical and ideological divides within and between GAFAM (Google, Amazon, Facebook, Apple, Microsoft) and BATX (Baidu, Alibaba, Tencent, Xiaomi) platforms. Start-ups like Telegram demarcate boundaries where – in theory – dialogue is no longer possible. This sparks the thought that quite possibly there is more than one economy, even if they sit on top of one another in layers: if there is no longer one market, what price its claim to universal knowledge? Automating the money system through cryptocurrencies is one way of restoring autonomy to the market by creating a new model for it. The ideal model for Bitcoin (Nakamoto 2008) proposed a system for managing transactions without trust or a trusted third party, be it a bank or the state, through a decentralised, automated and code-determined network. The turbulent history of Bitcoin and the 2022 collapse of the FTX crypto exchange show it is still vulnerable to the irrationally exuberant Ponzi moment, so much so that its protagonists called out for the kind of regulation that it was initially designed to pre-empt and evade. A counter-Hardin tragedy of self-interest appears here: not a Hegelian pre-determined fate but the tragic loss of what once touted itself as a new public sphere. The crypto crash demonstrates the impossibility of creating universal personal wealth, let alone welfare, on the basis of a shared determination to accumulate.

Profit is taken in the present but wealth is accumulated from the past. Whether language and land or code and computers, the media that channel wealth share with them their origin in the commons. Marx called this immaterial commons the general intellect, the vast resources of a shared legacy of those things no individual can function or exist without, but which no individual created or could create, such as language and mathematics (Marx 1973: 706–716; see Vercellone 2007, Virno 2007). The failure of crypto demonstrates a unique quality of money, the dominant medium of the twenty-first century: that unlike every other emanation of the general intellect, it no longer evolves. Wealth inherits cybernetics' structural paralysis in the face of change. Its terminal stillness is that of an imagined perfect autonomy, beyond desire, beyond society, beyond time, that has never and never could exist – which tells us a great deal about the status of wealth. Wealth is not imaginary in any psychologically or socially generative sense, in the way imaginary utopias can inspire change. It is instead the one thing that perfectly succeeds in its quest for existence. Everything lacks and yearns, everything hankers for a future, everything interacts – everything but money, which disappears into its own presence the moment it achieves its perfect stillness. This paradox poisons Hardin's inevitable, determinist 'Tragedy of the Commons', which fails, as neo-liberalism from Mont Pèlerin to crypto has failed, to create even the circumscribed satisfactions it promised. It is hard to escape the conclusion that, by erasing everything that preceded and created it (work, world), money is entropic, and the longer it persists, the less world will remain.

The commons remains, a lost culture for Indigenous peoples, and a future vista for ecological thought. Ecocritical aesthetic politics implies abandoning the anaesthetics of personal wealth. Because it is built on the privations of others, and because it cannot provide welfare and prosperity even for the vanishing self it promised to create and maintain, personal property can never be good. Private wealth is always deprivation, of others and ultimately of the self that accumulates it. Reducing communication to the circulation of economic information diminishes all it touches. To escape this sarcophagus of hopes and desires, we need at the minimum to acknowledge communication 'as a tissue composed of individual memories that form a collective memory by exchanging symbols' (Flusser 2023: 1), to understand that nothing individual or dividual exists that is not also collective, that exchange does not mean hoarding but sharing, and that history unravels selves not to hold them apart but to weave them together. To fare well and prosper, aesthetically and politically, in the senses and in common, we cannot presume that communication has not already been perverted by its fifty-year passage through cybernetic communications and economic systems and its new passage through encoding, the end result of the real subsumption of consumption and the monetisation of contingent externalities. It is no longer just employees who are human resources; every consumer is now raw material for the emergent data economy.

Contemporary economic life or, to give it its proper name, capital (accumulated wealth) has produced a self that is either locked into its vanishing possession or wracked with fearful anticipation of loss, or both. This unhappy ego is tied by privation to a miserable half-awake existence. What capital excludes – the noise of living life – is the remainder of information processing. It is the excluded face of communication, external and excessive, and it may yet lead to the palace of wisdom. For a privileged few – and they are otherwise the most oppressed and immiserated of all humans – there may be an Indigenous, pre-colonial commons to return to. The rest of us are 'in blood stepped in so far' (Shakespeare, *Macbeth*, Act III Scene iv) that we cannot presume such a return. The commons will have to be built, so that we can once more communicate beyond the information processing role that is all capital has left us by way of communication. Without communication, there is no community, and without community there will be no commons. Because we cannot presume there is a commons to return to, we must build commons in order to communicate, and communicate in order to build commons. First, however, there has to be a future beyond the wasteland of the vanishing present.

1.1 Posthumous

... an irretrievable image of the past which threatens to disappear in any present that does not recognise itself as intimated in that image

Walter Benjamin, 'Edward Fuchs', 262

After the End: The Divje Babe Flute

The end is all too possible to imagine in the early twenty-first century. A trope of science fiction (especially British science fiction reflections on the end of empire from Wells and Stapledon to Ballard and Brunner), the end dangles in front of us today as the logical outcome of environmental tendencies our species either cannot or will not change. The heat death of the universe evoked in the planetarium scene in Nicholas Ray's film *Rebel Without a Cause* (1955) has been overtaken by visions of ineluctable catastrophe at the level of species and planet. Against the vanishing present and its impending terminus, making culture becomes alternately frenetic, melancholic and visionary, in genres as disparate as TV wildlife documentaries celebrating deserted domains like Chernobyl and the deep oceans and formal music compositions designed to last longer than the predicted future of Earth. This condition is not without precedent.

Patrick Wolfe (1999: 2) is only one of those who have noted that, from the point of view of the colonised, invasion is a structure, not an event. The worst has already happened and continues happening. At time of writing in 2023, the failure of governments, agencies and economic powers to confront climate change places everyone face to face with life after extinction. What does it mean to make culture after the end, to make anything out of 'what it feels like to live in the psychological gulf that opens at the end of an era' (Hughes 1997: xi)? One answer comes from decolonial histories of what Anishinaabe writer Gerald Vizenor (2009) defines as 'survivance', and Canadian scholar Michelle Murphy (2017) as 'alterlife'. This is more than the ostensibly universal absurdity of the human condition described by another colonial writer, Albert Camus (1979), in 'The Myth of Sisyphus'. The colonial event – the catastrophe of genocide, epidemic disease, land clearances and in settler colonies replacing Indigenous peoples with imported slaves, indentured labourers and transported paupers, often enough from other colonies like Ireland – forced and continues to force First Nations into *sur*vival, living-on-after. We find ourselves in a parallel situation and therefore desperate to learn from Indigenous activists and scholars how to *sur*vive. But after stealing everything else from them, we white Westerners cannot carry on the theft by stealing even their suffering and their hard-won skills of living-on-after the end. As Max Liboiron (2021) argues, 'There can be a solidarity without a We. There *must* be solidarity without a universal We. The absence of We and the acknowledgment of many we's (including those to which you/I do not belong) is imperative for good relations in solidarity against ongoing colonialism' (Liboiron 2021: 24–25).

In the end, where the colonised have lived since colonisation and where we have only just arrived, any solidarity must be political, recognising differences in power, wealth and options. The colonised were noise to imperialists. The lives left over after subsumption and code are noise to corporations. Taking its name and measurements from the clatter of city streets and the noisome slums of the poor and excluded (Carmi 2020), noise has another history in the twentieth century, not as measure of exclusion but as a yardstick of survival after extinction. Sound, after all, is the most ephemeral of aesthetic experiences, no sooner heard than gone. Tracing an origin myth for music – noise's pair – might hear music as a magical response to the prefiguration of end-times in noise's inevitable diminuendo.

Modern humans only arrived in Europe about 45,000 years ago, so despite evidence that it was a Neanderthal artefact made by a now-extinct branch of hominids, archaeologists argued that a musical instrument discovered in a Slovenian cave in 1997 could only belong to rational, symbol-toting moderns. The provenance debate is settled now: the flute precedes modern humans' arrival in Europe. But a nagging doubt remains: if music is indeed an exclusive property of the moderns' symbolic reason, then this carefully made thing may not be, in this sense at least, a human artefact, made for ordering or communicating.

We will never know what went through the minds of the Neanderthal who made the flute from the femur of a now-equally extinct cave bear around 50,000 years ago. The instrument has two remaining holes and the traces of three more in addition to its open ends, tuned to a recognisable diatonic scale (Fink 1997). A recording of Slovenian musician Ljuben Dimkaroski playing a reconstruction is haunting and convincing: this was a musical instrument. Classic FM reports that it is evidence that even before modern humans, these cave-dwelling hunters were 'capable of such an abstract and uniquely human activity as creating music' (Rizzi 2021).

There should be considerable doubt about whether music is uniquely human. Ecological thinking and affect theory would suggest that if music exists, however defined, then it must flow through the world as harmonies and dissonances, rhythms and tonalities. The inference is that music discovered humans, rather than vice versa. A member of the dig team that unearthed the cave bear flute, archaeologist Ivan Turk, co-authored a descriptive and analytical paper on the find (Kunej and Turk 2001) in a collection (Wallin et al. 2001) of which half is devoted to 'Vocal Communication in Animals'. There is every reason to believe that rattling tail feathers and tail-slaps on open water may not only communicate or create social bonds, but for all we know make music – beautiful patterns of sound in time. Dimkaroski's rendition of an adagio attributed to the eighteenth-century composer Tomaso Albinoni shows that the reconstructed flute can hold a recognisably modern melody, 'abstract' in the sense understood at the latter end of the baroque. But what might making and playing the flute have meant 50,000 years ago (see Morley 2006)?

Cave bears were big, largely plant-eating, and there is little evidence that Neanderthals hunted them (a combination of climate change and competition with modern humans for cave space probably brought about their extinction). It is possible that the flute femur came from a kill, but as likely it was recovered from a natural death. The bone was separated from the carcass, cleaned and carved. The animal it came from was very definitely dead. If cave bears were, as the archaeology suggests, physically close to modern bears, they would not have made a sound like a flute; grunts and roars would be more likely. A flute could not imitate the animal. Instead, there is the tuning of breath. To blow, to breathe life into an inanimate thing, to re-animate a creature after its death – we cannot say what that might have meant then. It is hard enough to comprehend the mystery of music-making today. But there seems good reason to think that, in the cave at Divje Babe where the flute was discovered, player and perhaps listeners would have felt some more-than-ordinary reverberation. Call it magic.

Citing an idea of Marcel Mauss (1972), anthropologist Claude Lévi-Strauss described one exemplary form of magic: the idea of *mana*, the intrinsic power of objects and people in Polynesian culture. Such terms for an otherwise unidentifiable *je ne sais quoi* posit, Lévi-Strauss wrote, 'an indeterminate value of signification, in itself devoid of meaning and thus susceptible of receiving any meaning at all; their sole function is to fill a gap between the signifier and the signified, or, more exactly, to signal the fact that in such a circumstance, on such an occasion, or in such a one of their manifestations, a relationship of non-equivalence becomes established between signifier and signified' (Lévi-Strauss 1987: 55–56).

Mauss had set himself the task of debunking colonialist conceptions of magic as a primitive phase of human development. Lévi-Strauss argued that mythic thinking, like modern European science, was a method for understanding and controlling the world. A problem for this kind of thought was, he believed, that humans generate more meanings than there are things in the world to attach them to. This 'surplus of signification' (1987: 62) is what drives the non-equivalence between things and states of mind (signifiers and signifieds). Some third quality happens when dead bone and live breath meet: a new, magical occurrence, music, that escapes taxonomies of alive and dead, breathing and inert, without, however, creating a clear and definite meaning. Music is the excess of meaning, not just in the human but in the world. Spooky, magical, an unstable hinterland at the border of intellect, language, senses and world. The Neanderthal flutemaker may have identified this threshold between living and dead as magic traversing the undefinable *mana* of mortality, among a sparse human population perhaps already in the decline that would see them and the cave bears extinct a few thousand years after the flute was carved.

The Waste Land *and Other Non-Cochlear Sonic Objects*

The Divje Babe flute can stand at or near the start of the long procession of joyful animations of the inanimate from Pygmalion to Pinocchio; impious re-animations of the dead from the Golem to *Frankenstein*; and now the uncanny thrill of interfacing with AI – the magical force of Divine Creation, breathing life (*anima*: breath, soul) into clay seems to gather and sum a deep history, predating the written words that tell us the oldest stories. Even if the flute were, after all, not from an expired cadaver but made from a hunter's kill, and its role therefore to speak to or negotiate with the dead animal, its mediation of breath and bone would still exhibit an excess of affect over words and things. Something of that discomforting articulation of living and dead still hovers over contemporary self-operating systems, scarcely evolved from the haunted telegraphs exhumed in Jeffrey Sconce's *Haunted Media* (2000), and the far older strangeness of inert instruments of brass, wood and gut transforming air into melody with the power to bring back memories we never had and emotions we never felt.

An icon of English-language modernism, T. S. Eliot's 1922 poem *The Waste Land* is an early riposte to the language of noise emerging from communication technology labs. Voices and languages, snatches of song, church bells, a nightingale, wind, motor horns and a throbbing taxi distress its unquiet surface. A bored typist plays a record. From the river comes the sound of a mandolin. Bones rattle, a cockerel crows and dry thunder rolls across a desert. For Eliot, the modern sonic universe did not cohere as older traditions might have done. Almost incidentally, the poem challenges the belief that, because it is symbolic, communicative, socialising, ordered and rational, music belongs only to humans, and only to some of them.

Ralph Ellison connected *The Waste Land* with jazz in 1964 (2001; see Tracy 2016). Eliot was listening compulsively to his gramophone in the years of the poem's composition (Suarez 2001). His friendship with fellow poet Ezra Pound, the 'miglior fabbro' of the poem's dedication, may have made him aware of Luigi Russolo's futurist *Art of Noise* (1913) and George Antheil's player piano score for Léger's *Ballet méchanique*, compositions that invented or deployed new sounding technologies and granted them some degree of autonomy from composer's or player's control. Eliot had a gift for what other critics decried as 'pathetic fallacy', metaphors ascribing human feelings to weather and landscape, but the relation does not necessarily only go one way. Dry hills or driving rain can inflect our emotions as much as great sex can make the greyest morning sunny. Eliot wrote, 'These fragments I have shored against my ruins', hearing correspondences between soundscapes of industrial cities and inward states of the soul just when the Second Viennese School was starting to compose dissonance and silence. He was not more avant-garde than Arnold Schönberg and his pupils in Vienna in abandoning harmony or emphasising fracture over the integral work. *The Waste Land*'s sonics are significant because, in their collapsing categorial distinctions, they pitch the excess of noises over coherence, order, rationality or symbolisation. Reconfiguring noise as valuable and meaningful, *The Waste Land* conflates Shannon's double exclusions – of noise and meaning – and makes them available for an alternative culture.

That alternative way of hearing noise helped shape compositions like Barry Truax's *Riverrun* (1986) and John Luther Adams' *Become* trilogy (2013–2018), works that emphasise 'the world as a macrocosmic musical composition', in R. Murray Schafer's phrase (1994: 5). Schafer, in the words of his near-contemporary Pierre Schaeffer (2017: 263), sought 'to hear everything at the same time ... an active musicianly mode of listening, as if we were listening to an orchestra and trying to focus on all the sources at once'. This democratisation of every sound might suggest a reduction of hearing to the level of capital's universal exchange. To the extent that Schafer and Schaeffer, like Fluxus composer and sonic artist John Cage, wanted to create music out of this newly expanded listening, they can also be accused of extending the 'paternalistic rhetoric of "giving voices" to those who cannot represent themselves (traditionally children, women, the poor, the colonized, the disabled, animals, and other figures of marginalization) ... to inanimate natural objects such as glaciers and forests' (Pettman 2017: 66). Imposing a 'musicianly mode of listening' and 'giving voice' diminishes the sounds of waves and wind. On the other hand, imagining the geometry of the planets as universal harmony, inaudible to mortal ears 'whilst this muddy vesture of decay Doth grossly close it in' (Shakespeare, *The Merchant of Venice*, Act V Scene i), decentres anthropocentric listening – and defers hearing the music of the spheres to the afterlife. Even though the practice of music has long been a practice of abstraction, the re-tuning of hearing since John Cage's first assertions that his material was all-sound, not just intentionally made notes, encourages us to seek out sonic delight beyond human intentions or even capabilities; and to listen for what exceeds distinctions like Shannon's between signal and noise. This border between planetary or interplanetary reverberations and the organisational power of music is as ripe with animating power as the cave bear flute and is equally unclear whether we hear the bone or the breath, the world or our listening.

Writing about an installation artwork by Christine Sun Kim involving four subwoofers playing sounds at and below the threshold of human hearing, Caleb Kelly writes, 'the work is formed from sound waves that can be felt by people on the deaf spectrum, including Kim herself, who is profoundly deaf ... Conceptually, the work opens the potential for sound within the arts that is resolutely non-cochlear' (Kelly 2022: 98).

The strictly enforced sensory discipline that restricts 'hearing' to ears, excluding vibrations sensed through the soles of the feet, chest cavity and long bones, creates a hierarchy in the same way light sensitivity is disciplined by restricting it to what retinas can register, while ignoring how all skin responds to light. Schafer emphasised the continuity of the senses of hearing and touch, both sensitive to vibrations, both experienced as bodily and intimate, a continuum of body and world, sound and sensation and, in light of Mauss and Lévi-Strauss, of form and meaninglessness of the kind Eliot reached for with his 'Wallala leialala' and his 'la la'. The play of meaning/form and formless/meaningless extends to a second hierarchy, one that represses the body as a producer of sounds, and not just of percussion, articulate speech and song: the body that gurgles, farts, belches, yawns and sneezes, sounds we learn early on to suppress or mask. I can hear my own breath, heartbeats and digestion, even if others cannot. I may learn to ignore them but they accompany me as long as I live. When music immerses the body in amplification, it drowns out those sounds that otherwise tell us we are living. In its search for immortality, music always tends towards a posthumous condition, beyond death, recalling ancestors and anticipating afterlife.

With *musique concrète*, Pierre Schaeffer consolidated Cage's all-sound, but his tools were recording devices. Cinema had already embraced non-musical 'wild tracks' alongside dialogue and music. Using similar recording techniques but now without the ambition to amplify realism or promote identification with a listening character onscreen, Schaeffer realised the divorce of sounds from their origins effected by recording when he formulated the idea of 'sound objects', asking listeners not to listen for sources but to hear sounds themselves, divorced from whatever caused them *and* from the psychology of hearing. Reversing the process, Eliot's typist hears the gramophone, not Wagner or Marie Lloyd, as his poets hear 'jug jug' or 'tereu' in the nightingale's otherwise varied and liquid song. Beside the world lie technologies that may imitate or represent small fractions of the world – Eliot's gramophone records would have split *Tristan and Isolde* into a significant pile of 78rpm records – selecting sounds by microphone placement and direction, severing them from the sounding instruments they recorded, the bodies of the players absorbing and damping the sounds they produce and the ambience of the space where the recording took place, subordinating everything to disciplined and ear-centred listening to the detriment of the proximal sense of touch. This spatial discontinuity is a condition of recording, separating replay from event and, at the instant of recording, deferring playback to some future moment. The temporal pause between making and playing the cave-bear flute tells us such temporal disruption was already the case in the earliest musics we have evidence for.

The phrase 'live recording' may be an oxymoron, but we can allow for a certain co-presence of player and listener to the bone flute. Co-presence was also integral to Harry Bertoia's *Sonambient* sounding sculptures (Bertoia 2015), which keep their sounds and their source present to one another (although Bertoia also recorded his inventions). The throbbing taxi of *The Waste Land*, on the other hand, is only introduced in the line after the metaphor of 'the human engine', a body already tuned to the mechanical that in turn tunes the mechanical to itself. The throbbing between male and female (Wraith 2013) that traversed Eliot's Tiresias (who speaks this section of the poem) depends on the unique experience of hearing, there and then, the precise taxi throb, tuned to the vibrating body, prior to either recording or transliteration, as Eliot would have heard it in the early twenties – irrecoverable a hundred years later except as conscious, thus linguistically grounded empathy.

A different co-presence is apparent in compositions engaging improvisation and autonomy but subordinating them to temporal control, verging on the managerial, audible in minimalist works of the 1970s and 1980s by Terry Riley, Philip Glass and Steve Reich. Here the co-presence involves the phenomenal sounds produced by the players in compositions like Riley's *In C* (Cubitt 2023: 126–129) – a composition that allows for players of all abilities – with the presence of the score, particularly audible in this example because of the use of the Pulse, a repetitive high-C percussive beat. The score, as it were the intelligence of the music, is as audible as the notes vibrating in air, a script preceding its sounding, as deconstructive philosopher Jacques Derrida might have noted, specifically a script written for deferred performance and recording. If music prefigures the future rather than expressing the political, economic and social structures of its own time, when *In C* incorporated the random 'errors' of its performers into its design, it foreshadowed the subsumption of contingencies into profit-making facilitated by computer-driven high-frequency algorithmic trading.

Rule sets of the order of minimalist scores have been used for centuries to produce fugues and other musical forms. In computer-generated music, different again to Reich and Riley, algorithms must be formed as logical instructions. Electronic composer Laurie Spiegel derived the instructions for her 1977 composition *Harmonices Mundi* from Johannes Kepler's 1619 mathematical account of the relations between heavenly bodies. Combining computer logic with Kepler's geometry meant drawing on the deep legacy of rational systems, in much the same way that Eliot drew on the long history of languages. No one writer or programmer invented English or C++; both derive from millennia of Marx's general intellect: the commons of knowledge. Language, logic and maths are where we meet our ancestors.

Consciously, that is, in language, specifically in her title, Spiegel acknowledged the ancestral presence in her music through the reference to Kepler. Every logical expression, every instruction line, every aspect of the hardware is the congealed form of common knowledge that, in the West, we seal up in technological black boxes. The music of the Neanderthal flute is no more and no less magical in its dialogue with the dead beast than Spiegel's algorithmically deduced music in its dialogue with all the named and anonymous makers of computing, as well as all those, human and non-human, who, over thousands of years, have contributed to the evolution of music. Eliot's net drifts over two thousand years, Spiegel's over millennia – as far back as the Divje Babe cave and into the light years of interstellar distance foreseen for the *Voyager* spacecraft, both of which carried a copy of the Golden Record containing her *Harmonices Mundi*.

Voyager

Launched in 1977, the two *Voyager* satellites left the bounds of the solar system in 2012 and 2018. The Golden Record they each carry 'for the benefit of any other spacefarers that might find them in the distant future' (NASA n.d.) contains a remarkably diverse collection of sounds: weather, animals, machinery, languages and music, together with a selection of images of which many illustrate the sources of those sounds. They were designed to be heard in the far reaches of space, beyond the reach of living astronauts, and long after 'Earth is but a star that once had shone' (as James Elroy Flecker – a poet with a gift for the posthumous – wrote in 'The Golden Road to Samarkand' [1916]). Intended to make life on Earth decipherable to unimaginably alien beings, the *Voyager* discs evoke, simultaneously, two opposing emotions, hope and melancholy.

The melancholy is largely self-explanatory. The records have been made to travel the space ways after the human race is extinct, and our planet quite possibly denuded of life. Their premise is that there will be other consciousnesses that, in an indefinite future, can reconstruct our existence from the Golden recordings. Relating images to sounds may be problematic. Not only will future alien archaeologists have to work out how to extract them from the recordings and match the appropriate pairs, but they will need to piece together not only the connection between the written score of a Bach cantata, an image of a violin and some rudimentary instruction on human anatomy, but the presence of air as a medium and the precise range of wavelengths, overtones and harmonies humans find pleasurable. Most challenging of all will be acquiring some sense of the interplay of physical and psychological durations, recall and anticipation, and the very idea of organising sounds in time. Will they understand the etiquette of refraining from making sound, articulate or gross, during a performance? Or of when it is not just allowable but important to join in?

We humans are only conscious in language. Where language stops, we are in the Freudian sense *un*conscious, a space where bodily energies are shaped by the language they are excluded from. There are undoubtedly also *pre*-conscious operations of our bodies operating before and under the operations of consciousness: we breath and balance without conscious attention, but neither breathing nor balancing are subject to repression in the way other bodily functions are. Taking the 'pre-' prefix literally, there are components of the psyche that pre-date the emergence of the linguistically competent consciousness but maintain themselves, like breathing, into adult life. In Freud and Lacan, the exemplary pre-conscious state is neo-natal union with the mother's body, a lost ecological oneness we might yearn for or grow to fear but which accompanies us always. Sympathetic vibrations in immersive sound spaces tell us we are 'just being there alive, in and as the excess of sound' (Henriques 2011: xvii).

If ancestors are indeed present in language, logic and technologies, then there is also a *post*-conscious persistence in the world. Alongside all of these and threading through them is what Marie-Luise Angerer (2023) calls the non-conscious and N. Katherine Hayles (2017), in a different tradition but describing much the same thing, calls the cognitive non-conscious. For Hayles, cognition is a more broadly distributed capability than consciousness. Consciousness includes a sense of 'I', which implies the use of language or something like it among primates, marine mammals and others. Cognition she understands as an implicit intelligence below the threshold of consciousness, like breathing, and therefore shared with other living entities like plants. Angerer's non-conscious is more expansive, embracing 'technical, mental, and physical processes', not restricted to humans, but extending into, for example, the intelligence rain uses to find its way to an aquifer.

Proposing his 'sound object', an autonomous sonorous entity that cannot be reduced to physical existence or to psychology but operating in their interconnection, Schaeffer (2017: 69) writes, 'The ambiguity revealed by our brief consideration of the sound object – objectivity bound to subjectivity – will surprise us only if we persist in seeing "the workings of the mind" and "external realities" as opposites.' The ambiguity only increases, to the level of indeterminacy, in the light of the cognitive non-conscious. As cognition, vibrations in natural ecologies and technical devices are of a kind with the vibrations of conscious bodies and the mental processes they instigate. As extended cognition, hearing is the implicit intelligence of any sympathetic vibration, with or without consciousness or even life, dissolving any opposition between the workings of the mind and external realities. Hearing is the implicit, tactile intelligence of any sympathetic vibration, with or without consciousness or even life. Not only are we sounding and sounded objects: the world sounds through us, living or dead.

What might ancestral technologies be capable of if they are not constrained to the purposes of profit and control? We run a terrible risk if we let the ancestors loose; they have been imprisoned in industrial and digital technologies for centuries. They may be mad. The risk is as terrible as 'letting nature take its course'; whatever we mean or have meant by the word, nature has been so controlled and exploited, we rightly fear its capacity to devastate not only our species but itself. The only worse risk is not liberating nature and ancestors. Liberation might be dangerous in future; the alternative is catastrophic right now – species suicide at the hands of corporate government. A commons of ecologies, technologies and societies, of intellect, cognition and imagination, depends on the liberation of our ancestors and is our only hope. From the Divje Babe flute to the Golden Record, sonic cultures – so dependent on the dialectics of ephemerality and memory – realise hope by diving into the posthumous.

Preclusion

The imagination of the end haunts Anthropocene and post-Anthropocene cultures whose violent weather systems and burning landscapes are not only symptoms but cognition of planetary tragedy. Nineteenth-century aesthete John Ruskin's (1856: 201–220) critique of 'pathetic fallacy' dismissed the literary trope ascribing sympathetic feelings to a landscape that a poet might describe as weeping when she weeps or laughing when she laughs. When cognition and affect are no longer limited to consciousness, Ruskin's strictures reveal that they come from an equal and opposite *apathetic* fallacy: a now-foundationless belief that only humans, and only thinking, speaking humans at that, are capable of sensing and responding to the actions of the world. The implication of non-conscious sapience is, however, that even in the absence of observers, even in the gradually dissipating organisation of the cosmos as a whole, some vibrations from the deep past will continue to reverberate in a cooling universe. Zielinski's (2006) deep time and Parikka's (2015) even deeper geological time give some intimation of how models of the deep past now inform models for a deep future of the media – media which, as we imagine them persisting beyond the lifespan of either species or planet, we can legitimately call posthumous.

What kind of human is this, not post-human but posthumous? Like many other critics, John Berger (2015) saw in Charlie Chaplin's pratfalls a resilient refusal to be only himself: 'Each time he falls, he gets back on to his feet as a new man. ... After each fall the secret of his buoyancy is his multiplicity.' On the other hand, in *L'Idiot de la famille*, the philosopher Jean-Paul Sartre took Chaplin as the model of every human being 'reduced to impotence, reified, the human object [which] can only dream' but only on condition that it submits to being just an object (Sartre 1971: VI.B). Only once this human has learned to see itself from the outside, as object, can it exceed itself. For Norman Bryson, just as language speaks the speaking subject, so humans not only see but are seen by the 'gaze in the expanded field'. We fool ourselves into believing we are at the centre of the world when we exercise scientific or male gaze as mastery, but actually we are embraced by visibility that surrounds and watches us. 'Everything I see', Bryson explained, 'is orchestrated with a cultural production of seeing that exists independently of my life and outside it: my individual discoveries, the findings of my eye as it probes through the world, come to unfold in terms not of my making, and indifferent to my mortality' (Bryson 1988: 92). Looked at from the outside, every pratfall looks like the foreseeable consequence the little tramp never foresees. From within, on the other hand, every disaster proves the world is unforeseeable and therefore full of opportunity. Events happen to the Chaplin clown, not because of him; but only when he realises this will he have any chance of intervening in them.

Drawing on Sartre and Bryson, Vivian Sobchack noted that there is 'a different world – and a world of difference – existentially revealed through the nonanthropocentric gaze. This worldview is not menacing but expansive' (Sobchack 2004: 97). For Sobchack, it is possible to inhabit a world without forcing it to be an object, or ourselves to be its centre. Posthumous humans are no longer subjects or even objects. Without imitating or stealing the skills of *survivance* developed in response to the colonialism the West continues to visit on Indigenous peoples, it is possible to continue to inhabit a world in which the worst has already happened. For Hegel, becoming a self meant confronting death (Hegel 2018: 108-117) in a struggle for recognition that no one wins, the servant who succumbs to fear of death or the master who overcomes it. But there is no mastery except in the eyes of the servant, despised but ever watchful. Neither succumbing to nor overcoming but accepting death, the posthumous condition allows us to inhabit and be inhabited by the world after the death of the scientific, colonising, masculine master. Posthumous media, from the cave-bear flute to the Golden Record, are talismans against the long dark that comes after us. Posthumous, like our ancestral technologies, we can be embraced by our ecologies, able to hear without ears or brains. Like 'sustainability', inheritance only prolongs the timeless present. We inhabit posthumous time because the objectifying master is already dead. *Survivance* – to live on after the universal present – is only the first step. Beyond the ethical imperative to survive lies the job of devising a posthumous politics. Before that, however, there arrives the challenge of living with one another in the face of the end, as love has always flourished in the face of mortality.

2
Love

Human on my faithless arm
W. H. Auden, 'Lay your sleeping head,
my love' (1979b: 50–51)

The Liar's Paradox

Love takes time. Gratification can be swift, but, as queer semi-otician Roland Barthes (1978: 224) observed, in love 'There is not only need for tenderness, there is also need to be tender for the other.' The more time we spend curating selves on social media profiles, the less we have to spend on tenderness. With the rise of advertising-supported broadcasting, Dallas Smythe observed (1977), the majority of non-sleeping time became work time. The demand for attention to social media is even greater. Love requires leisure, the same way that the good life demands a basic quantum of food and shelter. The less leisure, the less love. Yet we feel intuitively and want to believe that love cannot be measured. Either you love or you do not and, even if rare or temporary, love is possible and we expect it to be total. Love needs time, but it promises to be timeless: a paradox.

The exemplary paradox is the liar's paradox – 'I am lying' – because it starts an endless chain of consequences: if it is true that you are lying, then you lied when you said you were lying, and so when you said you were lying you were speaking the truth, but if you were, then it is true that you lied, but then... To work, the liar's paradox depends on the claim that a statement is either true or false. One way of dealing with it is to deny the true/false dichotomy by insisting the liar's paradox is not a paradox but a contradiction. Picking apart the words in the sentence, the 'I' that states it may not be an 'I' at all; nor can you trust the 'am' that the 'I' claims for itself. This 'I' is a performer. Its implicit statement is 'I am too smart for you', which is not about the I's relation with 'you' but a statement by 'I' about itself. This is not a rare and brilliant philosophical conundrum but a sadly common state of affairs: I am lying to myself. I may even know I am lying to myself (perhaps that is what gets me through the day).

The liar's paradox is a challenge to dialogue. Like friendship and love, it confronts (and in this case fails) the challenge of the interpersonal: how to bridge the gap between people. We only need to bridge that gap because there are separate persons, but persons – anonymous, interchangeable humans – are not without their own problems, as the tentative solution to the liar's paradox – that the liar is lying to themselves – reveals. We only experience ourselves as persons because history has made us strangers – to ourselves as much as to each other. Social media prey on this estrangement, promising to heal broken souls with agglutinative friendships. We inherit personhood from a collective history of rule by division, privation and life stories at the same time as we are instructed to walk on our own apart from mother, family and clan. Individuality leaves us bereft of companionship, aching for more than the satisfaction of instincts, however modulated by biography and history. The same history that divides us makes us yearn to share. Even though it seems to be a statement about the present, as soon as it has been uttered, it becomes a statement about the past: when I said that I was lying, I was either lying or not lying, or both. But that was then.

Saying 'I love you' is the opposite of 'I am lying'. 'I' still remains uncertain – it might be speaking in bad faith – and even if it is sincerely said, there is no guarantee that the 'I' knows what 'you' are or may become. Where the liar only unpicks their past under the disguise of the present tense, love is a promise: it brings a future into existence where either 'I' will prove true and you will reciprocate, or either of those parts of the promise may fail, or fade, but in any of those cases, the words point forward in time. Friendship, affection and love respect the instability of self and other. I may not know who you are now or how you may change, or whether, when I say 'I love you', I will be able to live up to my promise. But I have already given you the right to judge if I truly care for you. As care, love is a particularly intense form of consideration, pledged not just to understanding but to its consequences. I do not just look out for you: I pledge to devote my energies and actions to your wellbeing, whatever the cost. When masses of people claimed to love the late queen of England, a psychoanalyst might have interpreted their care as projection or transference, and unreciprocated. Like the forlorn lovers sworn to be true in a hundred tales of mediaeval and modern romance, the crowd's loyal affection for the late monarch had a religious feeling, not just because its greatest expression was postmortem, but because of its resemblance to God's unreciprocated love for humanity, and the unreciprocated love of the devout for God: not a shared project but simple devotion, a quality which belongs to love, or something like it. To quibble over whether what these faithful-though-spurned lovers felt was love is to insist that love is coded as an emotion in a recognisable schema of possible and discrete sensations. But to define love, or to restrict it to a 'code of communication' (Luhmann 1986: 20), is inadequate. Even though, as Indigenous anthropologist Elizabeth Povinelli (2006: 17) asserts, 'If you want to locate the hegemonic home of liberal logics and aspirations, look to love in settler colonies', love cannot be explained by its political functions. Because it involves complex, vulnerable, fragile sharing, love is multilayered and symphonic, involving all sorts of affects – anxiety, delicacy, lust, anger, shame, consideration and care – and always mobile. Emotional codes help create love stories, but like any code, they miss the multiplicity and mobility of love as affect.

The liar's paradox stops being paradoxical as soon as we recognise that it is a true statement of duplicity. Although we speak of true love, nothing about love is certain in the way a liar can be relied on to lie. Lying belongs to the category of truth, as one of its negations. It belongs to consideration because it is inconsiderate. Love is true to the extent that it considers (thinks through causes and assesses consequences), but love subordinates the results of its considered assessment of the beloved to its care for them, and so we say that love is blind. Love stories are full of duplicity. Dissimulation is integral to love songs like Dolly Parton's 'I Will Always Love You', a hit for Parton in 1974 and 1982 and for Whitney Houston in 1992, with its opening gambit 'If I should stay, I would only be in your way, so I'll go', its theme of sacrifice for love's sake – and hiding the emotional toll – a constant of love stories in every medium. The truth hidden in falsification is rich grounds for comedy, and has been since the oldest stories we have. It reached a certain peak in *Bringing Up Baby* (Howard Hawks 1938). As Andrew Britton noted, comparing *Bringing Up Baby* with previous Grant screwball comedies *The Awful Truth* (1937) and *Holiday* (1938), 'The partners engage in roughhouse, epigram, and repartee; the anarchic consorts with the urbane; the infantile drives that precede maturity and civilization are suddenly definitive of them' (Britton 2009: 10). Other major film critics including Stanley Cavell (1981: 113-132) and Gerald Mast (1982: 133-187) agree, in Mast's words, on 'its essential thematic issues – human spontaneity, animal vitality, sexual fertility, childhood fun. Like *A Midsummer Night's Dream*', Mast continues, sharing with Cavell a sense of continuity with archetypes of comedy, 'the film's wildly fanciful and farcical action is the means to improve the amorous vision of its young lovers, so they can achieve a harmony both with nature and with themselves' (Mast 1982: 160-161). Remediating Shakespeare's bewitched young lovers in their moonlit Athenian wood, ecocritique must surely salute the assimilation of love to the woods of Connecticut where, eventually, the scales will fall from David's (Grant's) eyes. The motif is enriched, however, when Cavell, dwelling on the ambiguities of love, concludes that 'Nothing about our lives is more comic than the distance at which we think about them' and (reflecting on a line in the film about hypnosis) that 'if I am hypnotized by (his) film, rather than awakened, then I am the fool of an unfunny world, which is, and is not, a laughing and fascinating matter' (Cavell 1981: 132).

The critic's love of film – cinephilia – is as prone to being duped as any love. The corkscrew twists of plot, the reversals of emotion, the chaos and harmony, in short the duplicity of the beloved who is never quite who they seem and the lover who is never (or never consistently) who they think they are, are the stuff of comedy and love, but also of criticism and study (Rancière 2014: 1-15; Elsaesser 2005). The mismatch between the mesmerised experience of film and love has somehow to be matched with words: an account of the movie or a pledge of the love. Love, in Dylan's words sung by Joan Baez, is just a four-letter word, but it can never be reduced to letters and syllables. The repartee of *Bringing Up Baby* stems from the inadequacy of language to express love, just as its plot – difficult as it is to remember in the middle of the action – revolves around more words: the marriage vows that David never gets to make as a result of the night's adventures. If saying 'I love you' is a promise, it is one that can be made in error, that can be broken, that may be true now but not tomorrow. Alternatively, and this is not an intrinsic power of language but a function of the mismatched and misrecognised hinterland between language and affect, pronouncing the word love may make it happen.

Or the interplay may happen at the level not of words but behaviours or, in cinema, of acting. Compare two scenes from *Bringing Up Baby*. In the first, at night, after beaning Mr Peabody with a rock, at roughly the twenty-one-minute mark, Susan (Hepburn) is left alone in her car after David has announced he never wants to see her again (Figures 2.1a–f). As she turns her head from the car window screen left, her mouth open, her eyelids part closed, she seems to be taking his farewell as a challenge. Continuing the turn, her mouth begins to close and her eyes to narrow until she is looking almost down the lens, her bottom lip protruding pugnaciously, her face almost a mask except that closing her lips gives the impression of a decision made. Turning back to screen left, her eyes swivel faster than her face until her head catches up with them, the lower lip gradually receding, as she seems to plot her next move. That the shot depicts a moment of calculation seems assured not just by the key light and close-up framing (with some backlight to separate her from the unfocused background and emphasising her somewhat windblown hair) but by the way she moves back from the key light into shadow. Reversing the trope of the hidden face emerging into the light in noir cinematography, this last move effectively produces a

Love 69

Figure 2.1a

Figure 2.1b

70   *Good*

Figure 2.1c

Figure 2.1d

Love 71

Figure 2.1e

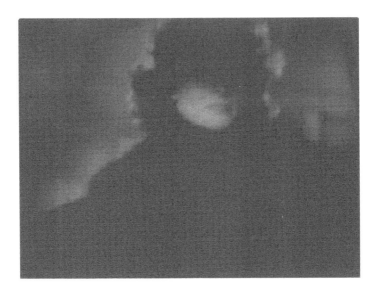

Figure 2.1f

fade to black, infusing Susan's zany persona with elements of film noir's femme fatale: dangerously alluring, alluringly dangerous. After David's last pratfall, the tonal variation from cunning and calculus to this fade into mystery, while it fits happily with the emotional swings and roundabouts of 1930s comedy, also evokes a darker patch in the moonlight.

Cavell's suspicion that he is becoming a (willing or otherwise) dupe of the film is at first borne out by this shot. But a second shot from the following sequence adds another twist. After a call from his fiancée, David gets another call, this one from Susan, who has just received the leopard. As she does her pratfall, David presumes she has been attacked, as Susan mimics the sounds of a leopard mauling down the phone wire (Figures 2.2a–f). Literally phoney, she uses several tricks from the Foley storeroom, upsetting a breakfast tray and dragging

Figure 2.2a

Love 73

Figure 2.2b

Figure 2.2c

74 *Good*

Figure 2.2d

Figure 2.2e

Figure 2.2f

the mouthpiece over a fire-grate to persuade him to race round to rescue her. Just after the last cutaway to David's end of the call, in mid-shot, Susan listens as David promises to come to her rescue. She is dressed in white in a white appartement in bright daylight, with a surprisingly neutral expression, made slightly haughty by the camera angle upwards from a few centimetres above the floor. Rapidly her expression changes to delight, illuminating to joy as she replaces the receiver and lies down, eyes closed, smiling broadly. This is love, not calculation anymore. As if to reinforce this new mood, there follows a crossfade to the equally brightly lit white hallway outside her apartment, effectively a fade to white.

It is striking that both shots, the close-up at night and the mid-shot in daylight, separate Susan from David: it is *her* transformation, from working out how to capture her man to a paroxysm of pleasure, that captures us. The comedy, as Cavell noted, may be an effect of distance – the distance of our observation from the film. But equally, across that distance, it is hard not to smile back in response to Hepburn/Susan's delighted grin. Is this a technical hypnosis, dazzling us with the flickering light on screen? Or is it that love is not necessarily an event or even a narrative but a tone, a chord, a floating zone the film has shepherded us into? Is love a world we navigate towards, one that pre-exists the people who fall into it? Is it, to use a term that is increasingly current in cultural analysis, an affect rather than an emotion? The literary critic Fredric Jameson offers a way to think this through when, noting 'the resistance of affect to language' (2013: 31), he writes, 'affects are bodily feelings, whereas emotions (or passions, to use their other name) are conscious states' (2013: 32), where consciousness is whatever can be expressed in language. Media and cultural analyst Marie-Luise Angerer (2023: 22) defines affect as 'the movements of connecting, interrupting, and translating between human and nonhuman', a definition she goes on to refine, very much in line with another cultural critic, Patricia Ticineto Clough (2010: 207), who describes affect as 'pre-individual bodily forces augmenting or diminishing a body's capacity to act'. Both want to distance themselves from the idea that affect is just a fancy word for emotion, while neither wants to restore the centrality of subjectivity after a century of Freud and post-structuralism that decentred (and often declared the death of) the subject. Bodies are at the heart of affect, not only because they had been largely omitted from discussions of consciousness before Freud, but because it is too easy to imagine mind as separate from the world. It is far harder to pretend that a body exists apart from the environment it ingests, inhales and inhabits. Affect is the world as it inhabits us.

For many working with the idea of affect, like Angerer, Clough and N. Katherine Hayles (1999; 2011), the 'nonhuman' points especially to the technological environments we find ourselves in: environments like cinema. Hollywood portrayed intensely individualist stories, but it was also a mass medium, playing to crowds, not domestic or personal viewers. In 1938, it had to make the whole picture palace roar with laughter, not just a target demographic or an idiosyncratic spectator. Its love stories had to reach out to and resonate with everyone who came to the movie. Resonating is a very affective word: thunder resonates when it makes the ground tremble, vibrating the air in your chest, shaking your feet and bones. An affect has to do something very similar: find some chord in you, in most or at least many of us, that will vibrate in sympathy with the movements of affect that sweep through a protagonist. Whether we fall in love like Susan or fall in love with Susan, the affect is *falling*. Hepburn performs a swoon that already existed before she swooned, a swoon that could be translated through the apparatus of camera, projector and screen so that much or all of her audience could share the fall. As medium of affect, film exceeds Deleuze's cynical moment, cited in the previous chapter, when a movie was only money, ferrying effects and affects across decades from its source capital to audiences outside the nexus of the cinema industry of 1938. The film works because swooning is already part of what we are and can do, and that is because, in turn, swooning does not belong exclusively to us humans but is a property of the world. And yet, 'I' and 'you' persist at either side of 'love', even if 'I' does not know who 'I' is, and because love, as relation, exists before and beyond its protagonists, 'I love you' always comes with the possibility that 'I am lying'.

The Intercostal Clavicle

The crowd became an object of fear in the fascist 1930s. Much of that fear was motivated by dread of communism, but the affect that whirled through the stadia of Spain, Italy and Germany was no less real for that. The fascist apparatus of performance, costume and amplified emotion was in its way highly cinematic. If it strikes us as a perversion of the naivety and charm of characters like David, it is partly because the roller-coaster reorientations of love as a movie affect are so unlike fascism's narrow range and targets: only hatred, aimed only at very specific classes of people like Jews and homosexuals. Though there are differences between 1930s fascism and twenty-first-century neo-fascism, both distinguish love as affect from hatred as emotion. Neo-fascism is characterised by its anger; its refusals (*anti*-abortion, *anti*-'woke', *anti*-migrant...); its masochistic self-portraits ('involuntary celibates', 'the great replacement'); and its devotion to symbols like the Flag and abstractions like Christianity (an idea rather than a religion) and the supposed 'right' to bear arms. In place of the wriggling pleasures of quick-change gags in screwball comedy, neo-fascism seeks uniformity so static that individuality disappears at the moment of its massification, just as money does in accumulation. True, fascism likes fancy dress. From boy-scout uniforms at Nuremberg to biker chic at the 6 January riots, even its crazier fashion statements are integrated into styles of dress, demeanour and discourse that proclaim that each pseudo-individual is indeed one of us.

Individualism is integral to neo-fascism, which differs from its 1930s counterpart in embracing individualism as an ideology. Not individuality but an '-ism': neo-fascism demands conformity with codes of dress and slogans, shared rage at common enemies, not free-floating, idiosyncratic and unpredictable personalities. *Bringing Up Baby* is surely premised on individuals, but screwball comedy works because its protagonists are as emotionally dynamic as its audiences. Characters who conform unchangingly, like Peabody, are unrelentingly lampooned and rightly biffed with bricks. For all their fancy dress and shock jocks, neo-fascists are boringly predictable. They even attempt to legislate against love, from California's anti-miscegenation laws that banned James Wong Howe's marriage until 1948 to 2020s Republican gay-marriage prohibitions. These attempts to force love to obey norms, to become predictable, all fail. All the evidence points to love being unpredictable, and people can indeed love anything and anyone. *Bringing Up Baby* shows love as an unforeseeable storm of sensations flooding through people which, like organised hate, can sweep them away. Like hate, love predates and shapes the one who hates or loves. Like a tidal wave – which may well be what it is – love does not offer a choice. The one who loves, swept out to sea, grabs hold of a floating spar and clings to it, without choice, because of the imperative demand of shipwreck. There is no market to visit where you select who or what to love: love arrives, or we arrive at love, when we are too weak and exhausted to resist. Freedom, if such a thing exists at all, has nothing to do with love – or hate.

Despite the stories we like to tell about how much less control contemporary societies try to exercise over love, no progressive history of freedom will explain the comedy of *Bringing Up Baby*. It seems humans are as weak in relation to their passions now as they were in 1938, or in 1595, when Shakespeare was writing *A Midsummer Night's Dream*. There is little to suggest a before-and-after in the history of love. On the other hand, even if, as affect, love rolls through the world and its inhabitants pretty much as it always has, the human world it rolls through has changed. Even if love is trans-historical, we experience it as historical beings, shaped by social and biographical experiences, mindful of causes and consequences, and most of all conscious of our alienation from one another and ourselves, so much so that we never know whether and how much a partner loves us, or how much and for how long we will love them. Alienation only makes love more difficult to understand. Not even knowing whether we are capable of loving ourselves now or in future, riven by internal uncertainty, any two find it hard to meet because both inhabit multiple versions of themselves. Since neither of them is one, they cannot meet *one* another. If lovers exist outside history, love precedes them as affect and flows through both of them. Ahistorical lovers are never alien to one another. As long as they share love, they can never misunderstand or fail one another. Without the contradiction between ahistorical affect and historical people, there would be no love stories. This is precisely the contradiction that *Bringing Up Baby* exploits. This other power, love, afflicts me over here and you over there, but because each of us has our own history, both parties are profoundly unsure of what 'I' experiences internally, what you experience over on your side of the relationship, and what you and I might do about it, now or in an indefinitely extended future. In contrast with the unquestionable certainties of neo-fascist hatred, love, as we live it, is always unsure of itself. Love is much more than the opposite of hate and, compared to the aggressive masculinity of neo-fascism, richly comic.

Perhaps lovers' inward uncertainties belong to the conflict between the biographical norms we pick up as historically specific members of historically specific societies on one side and love's flux outside ordinary time on the other? But that opens another conundrum: whether love is a discrete affect among many others or just one flavour of a common flow of energy. Are there many affects or only one, a rainbow we experience only colour by colour, but where all colours bleed into one another? Do Susan's moods in the two scenes from *Bringing Up Baby* depict two discrete affects – one a will towards capture (evolving from her Puckish pleasure in mischief on the golf course), the other a tumble into sensory delight – or are they moments of a single pulsing tide? If they are aspects of only one tidal affect, then David's very different reactions – walking away wishing never to see her again and rushing round to her rescue – would also be components of the same pulse, not just expressions of discrete affects proper to him, unconnected with her, and with no obvious connections over time beyond the way the film arranges them in sequence. Capture pairs with walking away, swooning with running towards, and there has never been a guarantee that love's psychic play obeys rules or even sporting etiquette. Singular or plural, affect or affects, the two who experience it or them, who seem to us and themselves to exist separately, alienated from each other and from themselves, also appear, to themselves and to us, to fall headlong into a connectedness that precedes their separation.

Affect, when it arrives, affects them both, and simultaneously makes each aware that, whatever mirroring occurs, they are separate in how they experience the event. When David admits 'It isn't that I don't like you, Susan – in fact, I'm strangely drawn to you in moments of quiet', then instantly follows up 'But there hasn't been a quiet moment', he is observing the gap between raw affect and emotion recollected in tranquility. If Jameson is right that emotions are words, since language is what distinguishes consciousness from sensation, naming an emotion not only tames the wild power and instability of affect: it creates a gap between environment and consciousness. To call all these swirling emotions by the single name 'love' – and to organise them into a comprehensible narrative like *Bringing Up Baby* – socialises affect in the same way that acquiring a language tames and socialises the polyglot babble of infants. Affect, an airy nothing, acquires a local habitation when it acquires a name, becoming a property of a consciousness, a language-using individual. Separating the great swirl of affect through the world into named psychic states is an act of control, splitting the ego between rational and irrational parts at the same time as it separates the world into discrete named objects, some of which are emotions. The transition from affect to emotion belongs to the always incomplete construction of a self. At the same time, giving it a name no more demolishes the spirit of affect than calling the spirit of mischief 'Puck' stops mayhem exercising its ancient powers. Love is the social and linguistic construct that binds two (or more) individuals together despite their having been pulled apart by socialisation and language acquisition.

The ethical dimension of this simultaneous distancing and rapprochement occupied the philosopher Alain Badiou. He took his cue from the psychoanalyst Jacques Lacan who pronounced that the sexual relation is impossible, because each partner desires only their own pleasure. Badiou argued that love must then be something other than sexual. In his little book *In Praise of Love*, Badiou ventured this response: love, he wrote, 'is a quest for truth. What kind of truth? you will ask. I mean truth in relation to something quite precise: what kind of world does one see when one experiences it from the point of view of two and not one? What is the world like when it is experienced, developed and lived from the point of view of difference and not identity? That is what I believe love to be' (Badiou 2012: 22).

Following Lacan, Badiou leaped from the selfish pursuit of orgasm to the truth of a world lived in the light of difference. Both 'truth' and 'world' have very definite meanings in

Badiou's philosophy, pursued through twenty years and three volumes of his monumental *Being and Event* (2006; 2009; 2022). Badiou's truth is a project. Love is the truth of the interpersonal world, as opposed to other truths operating in other worlds of thought, art and politics. Love is necessary because sex cannot bridge the gulf that separates I and you. This fits neatly with the portrayal of love in Hollywood's overwhelmingly individualistic films, especially the adversarial gambits of *Bringing Up Baby*. It doesn't explain, however, how we all feel movies' weather shining or raining on us in front of a screen.

The steps of Jewish ethicist Emmanuel Levinas' argument, nearly fifty years before Badiou's book, are bound up in mid-twentieth-century European existential philosophy but they come down to a similar ground: the face-to-face encounter of two strangers. First, 'The I is not a being that always remains the same, but is the being whose existing consists in identifying itself, in recovering its identity through all that happens to it' (Levinas 1969: 36). Constantly battered by events and experiences, a self is a never-ending project of restoring and reaffirming a kernel of identity that may be lost or misunderstood but which never changes. Meeting an other requires that I exist as this self-identifying, self-recovering being; indeed, there is no other that is not defined by its difference from the self – 'Alterity is only possible starting from *me*' (Levinas 1969: 40, original emphasis). Levinas calls ethics 'first philosophy' because it is not an optional extra: relations with the other derive from and confirm my existence, but at the same time prove that I is fundamentally unstable in its loneliness. Language connects I with others, but it can only do so by emphasising what we share: whatever is the same. Levinas wants to emphasise difference: 'Thought and freedom [the basis of ethics for Levinas] come to us from separation and from consideration of the Other' (1969: 105). In an essay condensing the arguments of *Totality and Infinity*, Levinas writes that I bring the 'extreme exposure, defencelessness, vulnerability' of my face when I meet my Other who 'becomes my neighbour precisely through the way the face summons me, calls for me, begs for me, and in so doing recalls my responsibility, and calls me into question' (Levinas 1989: 83). My incompleteness is not completed by the other; on the contrary, as a more recent commentator puts it, the Other is 'infinitely demanding' (Critchley 2007). I am called into question because I never entirely recover from everything that happens to me, most of all this encounter.

There are three problems here. First, the alienation of I from the other lies at the foundation of Levinas' 'first philosophy'. 'I' is what makes the otherness of the other possible. Second, Levinas, like Badiou, imagined a self already capable of thought, therefore of language, but it would be absurd to think I invented an entire language, and that my others not only invented languages of their own but invented the same language that I speak. The medium of connection precedes any individuality based on thought or speech (or for that matter 'rights'). And third, for Levinas, the Other is a generalised and abstract entity which, however, is exclusively human (no non-human animals allowed) and I must meet it face to face, not online or as a photograph. But when Susan makes David come to her rescue by rattling the furniture, she makes her demand through the mediation of a telephone, and we experience her falling in love through the medium of film. I am proposing three things, then: that there are many ways to meet, not just face-to-face; that meeting always involves more than two (there is always a telephone, a camera, language...); and that I and you only exist as effects of alienation, not as primordial conditions. Mediation and connection come first. Everything is mediated – not just by technical media or language but by being connected to the world – and everything mediates. Just as the impossible leopard in Connecticut mediates Susan and David's love story.

You could argue that Levinas is off-topic because he wrote about strangers and ethics, not love. But we are always strangers when we love, especially if Badiou is right and love is the lifelong, unfinished and probably unfinishable project of the two. My contention is that love – and the oceanic affect of which it forms one possible movement – persists as a characteristic not of bodies or consciousness but of the world that, each in turn, individuals come to inhabit. We catch a glimpse of it when an infant snuggles in its mother's arms, a bundle of sensations flowing through it, not even knowing inside from out. Selves only exist once they have been hoisted out of the flux of infantile union with the world, separated from neo-natal bliss and made to understand that their bodies are separable things. Only after they have been subjected to social norms and alienated by the rules of speech do they become capable of experiencing love as conflict, drama, tragedy and comedy: stories that develop over time. The contradiction between an affective world and an emotional self is what makes misunderstanding and duplicity possible and ensures the path of true love never runs smooth, to the amusement of everyone involved and uninvolved.

Kickstarting the story and keeping it rolling when it threatens to resolve itself is the intercostal clavicle, the all-too-phallic bone that arrives on the morning of David's wedding day. Three animals enter the plot to ensure it never arrives at its destination: Baby, the leopard; George, Susan's dog, who steals and buries the bone; and the brontosaurus that it is supposed to complete and that is demolished in the final clinch at the end of the movie. The phallic joke is complete when the bone, by this stage, has effectively disappeared. The phallus is not the penis but a *symbol*, of obsessive significance for any society determined to preserve masculine privilege. Guns, cars and – as signifiers of male potency – women's bodies are phallic symbols for patriarchal regimes (as folksinger Melanie sang in *Psychotherapy* [1970], 'a thing's a phallic symbol if it's longer than it's wide'). In Lacan's psychoanalysis, the phallus symbolises a lack. The intercostal clavicle gag is that David misplaced what never existed. On the way, as Andrew Britton argued (2009: 10), he is progressively unmanned, infantilised by various indignities which reach a sort of mini-climax when he bounces round in a negligee shouting 'I just went gay all of a sudden'. This surrender to polymorphous perversity presages his eventual acquiescence to the love he has resisted throughout the film, a surrender of the social norm of dignity that he laid claim to early on, in favour of the tides of affect.

The struggle between dignity – call it 'self-worth' to emphasise the individuality it constructs – and affect is never over. The growing human does not become *more* erotically focused during puberty but less so. It loses its immersion in its senses when adult sensuality gradually reduces to erogenous zones. Childish enjoyment of the whole mind-body in play succumbs to repression, and sensory pleasure to zonal reduction. Sharing food, dancing, wine and roses are the last remnant of sensory play, albeit reduced to rituals of seduction. The processes of repression are, however, neither universal nor universally successful. Love is not only excluded from the sexual relation, as Lacan and Badiou argued; it is only possible to love because sex is such a narrow, repressed activity. Whenever it is selfish, whenever it focuses on orgasm, sex reveals itself to be the result of repression. Love emerges from the *failure* of repression. It is unending – which is to say, it is historical – because repression fails in so many different ways.

Zero Plus

Levinas described a relationship with a stranger, not a lover. The distinction may be moot – a lover may be as unknowable as a stranger – but it raises the spectre of a third interpersonal relation between ethical demand and love: friendship. In the *Nichomachean Ethics* Aristotle notes 'his friend is another self' (IX, 9: 241: the Greek reads *heteros autos*). Commenting on this passage, Italian philosopher Giorgio Agamben, disagreeing with Levinas (Agamben 2004: 6), wrote 'The friend is not an other I, but an otherness immanent to selfness, a becoming other of the self ... Friendship is this desubjectification.' A friend is inseparable from me, can only be thought of in the relationship of friendship and is known and trusted (as a lover is not). Agamben makes a play around the idea of friendship as sharing: what is shared first has to be divided, and that goes for the self as well as the other that it befriends.

Agamben cites, as Derrida does in his longer book on *The Politics of Friendship* (1997), a passage in Montaigne's essay *On Friendship* that illuminates this idea, when Montaigne writes of 'a love which terminates in friendship' (I, xxviii, Montaigne 1958: 96). In an effort to clarify this sense of ending, Montaigne offers a short parable from Cicero (1971, 10,35: 194). Laelius asks, ' "And what if [your friend Gracchus] had ordered you to set fire to our temples?". "He would never have told me to do that", answered Blossius. "But if he had", Laelius insisted. "Then I should have obeyed him", said he' (Montaigne 1958: 98). Montaigne, disagreeing with Cicero, is adamant that, even at risk of a judgement that might cost him his life, Blossius answered truthfully: that the friends were bound together in virtue, but they were bound together in friendship first, so much so that neither would need convincing since the motives of each would be entirely transparent, so deeply entangled is true friendship (Montaigne forces himself to juggle with Cicero's opinion that since friendship is good, it must also be virtuous, which presupposes the virtue of both parties).

A critical aspect of this tale is that it is hypothetical: what if your friend asked you to commit sacrilege? What if, in the fervid imaginings of Bloom in Joyce's *Ulysses*, his would-be friend Stephen wanted to sleep with Bloom's wife Molly – and Bloom let him? Bloom is fantasising (it is unclear which of the three roles – husband, wife, adulterer – he would take up). Montaigne's example of Laelius and Bossius is more strictly an act of fiction. In this technical sense, friendship is fictional; it is not necessarily wholly actual. It includes in itself something that does not and has not but might exist or occur. Bossius' answers translated as 'would' and 'should' are in the subjunctive form. If such were the case (where 'were' is a remnant of an old subjunctive verb form), Bossius should, would or could act accordingly. Fiction consists in this play around a state of affairs that does not exist but hovers at the edge of likelihood: certainly not probable, possibly not possible, but just about imaginable – a scenario, a hope.

The Two that Badiou prizes so highly does not start from or become One. It is closer to Zero as it was defined by the mathematical philosopher Gottlob Frege (1953). Frege observed that anything that exists is identical to itself, and therefore Zero, which by definition does not exist, can be defined as the non-identical. Agamben's 'becoming other of the self' is an admission that the self becomes, in Frege's language, non-identical. So friendship cannot be determined by the solid, prior existence of each friend. Each of the friends has become other to themselves, as non-identities. If Montaigne is right, then the closer two people are, the less each of them is (on) their own, losing the self-identity of One. Only as they approach the zero-condition of complete non-identity do they truly belong to one another. Frege goes on to argue that all the counting numbers (1, 2, 3...) can be derived from Zero. The implication is that friendship supplements each person's non-identity first as Zero + you, then Zero + I, then potentially an infinite series, every item comprising the Zero of non-identity in an endless list connected by non-identity. Zero, 'the nothing that is' (Kaplan 1999; see also Rotman 1987), non-identity, is the difference that combines, and helps us understand the duplicity implicit in connecting and combining. Affect is 'an airy nothing' because it is non-identical. True love would only be truly true if it never changed, never evolved and never generated stories, since truth, because it exists, is self-identical. Non-identity is not true in this sense. Instead, it generates this subjunctive mode between actual and fictional, that may never come to pass but might. This wavering between non-being and possibility is not a truthful mode of existence; it does not even truly exist. Perhaps humans invented myths and fictions precisely to draw out this quality of the world; and perhaps it is when we are immersed in the other that we are most immersed in the world ('perhaps' is another subjunctive word: Derrida 1997: 28–31).

The same fantasy which drives the duplicity of love and makes love stories possible is a feature of love as experience and affect. Fantasy inhabits multiple positions (Freud 1979), most of all the place of the beloved. This is why love feels so private, as an experience or observed among strangers. Love involves secrets that only lovers share. As Derrida observed, 'The classical concept of the secret belongs to a thought of the community, solidarity or the sect – initiation or private space' (1997: 35–36), though he goes on immediately to contest this secrecy from the point of view of a friend who only speaks to you from a distance, who loves solitude as much as love and who can therefore claim with some truth to be truly other. The paradox lies in the claim that lovers can share each of their secret loves of solitude. For fantasy, this is only a paradox, not a contradiction. As a lover, you empathise with and inhabit that withdrawal, as much as you feel your own desire to be close. A secret shared is not a secret; but the sharing is.

But then feminist activist Sara Ahmed writes, 'love also makes the subject vulnerable, exposed to, and dependent upon another, who in "not being myself", threatens to take away the possibility of love. Love then becomes a form of dependence on what is "not me" and is linked profoundly to the anxiety of boundary formation, whereby what is "not me" is also part of me' (Ahmed 2014: 125, citing Freud 1961: 48).

Because the lover is another, they can never be wholly trusted not to put an end to love, but distrust reveals that the one who loves can never wholly trust themselves. There is always the possibility that love's anxiety might turn into violence. In her analysis of hate groups that claim to love liberty, love their country and love their 'white racial family', Ahmed is at pains to understand both the reversals of love and hate in interpersonal (and political) relations, and the dissimulation of difference that every bland assurance that 'I love everyone' uses to hide oppression. Ahmed's focus on dependence and the anxiety triggered by the 'not me' that becomes part of me disquiets friendly or amorous idylls. A hate group that identifies itself through a non-transferrable marker like skin colour is doomed to the same kind of first-person language that dooms any love story as soon as it becomes a first-person narrative (it is notable that cinema has in general been inimical to first-person storytelling: Robert Montgomery's 1947 attempt to imitate the first-person narration of Raymond Chandler in *The Lady in the Lake* is generally deemed a failure; it is hard to understand even the most 'Romantic' avant-garde films – Brakhage's *Window Water Baby Moving*, for example – if you reduce them to the point of view of an 'I').

Non-identity, the strange medium between you and I that bridges and separates us, translates every paradox, including Montaigne's imaginary demand for something I cannot give: a friend or lover will only ask for what they know I would be ready to sacrifice. The *fact* is that I can entertain an impossible demand; the *trust* is that it will never be demanded; the *sacrifice* is that I will never demand anything like that; and the *fantasy* is that if ever it were demanded, I would give. The non-identity of fact, trust, sacrifice and fantasy is the *gift* – that keeps on giving because it is never realised. Catholics were right to insist on confession before communion, not because I must be forgiven, but because I have to speak from the isolation of my soul before I can pass into the mystery of community. I must name my shame before I can share. If the infant's first demand is always excessive, its first reaction is always shame that it has demanded too much. Nelson Maldonado-Torres writes that Goodness 'refers, not to the need for things, but to a desire for the Other that emerges beyond any complacency. Goodness means, in this sense, the gift of the self to the Other. By definition, evil refers, in contrast, to the emergence of a concerted effort to put an end to the paradox of the gift and to render ethics unrealizable' (Maldonado-Torres 2008: 239).

Maldonado-Torres identifies evil with the colonial refusal to recognise the claims of the Other. Such is a child's demand, deprived of the shame that follows it. The ethical alternative is not demand, which in its own way incorporates the possibility of the gift, but sacrifice: the more or less willing decision to forego desire altogether.

Sacrifice is a retreat from sharing. Only I can know my secret honour. In place of being incomplete, dependent, at risk but also capable of demanding and giving in an incompletable relation of exchange, this new-constructed I withdraws into its identity with itself. Demand, on the other hand, when undertaken in love or friendship, never demands sacrifice because that would imply withdrawal into a separate self. There is no such thing as self-sacrifice: every sacrifice is an assertion of selfhood. The demands a friend or lover makes are always gifts: they give the other the opportunity to give, to share their selves. Perhaps this is why children confide in teddy bears, trees and pets: because it gives inanimate things the opportunity to come alive. There is another reason why we practise friendship on cuddly toys: not because my shame is safe with them, but because creatures and places without language sit exactly at – and so deny the power of – an otherwise anxiety-producing border, this one the border between affect and emotion where, as the song goes, 'I can't give you anything but love'. Language meets its outside in a teddy bear, the pre-linguistic moment before anything like an 'I' existed, the extra-linguistic world where, even now, 'I' is a transitory and local effect. Much of what Susan and David say is lovable, but nothing so much as her gag with the lost shoe, or his resignation as his brontosaurus collapses. Whenever love comes up against non-identity – and that is always the case with love – it comes up against the limits of language, and thus of everything social and historical. Hegel traced social relations back to the master–slave struggle (Kojève 1969: 45–70) and the fear of death, of the void, of non-identity. Masters and slaves cannot love each other because they fear non-identity. They act as if death was universal, but because each love is unique, love is not universal. If Hegel was right, love is not even social.

Love does share with death an understanding that whatever might be universal occurs on the far side of consciousness and language, but also beyond the borders of arithmetic. A mathematical puzzle of some importance for ecocritique is the question of whether there is only one ecology or many. Do I inhabit a particular suburb or a planet? Is St Kilda one of many purely local ecologies? Or is there one planetary ecology, an ecosystem that includes and assimilates it? The question is proper to love because it is a matter of perspective. When I consider how my day is spent among local shops, streets, gardens, houses, pets, trees, insects and birdlife, I can feel myself a denizen of this place. But when I observe the building materials, traffic, passing aircraft and docking ships, roofscapes of aerials and dishes, or note the weather approaching from the desert or the Southern Ocean, and chat with a neighbour about whether we will have El Niño or La Niña next year, I know I am a citizen of at least a hemisphere, and very probably of Earth. Clearly there is no single, unified ecology but a multiplicity of connecting and interacting energies and agencies. Even before the Anthropocene, nature has never been at one with itself. As feminist philosopher Luce Irigaray (1985) has never ceased to argue, there are always at least two. If nature as affect is non-identical, it would be tempting to see the human – singular or multiple – as the One that opposes it. But Frege's logic suggests that the first relation ecology establishes beyond itself, to the extent that it has a beyond, is not one, since there is never one, but the plus sign +. The plus sign indicates that even nature is incomplete, that it too always seeks a supplement and that like human lovers, addition never concludes the process of reaching out for the other which, like the blank space after the +, is no more self-identical than the ecology is. For obvious reasons, words cannot name the multiplicity that precedes and exceeds language. Equally numbers cannot count whatever precedes and exceeds numbering. So when sages say 'all is one' they very probably mean there is an endless flux of energies restlessly changing in multiple ways, directions and dimensions. Then again, whatever is defined by being not-language and not-maths is already in a pair, perhaps a love affair, with the more-than-one. The implication is that both planetary and local ecologies are incomplete, that they yearn for a relationship with something beyond them, that they may love us as much as we love them.

Connecticut

Because humans are alienated, singly and collectively, by histories of separation and loss from themselves and their world, places reach out for humans in the same way they reach out to every evolving creature seeking a niche to fit into. The problem is that humans, in the process of acquiring language and manners, have been repressed so deeply that they can no longer be trusted with the instincts that have been profoundly mangled in the process. If it is true that our first reaction was shame, we need some sort of commons to rescue us from shame or we would destroy ourselves. This is the role of confidants, be they lovers, friends, toys or places: to be the playground that teaches infantile fantasy to become communicable imagination. Billionaires, on this reckoning, are spoiled children who never learned to be ashamed. We need the commons to protect us against their monopolies and monomanias.

Not everyone can share my secret shame. We cannot and do not all love the same person. We do not and cannot all love the same place. The Connecticut woods of *Bringing Up Baby* have played no part in my life, and the river I played in as a child has never featured, to my knowledge, in any novel or film. At the same time, the commons is not privative: there are places enough to go round. Even common places that have already been ruined are deeply social, inclusive not just of ecologies but of people and their things. A vision of place like the imaginary villages of the nationalist right cannot be common because it is exclusive, welcoming only to 'people like me' who speak 'my' language with 'my' accent. The ecology of my place inevitably includes me, and I can share my love for it, but only up to a boundary where sharing reverts to exclusion, the moment when fascism mutates love into hate. Within those limits, love does not conserve place: loving it, I inevitably interact with it, walking and breathing. Ecologically, love is entropic. Thermodynamically speaking, it is inefficient. But it is extremely particular. Fascism's fantasy village is the face of an abstraction too pure to be real: a hyperobject, as Timothy Morton (2013) calls things we believe in and that affect us but are too vast, slow, numerous or swift for perception. Fascism's fantasy of consensus welcomes anyone who conforms. Love, on the contrary, rejects the abstract generality of 'anyone': it is particular, as in 'my particular friend', each love utterly unlike the one next door. Hyperobjects like 'race' or 'liberty' definitely exist – we feel their consequences minute by minute – but their existence entails forgetting the particularity of demand, risk and imagination that propel the gift of love and friendship. Only giving allows difference back in, thwarts the indifferent, expresses the non-identical. Everything else is just efficient.

Of course there was no Connecticut in *Bringing Up Baby*: the film was shot almost exclusively in studio. Connecticut is a state of mind, a shared fiction. Because this wood is fictional, it makes possible the magic of the night, where lovers lose and find each other on Venus' 'tolerant enchanted slope', evoked by the poet Auden (1979b: 50) a year before *Baby*'s release. A state of mind, as Auden says, 'Of supernatural sympathy': an ecology that binds together lovers, place, the spirits of the country and the ancestral power of language. *Baby*'s director Howard Hawks uses similarly ancestral techniques – in his case language, framing and lighting, performance and cutting – to create the dream-world of Connecticut, a placeless place which nonetheless reserves some socio-cultural and ecological reference. It is a place in the same way that Hepburn is at once an actor born on 12 May 1907 in, of all places, Hartford, Connecticut, and the luminous shadow-player we watch and hear onscreen, displaced and out of time. That interplay of embodiment and fantasy that lies at the heart of stardom is both an expression and an ingredient of the simultaneous specificity and abstraction of ecology as a concept and a felt reality.

At the same time Connecticut was a real place represented onscreen in its name and cultural attributes: a place from which golf-playing graduates of Bryn Mawr come (the elite women's college Hepburn attended), where rich aunts dwell, and where there are no leopards (a fact that delighted Cavell) – except that there are two, actually played by one leopard, although Susan says her brother captured it in Brazil, where there are also no leopards, only jaguars. Just as Connecticut is played onscreen by various Californian locations, David's Museum is identifiable by an exterior library shot of the American Museum of Natural History in Central Park, New York (to explain why a road trip to Connecticut is necessary and possible). Just as Susan is not Susan but a Hepburn performance, the trained leopard playing Baby and its wild twin is displaced, severed from its African roots, doubling as an explorer's trophy and an escaped circus animal, and attributed to Brazil despite being an Old World cat. The specific inheres and subsists within the fantastic, in the same way the road rear-projected behind Susan and David on the way to Aunt Elizabeth's has been at some point a real road, even if no one remembers now where it once was. To love a place is to understand these multiplicities, its ability to be itself and elsewhere, to infuse me with its existence while I infuse it with mine, to affect me as I am and as

I might be or have been or – surely the case with love between humans too – what I might be in the process of becoming.

Humanities scholars of my generation came up, by and large, through the schools of structuralism and semiotics, the former emphasising the power of structures to shape the world, the latter of signs to form it. The burden of semiotics was that the real disappeared under the weight of all the signification piled on top of it. For ecocritique, the real not only survives but permeates all signs. The burden of structuralism was that structures persisted, unchanging, as real things. For ecocritique, the real never sits still, even though structures sit on top of it and signs guide how to understand and interact with it. The difference hinges on the reality of things and our fondness for them. It is almost redundant to point out that this demands a look into what structuralism and semiotics were always accused of omitting: the question of what is and is not real.

Alain Badiou offers, in a book that rejects everything on it, a list of things that 'we usually and universally understand as "happiness"' – namely

> a quiet life, the abundance of little everyday satisfactions, interesting work, an appropriate salary, an iron constitution, a happy couple, memorable holidays, lovely friends, a well-appointed household, a comfortable car, a sweet and faithful domestic pet, trouble-free and charming children who are successful at school.
>
> (Badiou 2019: 34)

The domestic banality of the list presumes a wider world. One: salary, house, car and holidays, even schooling are marks of affluence, accoutrements of wealth. Two: as feminist activist Sara Ahmed (2010: 6) notes in her introductory survey of the wellbeing industry, 'One of the primary happiness indicators is marriage': Badiou's couple with children privileges marriage and reproduction. Three: the adjectives – everyday, interesting, appropriate, memorable, lovely, comfortable, faithful, charming and above all successful – reverberate in sympathy with every advert you have ever seen, from cameras that make holidays memorable to pet food that makes animals sweet. Four: success is locked into private property while friends, children and pets become symbolic possessions. Five: the closed system of successful happiness and happy success excludes the remainder of the world, which, like the schools that provide children's success and the roads a comfortable car requires to run on, are reliably provided from somewhere beyond the quiet life of the happy couple in their well-appointed household. Where social goods like roads and education can be taken for granted, there is no need to visit the world, let alone to change it. Badiou's list is as privative as any other form of private wealth.

A doctrine of individualism pervades writing about lovers, including Badiou's, tending to imagine they existed as discrete individuals before they entered into the loving relation. The obvious counter-argument is that David and Susan do not exist other than as lovers. We never meet them as individuals before they meet, except for David's back-story as fiancé and scientist which, when we meet him, is already in the past. Whatever individuality he has he experiences as a historical imposition. In the love story that ensues, imposition and individuality crumble as David undergoes his humiliations and disorientations, while Susan, as we have seen, moves from schemer to dreamer. Nonetheless, throughout the film, even in the final scene, each appears to the other as other. The impossible project is to overcome that separation. The night in Connecticut appeals to a prior non-identity which David in particular has lost by becoming a marriageable object. The woods are a utopian 'beyond' where boundaries no longer exist. Except – here the necessity of love as story asserts itself again – love of the kind we watch develop in *Baby* would not exist without borders and boundaries between the two lovers. David clearly and Susan implicitly experience this sense of an edge that separates an individual from the world not only externally but internally. Through their shared story, marked by the failure of individuality to create a coherent subject, both have to overcome their self-possession.

Love is always a struggle, political philosopher Cindy Zeiher argues, because 'love has a clear function: to teach us about lack and uncertainty'. For Zeiher, however, love does not create a bond: 'when in love with someone, we are all the while faced with our *alone*-ness'; love 'is a struggle one faces alone'. She does help with the problem of transcendence when she says that 'struggle renders love as both an empirical reality and a transcendental aim manifesting in the most ordinary aspects of life' (Zeiher 2017: 304, 303, 307, 305). Love is real, but also imaginary. It happens to a lonely 'I' that only realises how alone it is when it falls in love. Staying in love is a struggle because it makes me face up to my own unhappiness. And yet, to disagree with her findings, love is not limited to what happens between two lonely people. It also involves something older and stranger, preceding and beyond the limits of these selves. This beyond is what I have been calling variously affect and mediation – a mediating world that predates the formation of the selves that have been coagulated out of it over the course of historical and biographical time. There is love first, and only later people who fall into it. There are the woods in Connecticut, and only later the lovers who find each other in them. Flight from self-alienation is only half the purpose of falling in love; the second half is recovering the place where lovers meet, the affect that flows through both of them.

Zeiher's insight that love teaches us about lack is more historically specific than this oceanic mediation. Martiniquais poet-philosopher Édouard Glissant (1997: 8) illuminates his statement that 'Relation is not made up of things that are foreign but of shared knowledge' by telling us that 'the experience of the abyss can now be said to be the best element of exchange'. The abyss he writes of is the Middle Passage, the depths of the Atlantic where African slaves were thrown overboard on their way to Caribbean plantations, but his phrase evokes the void that engulfs all accumulated possessions, an emptiness that belongs specifically to the era of capital. Whether the owner of accumulated wealth, or the slave whose body was possessed, possession creates lack, a void, an abyss. So Zeiher's 'transcendental aim' does not transcend history: wherever it springs from, it is always shaped by specific conditions, in our era the great void of lack that gravitates around the black hole of wealth. But she is correct when she implies that the aim is transcendent because, against the grain of history, when it manifests 'in the most ordinary aspects of life', a stronger and longer-lasting flux emerges into the everyday. This 'transcendental aim' to escape lack and pursue wholeness permeates aesthetics as it permeates the everyday struggle to love. Like the liar's paradox, the conflict between transcendence and actuality only appears paradoxical, but it is real enough for love to hurt as much as it sometimes does. The real contradictions emerge at a border between selves, internally and externally alienated, and the ocean of affect. Like the sea, love precedes and exceeds whoever falls into it. But those who fall are still real people. Love intercepts but cannot cure the historical and biographical fate of individuality and the self. Nor is affect uniformly pleasurable: it is as likely to be experienced as unpleasant or even fatal as it is to be felt as joyful or sublime. Venturing to describe the indescribable (and love surely falls into that category), the only affect is difference. Like white light splintering kaleidoscopically, affect is constantly refracted and diffracted. In love, that rainbow of perceived and unperceivable wavelengths suffuses the encounter where the non-identical meets the unhappy identities of I and you, shows them how unhappy they are, and gives them a project to create something new that is neither of them, and both, and more.

Political philosopher Hannah Arendt (2006) floated the idea that, once upon a time, nature was immortal and only men were mortal, driving the Greeks to seek their own form of immortality through poetry and historiography. You could say they sought something like the endless repetition of nature in the endless repetition of their deeds and words. For us moderns, the boundless ocean of natural affect and non-identity is immortal, and love is our alternative to the Greeks' poetry. A love poem, after all, is only evidence that someone loved. But love as experience is a trajectory across time, an unnatural line through the natural cycles, aimed at a goal beyond them. Not infinity, necessarily: perhaps just a star to wish upon which sets us on a path that, without conclusion, is irreducible to the indefinite repetitions of nature and, at least to that extent, exceeds the mortality it comes from. Lack, the insufficiency of selfhood, its internalised exile from the world, urges the self beyond itself in search not of a better life but of life itself, more life. Staying still is not an option: lack makes the self chase itself around in its own circles like a headless chicken, incapable of kickstarting a trajectory. So when two run into each other, an event – of falling or stumbling into love that sets a line through the existing chaos – ties a kind of knot, a co-incidence of two pathless voids that makes the braiding of their energies inevitable. Feminist decolonial philosopher María Lugones described these energies as 'the playful attitude' which 'involves openness to surprise, openness to being a fool, openness to self-construction or reconstruction and to construction or reconstruction of the "worlds" we inhabit playfully' (Lugones 1987: 17). My energy comes from playing in your world, and yours from playing in mine, even though neither of us fits wholly in what passes for our own world, and each of us inhabits several, sometimes many different worlds – of workplaces, families, communities, artworks and love stories. It remains only to reverse the valence: in love and friendship, other worlds inhabit us.

This quality of love is not exclusive to human beings. Imaginary and subjunctive objects can become objects for love. That goes especially for intellectual constructs that fail to exist properly but provide the basis for experiments with actuality. Software is a prime example of this kind of subjunctive object. Cultural critic Wendy Chun describes software as 'models' and she asks: 'How can we emphasize [models'] relationship to hypotheses and other forms of reasoning that lie beneath, that are less than reality, but not for that reason less important and scientific? Perhaps one way forward is to embrace Latour's insight that "if something is constructed, then it means it is fragile and thus in great need of care and caution"' (Chun 2015: 692–693, citing Latour 2004: 246).

Chun evokes, in order to dismiss, the postmodern term 'hyper-real', used to criticise the construction of appearances that hid, buried and ultimately destroyed any possible reality. On the contrary, she calls on philosopher of science Bruno Latour to appeal to imaginary relationships – hypotheses or models – 'not simply to amplify or pre-empt human behavior but rather to change it' (Chun 2015: 697), 'to make decisions and coalitions beyond our natural sympathies – and, by doing so, invent new relations and futures' (Chun 2015: 703). This may well be how we should approach friendship: not as an actually existing entity, nor as a fantasy in need of tearing down and exposing, but as a dive under the fabric of the world to see what good there is in it, especially what friendships we can strike up with the non-human world that, thus far, we have for the most part only exploited and destroyed. The One that speaks scientific truth dissolves in the tides of non-identity. Against the hyper-real, where 'hyper' indicates something over or above, Chun suggests the 'hypo-real', whose prefix suggests under or below, an underlying condition assumed in every hypo-thesis. This surely is what has happened a billion and one times in the dark of cinema auditoria or in the flickering light of electronic screens. The actors, hypo-dermically under our skin, those airy nothings haunting imaginary moonlit woods, in *trompe l'oeil* reflected light as thin as quantum froth, scattering through neural pathways at the fringes of scientific or any understanding, enchant us, both because they seem so familiar and because we know they are entirely illusory. And so are the skins we imagine protecting our interiors from the threatening and alluring outside.

The illusion that we exist as separate beings is undercut in Chun's (and Latour's) phrase 'care and caution'. Love can be destructive. It is not only that our precarious psyches can flip from a feeling to its opposite. We might care for someone or something so intensely or sloppily that we destroy them (as the poet Philip Larkin wrote in 1971, 'They fuck you up, your mum and dad. They may not mean to but they do'). Care for place does not have to be driven by profit or hate to end up wiping out local species by replacing them with gardens and crops. The missionaries that destroyed so many lives and cultures no doubt did so from a deep sense of care for souls, even though it meant destroying the very people and things they came to save. Recalling the kind of care that motivated missionary schools' devastation of Native American lives and cultures, Indigenous scientist Max Liboiron argues that 'Care is not inherently good' (Liboiron 2021: 115), looking instead to solidarity across 'the incommensurabilities of different worlds, values and obligations' (Liboiron 2021: 25). Creating a 'we' out of the inconsistent multiplicity that I am and you are risks abuse. Gendered or simply physical power can infect and inflect love, not out of spite or anger but excess and misdirection of care. When Crutzen and Stoermer (2000: 18) ended their paper introducing the word 'Anthropocene' with a call to 'the global research and engineering community to guide mankind towards global, sustainable, environmental management', they were exercising care for a damaged world, but that care is a terrible gamble with ecologies already shattered by their exploitative encounters, now faced with the ministrations of more well-meaning outsiders. Can we trust ourselves, broken as we are, to be kind to broken ecologies by using technologies formed by raiding ecologies and imprisoning the creativity of ancestors?

The aesthetic politics of cinephilia has its own transcendental aim: to open the isolation cells of industrial technology, inviting at least one class of machines to participate in becoming otherwise. As the archetypal industrial art, the apparatus of cinema (cameras, producers, projection) can open channels of communication with the abandoned dead: the stars of old movies, the ghosts of old lanternists that haunt projection booths, and at last the anonymous thinkers and makers whose dead labour makes the whole technology possible. The care we cinephiles lavish on the medium absolves us from the guilt of all that we continue to exploit. Angst about artificial intelligence in the 2020s returns to the haunted media of the late nineteenth century: the departed who learned to tap tables after Samuel Morse introduced his telegraphic code; the radio wavebands where spectres howled; and the experimental gramophone records and filmstrips that reanimated the deceased (Sconce 2000). Machines were never inert until they became the complex implements of industrial capital. In media technologies, the repressed ancestral labour congealed in those devices returns. I call it love because we love even inert objects, but we love them in complex and nuanced interactions, of the kind the poet W. H. Auden observed in his elegy for another poet, W. B. Yeats: 'By mourning tongues The death of the poet was kept from his poems' (Auden 1979a: 80-82). Breathing life into the written words of the dead overcomes what we most dread about mortality: the separation that sad Western traditions assure us is the fate of the deceased. The love of things, of place, of each other oversteps the imposed loneliness of modernity and the centuries-long separation of humans from their natural and artificial worlds.

Caution is not a reason not to love. Love means always having to say you are sorry: always modifying what you say, do and think. Love is never reciprocal. It demands submission because, in love, nothing is commensurable. Not even the self, confronted with its own illusory existence in front of the movie screen, can be measured against itself, or even against the machines that it loves. Love is given: it cannot be exchanged. That is why, without love, there is only the marketplace and the angry self-assurance that fascists seem to enjoy so much. Extending love beyond the human to places, animals and machines brings deep feelings and greater obligations. Loving neighbours across the threshold between worlds makes it possible and necessary to change. True, there is unknowable risk involved. Excessive, misdirected care can be hurtful and harmful. But it is better to take that risk than accept the absolute certainty that refusing love and its changes will condemn you to endless loneliness, anger or, worse still, apathy.

2.1 Apathy

Charity, community, duty and struggle are good: not only sanctified and rewarding but good in themselves. And yet the evidence is that they are being replaced by social pathologies, social media bubbles and echo-chambers, trolls and splenetic outbursts. Fury appears to be the dominant emotional state of our times. More reflective commentators, including William Davies (2018) and Joseph Vogl (2023), acknowledge the same condition where 'knowledge becomes more valued for its speed and impact than for its cold objectivity, and emotive falsehood often travels faster than fact'. It can also generate another emotional state in which 'otherwise peaceful situations can come to feel dangerous, until eventually they really are' (Davies 2018: 3). As Davies has argued, we live in a reaction economy, whose most suspect citizens are the apathetic. Today, the opposite of hope is no longer despair: it is apathy.

Probably reflecting on the planned economy of Soviet-era East Germany, Bloch (1988: 16) insisted that no future can be planned because implementing a plan forged in the present maintains the present, but the future is by definition different from what we have now. Utopia, or any future worth having, cannot be imagined using the wits of the present. It must emerge, unforeseen, in its own right. To hope is to abandon any claim on what the future must look like in favour of trust that it will appear, it will be different and it will be better. The *locus classicus* of this form of blank utopianism in Bloch's Marxist tradition appears in chapter 48 of the third, unfinished volume of Marx's *Capital*:

the realm of freedom actually begins only where labour which is determined by necessity and mundane considerations ceases; thus in the very nature of things it lies beyond the sphere of actual material production. ... Freedom in this field can only consist in socialised man, the associated producers, rationally regulating their interchange with Nature, bringing it under their common control, instead of being ruled by it as by the blind forces of Nature. ... But it nonetheless still remains a realm of necessity. Beyond it begins that development of human energy which is an end in itself, the true realm of freedom, which, however, can blossom forth only with this realm of necessity as its basis.

(Marx 1959: 820)

Marx's 'realm of freedom', which receives few other mentions and no further detailing, grounds Bloch's futurology by refusing to describe what the realm might look like or how it might be recognised. On the other hand, Marx does specify, in the next sentence, that shortening the working day is the necessary first step, and in the cited passage is clear that the social regulation of work, rather than its exploitation by capital, is the first political goal. We have no idea what freedom might be like, but we are obligated to make the first moves towards it.

It is precisely this first step that seems so impossible to take when wealth and power tirelessly promote the idea that no change is possible or desirable. One technique is the neo-populist policy of blaming powerless enemies for creating unhappiness and anxiety. A second is to shift the blame from the industries that produce pollution – plastic bags, fertilisers, industrial meat production – onto consumers. The most extreme and most researched offenders in this activity are fossil fuel companies (Lopéz 2023). The process began, at least in its contemporary form, in the year 2000, when 'British Petroleum, the second largest non-state owned oil company in the world ... hired the public relations professionals Ogilvy & Mather to promote the slant that climate change is not the fault of an oil giant, but that of individuals' for a prize-winning campaign that popularised the phrase 'carbon footprint'

(Kaufmann 2020). Together, the five major oil companies spent more than USD 3.5 billion on advertising between 1986 and 2020 (Brulle et al. 2020). In a particularly egregious case of hypocrisy, Exxon spent millions on climate research but millions more on paid advertorials in *The New York Times* denying climate change and blaming consumers (Supran and Oreskes 2021; see Hartmann et al. 2023). Even the most influential media events, like the much-garlanded movie *An Inconvenient Truth* (Davis Guggenheim 2006), with Al Gore's famous PowerPoint presentation, can scarcely hope for the kinds of reach and impact that this scale of advertising spend, backed up with access to and influence over politicians and political parties, can have on setting agendas, stifling contrary opinions and promoting an overwhelming sense of guilt that, as individual consumers, nothing we do or can do seems to make a difference.

Disaffected consumption is matched with a series of more directly political modes of disempowerment. Distrust of journalism – largely borne out by the immorality and triviality of celebrity-watching and much crime reporting as much as by the readiness to accept advertorial spend, kowtow to advertisers and seek, like the fossil fuel or any other major industry, the succour and support of governments – meets the old joke, 'How can you tell when a politician is lying? Their lips move'. A growing belief that all politicians are corrupt not only protects those caught *in flagrante* but stains all members of the profession, down to the most downtrodden public servants. The old anarchist gag, 'It doesn't matter who you vote for, the government gets in' has now become a truism for millions of disaffected citizens. Most distressing of all is the economic, political and increasingly cultural turn away from the obligation of hospitality to migrants. In a culture of victim-blaming, migrants are credited with heinous assaults on the values espoused by the new Right. The 272 million people, or 3.5 per cent of the global population, living in countries other than those of their birth by 2019 pre-pandemic figures, not including those 'internally displaced' by war, famine and environmental collapse, are among the most powerless, despite being blamed for a range of ills over which they have no control (Sassen 2022).

These relatively limited cases – of consumers in the wealthy parts of the world, of migrants and other victims of abuse and discrimination and the large section of the citizenry that has given up voting – can account for a substantial part of the social generation of apathy. There is little to gain from blaming the innocent for their apathy. It is more important to ask why apathy is an available stance for everyone, temporarily, eventually, sometimes. Some people are apathetic all the time, but all people are apathetic some of the time. What social formations can explain why, alongside the 'resources of hope', there are also, everywhere, resources, if not of despair, at least of disaffection? There are at least two interacting sources of apathy, the first political, the second economic.

Concluding an essay on 'slow death', 'the physical wearing out of a population and the deterioration of people in that population,' Lauren Berlant writes that, while some find activist routes out of the condition, 'for most, the overwhelming present is less well symbolized by energizing images of sustainable life, less guaranteed than ever by the glorious promise of bodily longevity and social security, than it is expressed in regimes of exhausted practical sovereignty, lateral agency, and, sometimes, counterabsorption in episodic refreshment, for example, in sex, or spacing out, or food that is not for thought' (Berlant 2007: 754, 780).

'Practical sovereignty' refers, loosely, to the lived experience of being ruled and 'lateral agency' to 'an activity of maintenance, not making; fantasy, without grandiosity; sentience, without full intentionality' (Berlant 2007: 759). Her essay might be read as a response to an earlier and far less precise meditation on the silence of the silent majority by the French sociologist Jean Baudrillard: 'traditional resistance consists of reinterpreting messages according to the group's own code and for its own ends. The masses, on the contrary, accept everything and redirect everything en bloc into the spectacular, without requiring any other code, without requiring any meaning, ultimately without resistance, but making everything slide into an indeterminate sphere which is not even that of non-sense, but that of overall manipulation/fascination' (Baudrillard 1983: 43–44).

Berlant's 'spacing out' describes a condition very like Baudrillard's meaningless fascination, but Berlant advances on Baudrillard with her insistence that Left/Green utopians – and perhaps all who believe in the final justice of the Last Days – cannot afford to turn away from resistance, however attenuated socially and economically. This is not silent passivity but an active refusal. Working-class pleasures (junk food, booze, recreational sex) are consumed in accordance with the disciplines of contemporary capitalism, but the carnival of overconsumption actively refuses advertising's promises of perfect bodies in perfect homes in perpetuity. Capital asserts the responsibility of each individual consumer for their own health and wellbeing. Overconsumption, consumers consuming so much they cannot work, is an act of resistance by a population that is emotionally and physically drained, and which sees no alternative to – no new socialisation that could mobilise for change in – the cycle of labour and consumption.

The political sources of apathy (overconsumption, self-harm and nihilism) are experiences of empty, unmoving and immovable time, which brings us to the theological aspirations of contemporary economics. Philosopher Theodor

Adorno noted that the 1755 Lisbon earthquake 'sufficed to cure Voltaire of the theodicy of Leibnitz' (1973: 361), the belief that God's mistreatment of humanity could be vindicated as part of a greater plan for salvation. Bereft of a guarantee that everything will end well in the Last Days, there remains only Bloch's indescribable utopia: hope for a future when the profit motive is not the sole arbiter of value, with no picture of what Marx's 'realm of freedom' should look like. A twenty-first-century principle of hope (Bloch 1986) requires not only a refusal to repeat the present but also, faced with imminent apocalypse, some kind of faith that there will be a future at all. The immense inertia of the oil and other industries and the political forces that support them are core engines of apathy. Their survival depends on there being no alternative to the present regime. Historian of economics Joseph Vogl argues that current economic theory replaces Leibniz's theological doctrine with an economic one he calls 'a liberal or capitalist *oikodicy*, a theodicy of the economic universe: the inner consistency of an economic doctrine that – rightly or wrongly, for good or ill – views contradictions, adverse effects, and breakdowns in the system as eminently compatible with its sound institutional arrangement' (Vogl 2015: 16).

Like its theological forbear in Leibnitz, *oikodicy* is a variant on the doctrine of predestination.

Vogl stresses the central role of the market in futures. Futures began as planned investment in products that take some measurable time to reach a buyer – how much to spend on planting next year's barley, for example. By the mid-twentieth century, futures markets were auctioning already signed contracts between suppliers and investors. The risk and rewards depend on successfully guessing what the future price would be, given there is no way to foretell them. The major challenge for economic thought, then, was 'to find a formula that makes the transition from present futures [that is, the price paid at auction in the present for the right to sell on in the future] to future presents [i.e., the moment in the future when the product is sold, not for an imagined or planned price but for a definite sum] both predictable and likely, transforming what lies in the future and therefore differs from the present into something that resembles the present' (Vogl 2015: 68).

The miracle duly appeared in the form of the Black–Scholes formula (Black and Scholes 1973), a mathematical equation for hedging bets on future prices. The *oikodicial* aspect of this is then that present expectations and future actualities can be reduced to a single number. After Black–Scholes, according to Vogl (2015: 78), 'in the long run, homogeneity between the future present and the present future is more or less guaranteed to prevail'. Today this apparently arcane cog in the machinery of financial markets is buried invisibly in the algorithms underpinning high-frequency, computerised ('algo') trading systems. Unlike the individual traders playing it, the Market (with a capital M to indicate its unity, mystery and pseudo-divine control) 'knows' the future. Individuals can bet successfully or lose their shirts but the Market, according to *oikodicy*, always comes right. Language speaks us, according to Lacan, but it would not exist if we did not speak it. Similarly the Market guarantees every trade, but without trades, the Market would not exist. Futures trading ensures that the Market continues to exist, now and in the future, indifferent to differences, indeed ensuring that no difference can emerge (Pryke 2010). The power of this projection of the present into the future, this equivalence of now and the future we hope for, destroys any possibility that the unknown and unrealised future of Bloch's formulation can ever come about. There is no future other than the indefinite extension of the present.

The chaos of the collapsing derivatives market (which includes the market in futures) in the Global Financial Crisis of 2007–2008, continued in the 'cost of living crisis' of the 2020s, does not disprove this thesis. As economist Elie Ayache (2016: 243) writes, 'Traders don't use derivatives to trade the underlying; they use derivatives to make volatility tradable.' The derivatives market not only turns disasters into profits (Klein 2007): it actively seeks out unpredictable trends and events ('volatility') as sites where the most exploitable differences between prices are likely to occur. The sad truth is that many traders made a killing from the market collapse. Now that everyone can afford computers capable of risk management, the most advanced computer trading systems rely on their capacity to seize upon instabilities faster than their competitors. As anthropologist Arjun Appadurai (2016: 95) says, risk 'is simply immeasurable by any quantitative means. This amounts to saying that in regard to such trades, risk and uncertainty have no practical difference.' Now that risk is a tradable commodity in its own right, any uncertainty about the future, any possibility of its being different, is already calculable in terms set in the present. Even the unknown, reduced to a calculus, has become tradable in forms that never change. There is no future.

It is then not only that there are cultural factors pushing many sectors of the population towards exhaustion, disaffection, alienation and apathy, but that the one thing that might motivate them, the mere possibility of a condition other than the one we all occupy, has been erased. In theodicy, no matter what terrible events occur, God will redeem everyone in the end. In *oikodicy*, even if we strung up the last capitalist in the entrails of the last oligarch, the system would still prevail, and the planet still spin inexorably through the eternal return of the same. Some factors from the past drive people towards apathy, but there is also this blank wall of the present where not even the greed of corporate CEOs is to blame, anger is of no avail and there is no point wasting energy on a nervous breakdown.

Apathy is the negative of empathy and sympathy, but it is not the same as selfishness. It is the absence of feeling, disengagement lived out as inaction. As one of the Seven Deadly Sins, it goes by the name of Sloth, in Latin *acedia*, the negative of *cedia*, care, which at the time sloth was defined meant care for Christian rites and obligations. In ancient times, it had been a virtue: to be free from cares was to be free to contemplate the highest good. Today we should conjugate its etymology as a descent from carefree to careless to uncaring. Contemporary apathy recognises no future because it is the offspring of contemporary capital's eternal present. It is a state of the soul that demonstrates how much the soul, as it already appeared to W. E. B. DuBois (1961), is a collective reality, not the protected and protective inwardness of an individual. Apathy does not describe the despair of those (like the inmates of the Nazi camps described by Primo Levi [1988]) who have already survived the worst and entered the time beyond history and therefore beyond action. Apathy is a banal, everyday emptiness. It is not belief that action is impossible, or even that nothing matters – it is neither fatalism nor nihilism – but the feeling that action cannot effect change. It is not a psychological affliction but a social condition, reflecting how the sharp edges of social control, which used to allow us to know suffering, have been smoothed to glossy digital surfaces.

There are creative reactions to this condition. Some accept the current state of affairs and work with it. In England in the late 2000s and early 2010s, you could see everywhere mugs, posters and cards with variations on the motto 'Keep Calm and Carry On', deliberately citing the design and font of public service messages during the aerial bombardment of London in the 1940s. Calling up the even-tempered, jokey Blitz spirit once required to survive the trauma of bombing, the chipper slogan now served as a meme for surviving the banality of the everyday. Carrying on, continuing to perform the necessary tasks good-humouredly, ironically or grudgingly, is not action – oriented towards changing the world, for political or personal reasons – but empty activity. It is a righteous and admirable response to the failure of meaning. The most widespread symptom in the media arts is social media photography, not inaction or isolated individualism but activity – careless and cheerful sharing, sharing even though we know that what we share – image and connection – only profits vast corporate databases. That knowing quality, its 'Keep Calm and Carry On' ironic stance towards its pointlessness and subordination, is its own form of resistance even as it is subsumed into the colonisation of emotion by affective computing (Wang et al. 2022).

Beeple's *Everydays* project (2007–), notorious for selling its associated non-fungible token (NFT) for USD 69.3 million in 2021, can be read as an exemplary form of activity circumventing older (ethical, political) aesthetic claims for art as action or event or encounter. Making a new work every day is work, in the model of the disciplined factory labour first described by Marx (1976: 544–553) in the 1860s. Beeple says on his site – beeplecrap.com – that 'he makes a variety of art crap across a variety of media. some of it is okay, but a lot of it kind of blows ass. he's working on making it suck less everyday'. Linking through to the *Everydays* project, we read, 'The purpose of this project is to help me get better at different things', giving as an example, 'This year I'll be doing a render everyday using Cinema 4D and mostly Octane, instead of trying to learn new software, will be focusing on some of the fundamentals like color, composition, value etc' (Beeple 2021; original orthography). The discipline of working every day, not to produce a finished product using commercial software packages repetitively, has two incommensurable but synchronous messages. First, producing something every day is a performance, but it also imitates the work that capital demands of disciplined labour. A generous reading would be that Beeple is striving to subordinate himself entirely to realising the software he uses, devoting himself to its potential rather than his own. Alternatively, Beeple is employed in perfecting his skills in the manner of Foucault's 'entrepreneur of the self', 'being for himself his own capital, being for himself his own producer' (Foucault 2008: 226). Foucault noted the proximity of these forms of production to the then-new stakes of consumption: that pleasure comes as much from learning to consume-produce as it does from the things you make. Beeple's *Everydays* are in this sense exemplary of the discipline, not of the factory, but of consumption at a time when it has become central to the new reproduction and expansion of capital.

As John Roberts (2007: 51) highlights, the artist's acquisition of skill(s) no longer transcends the social and technical division of labour in capitalist society, if indeed it ever did. The task of 'sucking less' is not about developing skills, which have vanished into the technology, but of adapting to its standards. Beeple's dexterity aims to exceed the increasing standardisation of digital imaging, but any innovation he creates is more or less instantly subsumed into the software he uses. Every patch and update congeals a little more labour, skill and knowledge as computer code. Roberts proposes that the free and subjective labour of the artist rescues their materials from the grip of capital and turns them towards a kind of autonomy capable of unleashing the ancestral subjectivity of generations of workers towards non-dominating ends. Beeple's everyday efforts to keep pace with the cutting edge of graphics software do not clearly fall on either side of this dialectic of subservience and autonomy, but his aesthetic category of 'art crap' points towards a desire to break out of the productive sphere and to pursue other ends, even if – limited by apathy – those ends might fall short of art's utopian promise.

In the apathetic optic, the difference between days on Beeple's Sisyphean treadmill is minimal: an embroidery of images over the void of pointlessness. As clever and witty as Beeple's ironic submission to the new conditions of exploitation is, note too his self-deprecation, much of it expressed in the language of defecation. The reference to shit evokes Piero Manzoni's infamous *Merda d'artista* of 1961: a limited edition of cans purportedly each containing thirty grams of the artist's shit, and further back the grandfather of neo-conceptual art, Marcel Duchamp's *Fountain* of 1912, a urinal laid on its side and signed 'R. Mutt'. One of Duchamp's first forays into 'post-retinal' art, the *Fountain* was not so much to be seen as to be puzzled over: is any old thing art? Is art any old thing? The lavatory as binary pair of the privileged artwork depends on a system which consistently marks excreta as dirt, 'matter in the wrong place', as Mary Douglas defined it, noting, 'As we know it, dirt is essentially disorder. There is no such thing as absolute dirt: it exists in the eye of the beholder ... Dirt offends against order. Eliminating it is not a negative movement, but a positive effort to organise the environment' (Douglas 1966: 2). The rhythm of Beeple's production, and his claim that any one image is worthless, suggests then that each product is an excretion and their regularity is not that of the factory but of bowel movements. The actual art would then be not the visual images but the process of 'getting better', indeed of calmly carrying on.

Collectively, these images are, to take his declaration literally, a pile of shit. At the same time, however, he already mobilises the contradictions of Manzoni and Duchamp with his term 'art crap', and so places his excretions in a distinctive aesthetic impasse constitutive of contemporary art (Smith 2009). The co-presence of the highest and lowest values is an aesthetic statement, an artwork, even as the artist's labour becomes the significant value, rather than the objects it produces – rather in the way that Duchamp's act of selecting the vitreous enamel is more significant than the object itself. At the same time, these devalued objects function at the threshold between the art system and its exterior. The fact that Beeple exhibits these cast-offs on his site and elsewhere maintains their ambiguity, somewhere between artistic statements and oily rags cast on the studio floor. Their ambivalence – literally their double value – knowingly, even wittily and certainly ironically, undermines the coherence of putting matter in the right place: separating art from non-art.

Douglas insisted that dirt's definition depends on its beholder, but so too does the aesthetic significance of art. Beeple's art is activity without action. It does not attempt to break the art system, only to show the fragility as well as the power of a system whose margins it operates on. Its success derives from the ambivalence of consumption and production in working with software packages, allowing that to permeate the iconography of the daily pieces: ironic, often dark parodies of pop-cultural iconography from cartoons to Donald Trump, all reduced to the same level of caricature, glossy (in recent years) like the shiniest of industrial commodities, and as prone to an absolute equality founded on the relentless truth of exchange value. Like Andy Warhol's and Jeff Koons', Beeple's imagery is a droll commentary on the commodity status of art that nonetheless – through the huge price tag on its NFT – rejoices in the commodity status it seems to parody.

The sale of *Everydays* established the ambivalent 'work' (labour, product) in a terrain where other markers of success, such as Beeple's commissions for Calvin Klein and Justin Bieber, have been sidelined in the production of the sale as news event. If Beeple's practice draws on an anti-aesthetic tradition in contemporary art, one that sutures the otherwise disparate fields of pop and high culture, then the production of art auction as meme is a particularly witty demonstration of the importance of activity, rather than action, as a cultural practice. Activity is not a goal, but a technique of *survivance*. In the dying embers of the 'post', especially after postmodernism gave way to the contemporary as dominant cultural category, screen and audio media permeate biennials, and the once warring factions of Mainstream Contemporary Art and New Media Arts (Shanken 2016) have made their uneasy peace. This reconciliation has taken place as the significance of medium-specificity, once a touchstone of modernist aesthetics, dissolves. Contemporary art of any seriousness has to deal with the ubiquity of digital communications as they sink into the infrastructure of the 'everydays' of Beeple's title. This disappearance of digitality as a specific concern coincides with perpetual, indifferent, ironic and ultimately pointless activity. Incessant but directionless, Beeple's *Everydays* no longer turn towards that posterity that emboldened so many avant-gardes. It no more expects the future to redeem it than it sets out to redeem the past. It is as if the future that once powered the media arts has already passed, and we ramble through its ruins lacking both nostalgia (dismissed by the pastiches of peak postmodernism) and the revolutionary yearnings, spiritual and temporal, of the modernist avant-garde. The auction that netted the USD 69 million is just another occurrence, one that lifts the veil of indifference only long enough to reveal that wealth is the naughty secret of art, a secret which everyone has always known.

Tabor Robak's recent work exemplifies a second response to apathy, a situation that may be catastrophic, but is incapable of drawing itself up into a crisis. Robak's *Megafauna* (2020) is a large-scale interactive installation featuring elaborately detailed animated 3D creations ('magi') moving through darkness in a multi-channel projection system. The National Gallery of Victoria website (NGV 2020) observes that these magi derive, visually, 'from micro-biology, advanced robotics, data storage, and sacred iconography' and from several of the domains most closely associated with the development of artificial intelligence: 'geoimaging and cartography, military science and weaponisation, banking and healthcare'. Unlike Beeple, who has several short films on his site critical of US military spending and the mortgage crisis among other issues, Robak is not visibly critical of any of the practices that give him inspiration for the creatures he displays. Though they may draw on military and bio-technology, especially their syntheses in scientific visualisations, there is little sense that these are anything but abstract figures, leading the NGV's writer to describe the effect of the installation as 'like a sacred space or a monument'.

Robak's light projection is only a monument if ephemeral events like Albert Speer's searchlight columns at Hitler's Nuremberg rallies were monumental (and there is no question of Robak's installation having any totalitarian aspirations). Yet it does call up a sacred space that involves monumentality, like a temple or, because of its abstraction, a mosque. Robak is known for hyper-realist renders, often of ordinary objects heightened by their immaculate sheen to the level of abstractions which, even though we are always aware that they are digitally produced and therefore hollow surfaces, can ascend towards the kind of spiritual abstraction that Kandinsky (1977) and van Doesburg (1968) wrote of in the early years of abstract art. Unlike Beeple's self-constructed persona as humble seeker after skill, Robak is renowned for his consummate artistry. His is less an abstraction *from* oppressive sources in the technological industries, more an escape *into* a world apart from them. This virtuoso programming also differs from Beeple's in that *Megafauna's* wilful anonymity lifts the work out of the last references to social media or indeed the social world and into a realm where pure forms, freed of the Platonic task of grounding reality, evolve according to their own other-than-human logic. What intelligence they have, and it feels impressive, is the intelligence of a cherry stone that knows to grow into a cherry tree, precise yet malleable as it interacts with visitors. The impersonal intelligence of these artefacts makes them sacred. It would be incorrect however to think of them as in any way, individually or collectively, sublime. There is no holy awe. An angel manifesting in the sublunary world is an occasion of dread: these are moments of wonder which, because they have been called into being, lack the terror that marks the sublime for aesthetic philosophy (Kant 2000).

Instead, they only evoke the sublime, recalling rather than embodying it. The copywriter's line is precise: they are *like* sacred spaces without actually being sacred in the way your eyes may be *like* stars but are not actually distant balls of superheated gases fuelled by nuclear fusion. This is the clue to the magis' charm, like life without being alive. These similes make the work true to the contemporary moment, not because they describe it but because they escape from it through the alibi of resemblance. They live, but not in our time. In some ways they seem to figure out a future through the science-fiction images they also draw on, but the future they elicit is a memory of the future as it has been depicted, somewhere in the history that bridges the consumer fantasy of *Forbidden Planet* (Fred McLeod Wilcox 1957) and the retro-futurism of *Blade Runner*

(Ridley Scott 1982), a futurism of Detroit built-in obsolescence and chromium fins, the future that disappeared in the design of parodic science-fiction films as far back as *Barbarella* (Roger Vadim 1968) and the post-postmodern post-futurism of Julian Temple's *Earth Girls are Easy* (1988) and Tim Burton's *Mars Attacks!* (1996). Robak's futuristic designs are the residue of decades of decay kickstarted by capital's promise of infinite progress and its delivery of more of the same.

The particular fate of the future in the twenty-first century has been to lose anything but its ability to disappear, like Lewis Carroll's Cheshire Cat, leaving nothing behind but its smile. Robak's impersonal magi, future entities here right now, defuse rather than refuse capital's future of perpetual repetition. The *Megafauna* go into battle with the perpetual present which is the only time when capital can make profit. Robak's particular apathy, the cool, unfeeling circulation of impersonal creations, offers immersion into an alternative present. In place of dreaming of a future, it offers an elsewhere. In a technical sense it immerses its interactors in fantasy, occupying multiple positions in ambiguous scenarios: to be male—female and passive—active, and to experience pain—pleasure, permission and revolt all at once and in succession in wondrously knotted Moebius strips (Freud 1979). The fantastic creations of Robak's world are biological and mechanical in form, visual and tactile in sensation, objective presences and immersive experience, all at once, and in succession, inviting us to plunge into an endlessly fascinating round of activities that mimic and expand the realm of erotic and artistic fantasy. Other artists confront the harsh grounds of debt: Robak mimics its perpetual recirculations as it defers the final payment forever.

Unlike Beeple's disciplined consumerism, Robak's shimmering artefacts cast a consumerist spell where there is nothing to purchase, freeing consumption of the burden of turning a profit. There is no entrepreneurial improvement of the self. Transparently empty entertainments, with no grand claims to meaning or historical purpose, they float apart from the economies they draw on for investment, inspiration and structure: pleasures of the interstices where apathy appears as abstract play of forms, colours and light. Visibly coded, fictionally autonomous, they are vehicles of a delight that no longer needs the alibi of moral or political uplift. Beeple's apathetic activity submits to the apparatus: Robak's escapist play probes within its limits for meaning and information in the pre-ordained outcomes of his apparatus (Flusser 2011: 33–39). It is not that Robak reprogrammes or redistributes its field of possibilities but that, by inhabiting and allowing viewers to inhabit an aesthetic fiction apart from society, Robak warps the probability field of the apathetic society like a black hole warps space and time. *Megafauna* works because the form of the work binds it to the frictionless, flattened affect of the apathetic society from which it offers an escape. Robak's abstractions transcend the everyday by imitating the continuum of change without direction.

Something similar might be said of Refik Anadol's huge multiscreen work *Quantum Memories* (2020). On a square LED screen 10 metres on each edge and 2.5 metres deep, *Quantum Memories* deploys Google's AI Laboratory algorithms processing 200 million databased nature and landscape images to produce immersive abstractions and soundscapes. As Anadol's website explains, the work uses 'quantum computation research data and algorithms … to speculate alternative modalities inside the most sophisticated computer available, and create new quantum noise-generated datasets as building blocks of these modalities' (Anadol 2021). The underlying computation occasionally fills the huge screen; at others code and visualisations play out or enact the infrastructure of computation in subsidiary frames before the abstract forms of the hero animations burst back. As Bleeker and colleagues (2020) note of some earlier works by Anadol using related toolsets, 'These animated visualization techniques do not make the data legible as such; it does not invite a distillation of information, but rather awe from these spectacular and also enigmatic visuals.' That sense of awe is only increased by the scale, the quantity of source materials and the mysterious properties of the technology, which, as Arthur C. Clarke (1968) might have observed, appears sufficiently advanced to be indistinguishable from magic.

Overshadowing its spectators, *Quantum Memories* aspires to the sublime. But Anadol's tasteful renderings of processing as coloured waves of light and mass do not produce those sensations of terror that distinguish natural–spiritual sublime from human–artificial beauty. Interruptions of the 3D animations with raw code break the illusion of totality to suggest that visitors should be amazed not only by the end-product but by the human and inhuman work of generating them: the operation of technologies and their combination with humans, both donors of raw materials and the scientist-artists who collaborate in its working.

The sheer number of raw landscapes uploaded makes it impossible to analyse what characteristics they share, other than that those we glimpse at the start of each iteration are largely touristic shots, often of landscapes with some cultural value. As Adorno (1997: 65) observed, 'Natural beauty, purportedly ahistorical, is at its core historical.' Landscapes are emblems of nation, of political struggles; they hold the bones of the dead and the dreams of settlers, and even science proposes, along with its structured understandings of geology and ecology, some sense of the pristine, a word we almost never use unless in conjuncture with the word 'landscape'. The raw landscape images are then far from raw: they are, in Lévi-Strauss's (1969) partition, already cooked. A collection of user landscape images might well tell us about what constitutes 'landscape' at a particular moment (like Erika Tan's *The Syntactical Impossibility of Approaching with a Pure Heart* (2012), an animated collection of mountain views) or about the state of human understanding and care for land, romantic, scholarly or historical notions, family memory and geological time. Anadol's source images have lost all the histories, memories, cultures and formations of taste that shaped them and made them meaningful along with their authorship and histories of sharing and showing. *Quantum Memories* witnesses to the conversion of cultural materials into raw material.

Anadol's real-time generation of outputs strips its source images of any historical, political or affective content. In the language of Shannon's mathematical theory, Anadol's installation, including the interruptions of code and data visualisations, concerns efficiency in communication. Ten or fifteen years ago, interruption of signal was seen as a glitch: either the irruption of external noise that showed the system's incompleteness, or of noise internal to the system proving its incoherence. On that basis, glitching became a medium-specific aesthetic of electronics. More recently, as leading glitch artist and theorist Rosa Menkman noted: 'Not all glitch art is progressive or something new. The popularization and cultivation of the avant-garde of mishaps has become predestined and unavoidable. Be aware of easily reproducible glitch effects, automated by softwares and plug-ins. What is now a glitch will become a fashion' (Menkman 2011: 346).

In the intervening years it has become clear that glitches like the code interruptions in *Quantum Memories* are no longer accidents but symbols that function as signal, evidence that data systems now prove their authenticity through glitches. Beeple's devotion to a daily practice belongs to an older order of work, based on human labour, grounded in biological rhythms. When Anadol pulls back the curtain to reveal the artificial wizard orchestrating the scene, he is acknowledging that human labour is not the most significant aspect of contemporary production. Users supply images in untold numbers. This historically new condition – where human creativity becomes a resource for extraction – marks a movement in capital from colonial expansion and enclosure of Indigenous land to intellectual expansion and enclosure of intellectual property. While it benefits from this enclosure, *Quantum Memories* cannot be reduced to propaganda for information capital.

The particular quantum aesthetic that Anadol puts in play is the 'many worlds interpretation' of quantum uncertainty, which holds that that many worlds exist simultaneously, of which ours is only one. The animation displays a computer dreaming of alternative worlds. This utopian dimension to the work contains a second, dystopian premise: that the computer can dream new realities into being, new materials to be subsumed into information capital, extending the grip of digital control to what *might* exist. As with the work of Robak, Anadol reveals a warping of possibilities beyond any discrete calculation. Instead, Anadol deploys uncertainty. The fuzzy linguistics of dreams fades into the fuzzy logic of computing, where quantum modelling replaces the Boolean true–false (1 or 0) binary with the dizzying regression of infinitesimal real numbers between 0 and 1. Where human dreams are the psychic play of fantasy, ambivalence and multiplicity, computer dreaming is rigorously mathematical, even when nesting the universe of the infinitesimals inside true–false distinctions mimics the nested fantasies observed by Freud, sequential and simultaneous. The dreams of Anadol's quantum computer show that the programme is either so deeply inflected by its human interlocutors that it begins to exhibit symptoms of desire or, and perhaps simultaneously, that its desire is in turn a symptom of repression.

Repression, the ordinary action of restricting and controlling instinct, excludes nature not only externally as dirt but internally as uncontrolled affect in the wrong place. The recuperation and assimilation of glitches into the aesthetic of the most advanced modes of AI computing is the occasion for machine dreams. The therapeutic process of living with repression produces the anomalous structures where a machine intelligence is also capable of irrationality, because noise has become not only a raw material but an integral part of its processing. *Quantum Memories* is not the triumphal march of cyborg intelligence, the acme of the perfected Market idealised by finance capital. No: what Anadol shows us is a klutz tripping over its own feet as it tries to drink up the toxins computation has expelled in the effort to produce a pristine internal environment of pure data and pure signal. This is not a Marvel superhero movie: it is not even the prodigious equilibrium in the face of incompetence and accident that makes Chaplin's little clown such an enduring symbol of the human condition. For all its scale, grandeur, intelligence and beauty, this is a slapstick performance. This tension between total programming and hysterical improvisation is what makes this work work.

Google's image database is an example of the enclosure of the commons of the general intellect (Marx 1973: 690–711; Virno 2007; Pasquinelli 2019). Just as no one can speak without entering into the commons of a language, no code is free: it depends on the legacy of maths and logic as well as the underpinnings of computational history, to which it contributes, but that precedes and continues before and after the act of coding. In the twenty-first century, however, the rise of expert systems changes the relations between general intellect and expertise. Marx described the skills of the weaver assimilated into the functioning of power looms that from then on stood over against the workers whose capabilities it now embodied. Today we face the same process in the arena of emotional intelligence. Our affective engagement with social and network media, processed in the form of swipes, likes and shares, is converted to data and applied to the development of AIs that, in theory and increasingly in practice, respond to the evidence of emotion. No longer satisfied with the givens of geological, oceanic and agricultural resources, or with extracting the patterns of manual labour, relational databases and their intelligences mine cultural, social and interpersonal forms and place them over against the feeling, breathing beings that they have been abstracted from. As Luciana Parisi (2019: 29) argues, the human subject itself is reconfigured in its interpellation by artificial intelligence, returning only at the end of this recursive cycle of abstraction as 'an experiment in steering knowledge beyond what is already known'. Looped into the processes of information capital in this way, the human being is compelled towards a fixed, frictionless and ultimately apathetic state of computational being. Beeple's *Everydays*, Robak's *Megafauna* and Anadol's *Quantum Memories* make work in the confines of the new emotional landscape formed in the aftermath of data harvesting. They play upon the new polity of apathy as the instrument they have to hand, making complex, dynamic works from the contradictions of goalless real-time processes. Through their variations on capitalist realism, escape and glitch, they instruct us on how to survive, in a world that is unlikely to sustain itself, even while we dully contemplate whether it is worth sustaining.

These works, for good artistic, ethical and even political reasons, operate inside the systems they query and parody. The more successfully the system predicts behaviours, the less it is capable of originality. The system needs human invention to produce the random numbers it can no longer generate on its own. The risk for every aesthetic experiment is that it may become grist to the mill of capital. But we cannot go back to some pre-digital Eden: every news report on war and ecological disasters shows how devastating a life without digital infrastructures has become. The impulse to succumb to the structures we have inherited is great, especially when global systems are so complex that not only can no single human comprehend them: even the sum of all humans could not match the speed and granular detail of the AIs we deploy. And yet it is essential to think with what we have: the apathetic present. Hope is only hope when it exceeds not only the individual but the human collective. It has been clear since Marx that humanity can no longer be thought apart from technology. Apathy spreads into the non-human machinery that permeates the human. Collaborations with ancestral technologies must start with the drudgery capital has condemned them to. A post-human commons will only be built from the unwanted. Apathy is the enemy of politics, but no politics is possible without it.

3
Cosmopolis

> we are facing modern problems for which there are
> no longer modern solutions
> Arturo Escobar, *Designs for the Pluriverse* (2017: 67)

Legal Persons

Apathy beckons, a graveyard of hope as profit is the graveyard of presence. Into it disappear all the futures that love generates in its many guises, taking with them all the differences that make love possible. Digital capital makes all its participants equally indifferent and indifferently equal. At least since the French revolution of 1789, equality has been held up as a political good, a banner for slave rebellions, suffragettes and anti-racist movements. Dismissing equality is a high-risk activity. The one billion women and girls whose income is exceeded by the world's wealthiest 252 men do not have equality of opportunity. Birth and upbringing shape lives in profoundly unequal ways: as the old joke says, 'If I was going where you're going, I wouldn't start from here.' The rare exception, a Loretta Lynne making her way from coal-miner's daughter to Nashville superstar, does not disprove the rule. Because equality is not a natural condition but aspires to be a good, it must be constructed. Equality before the law without equality of opportunity implies careful construction of rights.

That construction, even if undertaken in good faith, had to start from some principle. For Marx (1973: 245), the principle was clear: 'the exchange of exchange values is the productive, real basis of all equality and freedom'. Kant's Western cosmopolis, on the other hand, was based on nation-states and their shared, rational principle of equality before the law. Projects for an alternative cosmopolis argue for multiple, queer solidarities beyond the binary oppositions of resistance (Indigenous/settler, male/female, Black/white), dismissing Kant's pious belief in one law for all. No cosmopolis can be built exclusively on concern about how 'we' should live, only on how others demand to live well. When 'we' opt to care only for fellow citizens, or only for citizens who look and sound like ourselves, care swiftly becomes violence. Liboiron's (2021: 115) critique of care demonstrates that, if we attempt to look after the needs of others by imposing our own ideas, however well-meaning, we will do them harm. My care for you works at the level of dialogue in interpersonal relations, but not at the political scale. Even the selection of who counts as 'other' is an imposition. This imposed care is inherent in the monoglot, universal cosmopolitanism extolled by Kant and his colonial successors, a singular, Eurocentric, international law. This Eurocentric law and the principle that everyone is equal before it underpins the discourse of human rights. Although it is almost certainly true that without the discourse and agencies enforcing human rights, things would be even worse, the practical implications of rights have proved a double-edged sword.

Drafted (and hotly debated) between June 1946 and February 1947 (Morsink 1999), the opening clause of the Preamble to the Universal Declaration of Human Rights states 'recognition of the inherent dignity and of the equal and inalienable rights of all members of the human family is the foundation of freedom, justice and peace in the world'.

The 'human family' is a telling metaphor. Article 16 defines family as 'the natural and fundamental group unit of society', a claim rebutted by feminists and queer activists. The exclusion of non-humans exposes the declaration to ecocriticism; the claim that equal rights are the ground of peace can be disproved historically; and there is a question whether freedom and equality are incompatible. Heteronormative, anthropocentric and ahistorical, the Declaration was framed by an organisation of sovereign nations to define the obligations of states to their citizens. Implicitly in this opening statement, explicitly elsewhere, rights belong to individuals, not collectives. The Declaration leaves out stateless people, the subjects of the 1951 Refugee Convention and subsequent Protocol of 1967 (UNHCR n.d.) who today inhabit the treacherous threshold between moral and political obligations at territorial borders. For good or ill, the Universal Declaration is thoroughly modern in Argentinian liberation theologist Enrique Dussel's (1995) sense of the word: the summit of the long colonial road of Western Enlightenment. The Western secular renunciation of God as the sole source of law oriented European history towards the construction of 'inherent' and 'inalienable' humanity, even before the French and American Declarations of the Rights of Man (and the writings of Paine, Voltaire and Rousseau that undergird them). Human rights, as historian Lynn Hunt (2008) wrote, had to be invented.

The philosopher Richard Rorty (1993) argued that individuals are not fundamental because community precedes individuality (an argument that also undermines Hardin's 'Tragedy of the Commons'). For philosophers Gilles Deleuze and Felix Guattari, individual and family ceased to be the fundamental units of society before the end of the twentieth century. For them, not even the crowd, that great figure of modern sociology and political concern, could explain the dynamics they descried emerging in 1980 when they first published *Mille Plateaux*. Instead, 'we must use another word, the Dividual, to designate the type of musical relations and the intra- or intergroup passages occurring in group individuation. ... a Dividual scale, a prodigious new chromaticism' (Deleuze and Guattari 1987: 342). The individual was defined by the indivisible unity of a singular and unique person. Dividuals on the other hand are already split, and their component elements, materials and energies, are not theirs alone but shared in *ensembles*, usually translated as 'assemblages' but in French evoking set theory and musical ensembles like the Ensemble Intercontemporain, founded by Pierre Boulez, whose compositions feature throughout *Mille Plateaux* (Campbell 2010; 2013; Lundblad 2022). The postmodern sociology of dividuals and rhizomes ('in which', according to Glissant [1997: 11], 'each and every identity is extended through a relationship with the Other') echoes, rather bloodlessly, Gloria Anzaldúa's (1987: 80) 'mestiza consciousness': 'though it is a source of intense pain, its energy comes from continual creative motion that keeps breaking down the unitary aspect of each new paradigm'. Glissant and Anzaldúa's alternatives to Eurocentric modernity recognise that anguish and struggle are unavoidable but also encompass utopian components of the post-individual condition experienced outside the imperial metropoles.

Perhaps it was recognition of such anguished utopianism that spurred Deleuze to observe in the 'Societies of Control' essay some years later how, when this cacophony of resonating molecules collided with managerial attempts to control it, 'We no longer find ourselves dealing with the mass/individual pair. Individuals have become "dividuals," and masses [have become] samples, data, markets, or "banks." ... which in no way attests to individuation – as they say – but substitutes for the individual or numerical body the code of a "dividual" material to be controlled' (Deleuze 1992).

Distributed subjectivity disseminates the old 'I', but instead of allowing it to seek new rhythms and harmonies with the ebb and flow of its non-human environments, emergent forms of digital control stripped dividual sensations of their meaning or emotional significance before submitting them to regimes of capture and accumulation. Older stories about individual heroes and older philosophies of desire based on narratives, like psychoanalysis, no longer held. Managed dividuals and their inter-relations, shuffling in random Brownian motion, had no future. Digital capture organised data-dividuals in kaleidoscopic but managed patterns across an endless present, indistinguishable from any other data source, technological or ecological.

It is unlikely the drafting committee of the Universal Declaration was complicit in the management of the new dividual. It is far more probable that their faith in individuals and households was already behind the times or fell behind rapidly after 1949. The rush of cybernetic, economic, environmental and governance inventions in the fateful year 1948 (Rosol 2023) may well have escaped them. The 'human' in human rights was evolving at speeds greater than lawmakers were able or wished to keep up with. William Whyte's 1956 best-seller *The Organization Man* was an early harbinger of the changes Deleuze observed in the 'Societies of Control' essay, but perhaps the most egregious evidence of a new organisational mode of dividuality under control is that corporations – vast cyborg agglomerations of computer networks with human plug-ins – were already recognised as legal persons. Even though individuality has become a polite fiction, the cosmopolis we actually inhabit – the planet-spanning consolidation of science, media, management and government – is built on the individualism enshrined in the UN Declaration of Human Rights. Whatever its authors intended and its critics dispute, individuality has become a privileged instrument of rule and exploitation.

The universality of rights is grounded in the universalism of European thought, derivable from René Descartes' reduction of existence to the one thing he could be sure of: the fact that he was thinking. Because no one can think except in a language produced in common, the proper expression would be 'I think therefore we are'. Thinking disproves its own isolation. Echoing Hegel's master–slave dialectic, Dussel made a more dramatic claim: 'Before the *ego cogito* there is an *ego conquiro*; "I conquer" is the practical foundation of "I think"' (Dussel 1985: 3 [1.1.2.2]). The colonial *ego conquiro* kickstarted capital with its massive influx of gold from the New World and opened modernity by expanding the late-mediaeval land enclosures to the new territories seized from their inhabitants by the colonists. It also, according to Dussel, made possible the idea of an 'I' that thinks, knows and surveys, an 'I' capable of owning, including ownership of knowledge and the capacity for self-possession. Every 'I' had these rights, even though they excluded slaves and first peoples from rationality, ownership and being an 'I'. The founding right of the discourse of rights was the right to conquer. Folded into it was the right to exclude, which not only demeans the conquered, but exempts rulers from the rules they impose, 'a regime of *privileges and immunities*' (Mbembe 2001: 50). Exclusion operated both ways: what could not be conquered was dirt beneath the conquerors' feet. But equally, universal rule was never universal. The discourse of rights that emerged among European Enlightenment thinkers like Hobbes and Locke began in the claim to individuality and remains associated with it. But individuality has always been limited: 'life, liberty and the pursuit of happiness' did not include the lives of First Nations, the liberty of women or the happiness of persecuted religious groups (Baier 1993: 152). We have only the rights we fight for. In the abstract, all rights come with their respective responsibilities: no right to speech without the obligation to listen. Historically, however, rights have always favoured the powerful.

Declarations

Universal rights, even though they are in the main general to the point of vagueness, are pronounced with the unambiguous force of the unarguable. Making indisputable statements is the work of legislators. Like Descartes' foundational *cogito*, any statement is a work in language. Descartes' omission of communal language from 'his' thought parallels the Universal Declaration's omission of the obligation to listen from the right to free speech. Omitting the other from the linguistic commons excludes colonial and ancestral others from thought. Reducing language to irrefutable statements is the same procedure that reduces ancestral skills and knowledge to the 'dead labour' congealed in industrial machines (Marx 1973: 706). The discourse of universal rights takes control and asserts ownership over language in the same way that property rights in the design and use of machines enclosed the general intellect. Both processes enslave ancestors in the unacknowledged infrastructure of capital, seizing ancestral processes for their own purposes and freezing their (r)evolutionary potential. Deprived of connection with ancestors, proprietary knowledge reserved for engineers and lawyers is constrained to produce what capital and the law require: profit and order. Severed from its roots, imposed on the colonised who are taught how to serve it, imperial language enacts the universal truth of Western modernity, and no good intentions can protect it from doing harm.

Discourses capture only carcasses and carapaces that language sheds in its restless evolutions. The discourse on rights conforms to an ossified layer of discarded language, the law – not laws like the rules of syntax or the laws of physics – sites where the word 'law' has gone for centuries to seek legitimation and universality – but law as in the legal system. Here law is language reduced as far as possible to immobility: law is language in chains. There is no poetry in law (for evidence, read Leviticus, the dullest book of the Bible). It has the power Gadamer (1989: 459) ascribed to tradition, evoked whenever we recall the past in order to interpret the present, including its absolute lack of 'prior freedom to select and reject. ... It cannot unmake the event that it is itself'. Judgements can be delayed and punishments evaded, but law itself can only be obeyed or disobeyed. Unlike law, language, even a 'dead' language like Aramaic, is generative and unstill, and never submits to power, even the power exercised through it. As one of Gadamer's major sources has it in a pre-echo of Chomsky, language makes infinite use of finite resources and can therefore say absolutely everything, even things that cannot be thought today (Humboldt 1988: 91). With its restrictive extra rules and strict definitions, law makes only finite use of language's resources. Unsurprisingly therefore, law is not free, and therefore nor are legal rights. Various constitutions assert the inalienable right to pursue happiness, where 'inalienable' has the strict legal sense of something that cannot be sold. Yet we know that we bargain away the right to pursue happiness for at least that portion of the week when we are at work pursuing someone else's idea of happiness. Article 1, section 1 of the Californian Constitution lists some other 'inalienable' rights, among them 'acquiring, possessing, and protecting property', a right to a historically specific form of possession that has not always applied, and does not necessarily apply to all who live in California today. The only positive aspect of the doctrine of natural law underpinning the idea of rights is that it makes it obvious that law is never free from natural constraints, and its practitioners and subjects are always dependent on the world they try to bootstrap themselves out of.

Where do rights come from, then? If, as the UN Declaration has it, human rights are 'inherent', then they are God-given birthrights. But giving is never a one-way action. A gift calls for gratitude. When we give recognition, as Levinas claimed we could not fail to, we want to be recognised in return. God, however, has remained obdurately silent: He gives but does not recognise us when we try to thank Him, let alone give something back to Him. In its implacable implementation, justice takes on the role of godhead, wanting and needing nothing in return. Legal rights are given to us by a narrow class of humanity who thereby claim control, initially within territorial borders. Boundary-making asserts the primacy of legality over cultural tradition, the mythical foundation of the nation or clan. Despite claims that states 'had defined themselves from Thucydides to Bismarck by their claims to sovereign independence' (Kennedy 2006: xiii), the idea of sovereignty within borders is far more recent. Standard histories trace the idea to the 1648 treaties known as the Peace of Westphalia. According to historian David Croxton (2013: 351–362), the Latin of the Westphalian treaties did not even have a word for 'sovereignty'. The formulation in Article 3, section 1 of the UN Charter – that 'the Organization is based on the principle of the sovereign equality of all its Members' – was the result of fierce negotiations between the victors of the world war and the rising coalition of non-aligned nations. In the face of decolonisation, the Great Powers asserted a sovereignty that they had not needed before (Mazower 2009). Enforcing geographical and class differences long predated the UN. The foundation of the UN and its Universal Declaration made the legal monopoly of nations over their territories and borders a formal and defining attribute of states.

On the upside, under the Declaration, nations had to take on obligations to their citizens. What constituted a citizen in the colonies and to a great degree in their independent aftermath remained moot. Modernity/coloniality begins with enclosure and exclusion – of barbarians and savages, of the poor, uneducated and outcast, of other living creatures and of land and water – as externality, environs and resource. Kwame Nkrumah had demonstrated that, when imperial powers ceded sovereignty to their colonies in the period following World War II, they did not cede power. Postcolonial borders, set by the imperial powers, imposed a mode of sovereignty that could be exploited in purely economic form without the costs of administering a state or recognising its citizens and their rights (Nkrumah 1965: ix). That this condition still holds in the twenty-first century is clear from Colombian political anthropologist Arturo Escobar's complaint that so-called 'third world national perspectives … often emphasize sovereignty over natural resources' (Escobar 2008: 282) – to the benefit of neo-colonial extractivist corporations and the detriment of Indigenous inhabitants. Historian Giovanni Arrighi puts flesh on the bones of this argument when he clarifies that the post-war period brought to an end 'a governance which Britain was able to exercise by virtue of its control over the European balance of power, over an extensive and dense world market centered on Britain itself, and over a global British empire'. In its place, at exactly the time that the UN Declaration solidified and universalised the 'Westphalian' system, the rising US hegemony pushed sovereignty into crisis when 'constraints and restrictions on state sovereignty came to be embodied in suprastatal organizations' (Arrighi 2010: 76), like the UN's system of international legal obligations ('the international order'), risking not only the colonial mode of production and control but the capitalist system itself. Despite the obvious fact that migration, globalisation, computation, pandemics, climate change and bio-engineering – in fact all the hallmarks of the twenty-first century – are no respecters of borders, nation-states define themselves ever more aggressively by and at their boundaries.

As moral philosopher Annette Baier observed, 'We are a species who claim and contest rights, and the contest is especially great when claims are made about universal rights, but we are also a species who trade rights, who relinquish old ones for new ones, who circumscribe some in order to extend others' (Baier 1993: 152).

The trade in rights is fundamental to capital: I sign away some of my rights every time I click 'Accept'. The rights and obligations of states and the global 'rule of law' here meet a typically capitalist solution, one that ignores citizens' and non-citizens' demands. MacIntyre's sceptical approach to rights and freedom drove him to ask how to articulate the contesting energies of demands for rights from below with institutions enforcing rights from above. He believed that struggle is internalised as an amoral contradiction:

each of us is taught to see himself or herself as an autonomous moral agent; but each of us also becomes engaged by modes of practice, aesthetic or bureaucratic, which involve us in manipulative relationships with others. Seeking to protect the autonomy that we have learned to prize, we aspire ourselves not to be manipulated by others; seeking to incarnate our own principles and stand-point in the world of practice, we find no way open to us to do so except by directing towards others those very manipulative modes of relationship which each of us aspires to resist in our own case.

(MacIntyre 1981: 68)

MacIntyre's quandary can be posed as a psychic consequence of the collapse of British hegemony after World War II. More usefully, we can understand his contradiction as the driver of decolonising demands. Rather than producing guilty consciences, the internal contradictions of rights drive 'the basic, most fundamental, decolonial task ... in the domain of knowledge, since it is knowledge that holds the [colonial mode of production] together' (Mignolo and Walsh 2018: 177). Summarising this alternative thesis as the 'epistemological decolonial turn', Puerto Rican sociologist Ramón Grosfoguel places the struggle for knowledge in the context of the values imposed by the 'European/capitalist/military/christian/patriarchal/white/heterosexual/male' colonist. Attacking the presumed privilege of Western modernity of necessity implies attacking the binary hierarchies they are based on. Decolonial epistemology – the politics of knowledge – demands an end to

- an epistemic hierarchy that privileges Western knowledge and cosmology over non-Western knowledge and cosmologies, and institutionalized in the global university system.
- a linguistic hierarchy between European languages and non-European languages that privileges communication and knowledge/theoretical production in the former and subalternize the latter as sole producers of folklore or culture but not of knowledge/theory.

(Grosfoguel 2007: 217; citing Mignolo 2000; 2003 and Quijano 2007)

He concludes that 'Anti-capitalist decolonization and liberation cannot be reduced to only one dimension of social life'. For Grosfoguel, rights are never equal: they are always structured in hierarchies. Rights exchanged in an ostensibly equal market are always going to be exploited. Grosfoguel's alternative is 'liberation' (Grosfoguel 2007: 219).

Jackson Pollock, 1949

Liberation is not the same as freedom. Just as equality was once the political opposition to feudal hierarchy, but became the economic principle that all citizens are alike and interchangeable, so liberation, driven by anti-colonialism since the Boston Tea Party, became the legal category of free economic agents. Community and commons, like liberation, belong to the ontological truth of affect and mediation. Equality and freedom belong to the historical divisions of communication – the alienated actuality Levinas mistook for a universal condition. Grosfoguel's liberation requires 'transformation of the sexual, gender, spiritual, epistemic, economic, political, linguistic and racial hierarchies of the modern/colonial world-system', a list which is not only restricted to humans but includes elements that are all too easily positioned as psychological. Crucial to that transformation was the construction of the autonomy of art (Eagleton 1989) and, eventually, the freedom of the artist.

Martha Holmes' shots of the painter Jackson Pollock in action for *Time Life* in 1949, followed by two more photoshoots, by Rudy Burckhardt and Hans Namuth, in 1950 and Namuth's film of 1951, including a sequence, shot from below, of Pollock painting on glass, 'helped transform Pollock from a talented, cranky loner into the first media-driven superstar of American contemporary art, the jeans-clad, chain-smoking poster boy of abstract expressionism' (Protzman 1999; see Barber 2004). Looked at from a distance, the looping hieroglyphs of black paint along the 5.5-metre length of *Summertime 9a*, painted in 1948, look alternately like a lost script or stylised dancers in some wild forest rite. Organic, indefinite scrolling lines and pools of gray underlie the black, some of them fine as web silk. In places, spaces between them have been picked out in yellow, blue and mauve brushwork to foreground the irregular geometries of accident. For the most part, the bolder gestural lines keep within the frame, but here and there they pass beyond its edges. Stepping closer, walking along its length, spots of green and blue and short, curved brown marks pepper the edges of the canvas, then you see more of them across all of it. Closer still and you can see how the paint has soaked into the raw canvas, finding its own resting places, and how even seemingly more controlled areas of brushwork have been smudged, colour dragged a centimetre or two, the colours less pure and the canvas less clean than they seemed from further back. Close up, design gives way to chaos. You see how some of the thicker applications of black have dried with a rumpled skin. Like listening to a jazz riff, you hear the melody first, then the timbre of the saxophone reeds and at last the rasp of the players' breath. However celebrated his process, Pollock's *Summertime* is a painting, on a wall in the Tate Gallery. Like much early modernist painting, it opposes formal purity to 'primitivism' (Rubin 1984), clean lines to dirty surfaces. Its observance of the frame battles with the energy of the draughting to create a tension you could interpret as the struggle between making art that a gallerist could recognise, and liberation from all constraint.

Pollock became a press (and later diplomatic) icon of American freedom, strongly gendered – the artist as cowboy – and racially specified – bebop improvisations of Charlie Parker and Dizzy Gillespie brought back to white America. Most twenty-first-century comments on the imagery of Pollock at work emphasise his intense concentration, but the drip paintings also attracted 'My child could do that' comments, easily pilloried as philistinism, but also tributes to a democratic principle of equality: anyone, with a modicum of energy and determination, could indeed achieve similar fame and fortune.

Sadly fame and fortune are what economists call rivalrous goods: the more rich and famous one person becomes, the less wealth and celebrity – limited by supplies of attention even in the social media age – is left for everyone else. My freedom to succeed depends on depriving you of the same success. We can be free or we can be equal, but we cannot be both. Equality is indifferent: it de-differentiates all identities because, in a world of equal exchange, any identity is equivalent to any other, any vote is indistinguishable from any other and a dollar is a dollar. The equal weight of every vote, reduced to an abstract exchange in winner-takes-all democracy, consistently devolves into two-party systems that do no justice to differences between and within people. Equality's consistency makes the inconsistent ambiguities and ambivalences everyone feels about politicians and policies irrelevant. Equality comes at the cost of the freedom to live, act and think differently, to be inconsistent, even to oneself: consensus is the politics of consent. Even what is admirable in the ideal of equality before the law is denied by experience and reports. The freedoms that accrue to power, wealth and fame overwhelm aspiration to equality.

Alter-Cosmopolis

Previous chapters argued that a void in the heart, which wealth only aggravates, drives its flawed and deprived victims towards love and ethics. Mediation and affect provide the means to reconnect, but in the process love must re-open the wound before the tidal flux of mediation and affect can suture it back together. Wealth and love proliferate differences: equality erases them. Love, including the love fans bear towards stars and the love of wealth, however ultimately unsatisfactory, overwhelms the indifference of equality. We blame 'society' for the norms that force us to become anonymous quantities, and we strive for personal freedom to distinguish ourselves from social anonymity. But when we demand the freedom to love, we are looking for a new way of socialising, and when we demand freedom of speech, we want to speak to the society we otherwise wanted to abandon. Driven by privation, pulled by affection, the pursuit of freedom is haunted by contradictions. They become painfully clear if we understand the competition is not between freedom and equality but between freedom and the social and political ideal of cosmopolis.

Setting aside Kantian colonial cosmopolitanism, cosmopolis as world-city idealises the political-economic world as it might or should work in future. Greek-Australian cultural theorist Nikos Papastergiadis described cosmopolitanism's main attributes and instruments as 'denationalization, reflexive hospitality, cultural translation, discursivity and the global public sphere … a commitment to the process that Anthony Appiah described as the "imaginative engagement" with the other. Ethical relations with the other, political networks for activating social change, and cultural platforms for facilitating exchange' (Papastergiadis 2012: 9–10, citing Appiah 2006).

American philosopher Martha Nussbaum (1996: 4) gave a similar definition of the cosmopolitan as 'the person whose allegiance is to the worldwide community of human beings'. Anthropologist Bruce Robbins emphasised that there is not only one community and one, undifferentiated humanity: 'Like nations, cosmopolitanisms are now plural and particular. Like nations, they are both European and non-European, and they are weak and underdeveloped as well as strong and privileged' (Robbins 1998: 2). Revisiting the idea twenty years later, Robbins described a shift from the 'normative ideal' of Nussbaum's cosmopolitanism, 'from cosmopolitanism in the singular – an overriding loyalty to and concern with the welfare of humanity as a whole – to cosmopolitanisms, plural, which were now seen to be as various as the sociohistorical sites and situations of multiple membership from which they emerged' (Robbins and Lemos Horta 2017: 1).

Thus Cameroonian political theorist Achille Mbembe (2021: 215) makes the case for Afropolitanism, embracing 'the foreign, the foreigner, and the far-off, … to recognize one's face in the face of the foreigner and to valorize the traces of the far-off in the nearby' entangled in the histories of African diasporas and the centuries-long interchange with Phoenicians, Romans, Greeks, Indians, Arabs and more recent settlers. One of the great figures of the Afropolitan diaspora, Frantz Fanon, the Martinique-born fighter in the Algerian war of independence, wrote, 'So, comrades, let us not pay tribute to Europe by creating states, institutions, and societies which draw their inspiration from her' (Fanon 1991: 314), espousing a distinctive Afropolis of the kind Mbembe promotes. The idea of a universal cosmopolis reflects, in the very consciously gendered words of Puerto-Rican philosopher Nelson Maldonado-Torres (2008: 114), a condition when 'Imperial Man claims right of ownership everywhere. His cosmopolitanism works in the function of his power.' From the multiple perspectives of decolonising and feminist cosmopolitanisms, the old, normative 'worldwide community of human beings' appears as a typically universalising Eurocentric claim.

In reply, Papastergiadis (2012: 12) argued that such criticisms 'not only overlooked the aesthetic processes but also diminished the scope of the idea.' He returns instead to the ancient Greek dream of world citizenship among 'the early Stoics, who saw the cosmopolitan ideal flowing from the animating force of love that is present in every person,' rejecting the enclosure of the city-state, defining community as common humanity, adopting 'a non-hierarchical vision of cultural value' and encouraging 'an attitude of self-awareness through genuine curiosity and open exchange with the other' (Papastergiadis 2012: 82), adding that the Stoics 'asserted that human rights were not constrained within geopolitical boundaries' (Papastergiadis 2012: 82). According to Scottish American philosopher Alasdair MacIntyre (1981: 69), the Stoics could not have talked about rights because 'there is no expression in any ancient or medieval language [including Arabic and Japanese] correctly translated by our expression "a right" until near the close of the middle ages'. MacIntyre's belief that language determines thought is backed up by the power of imperial languages like English, French and Spanish to shape the sciences and cultures of the people they colonised. Against MacIntyre, 'if language can be employed as a symbol of nationality by a dominant group, dominated groups may, of course, exert the same logic and make political claims based on their linguistic identity' (Coulmas 1988: 11). Reviving Indigenous languages and evolving creole dialects shatter colonial languages' attempts to suppress the demand for rights. Only the colonist is trapped in language: the colonised are polyglot, and their linguistic diversity can explode into political alternatives at any moment. It may well be that, even without a word for 'rights', the Stoics could indeed believe that the rights they might demand and exercise could be different in different times for different people.

Twenty-first-century migration makes it impossible to ignore the intensifying power of geopolitical borders (Papastergiadis 2000). The interstate system that emerged in the wake of Europe's colonial expansion after 1492 created 'not only rank order [of the imperial powers] but sets of rules for the interactions of states with each other' (Quijano and Wallerstein 1992: 550). MacIntyre critiques Kant's (1983) assertion that shared principles of law, freedom and equality tied nations to a cosmopolitan 'intent', even before cosmopolis itself could be realised. Like Hegel after him, Kant clearly felt that history had a goal, in Kant's case universal peace. Political philosopher Cornelis Castoriadis (1987: 184), passionate eulogist of creativity and autonomy, refused that view, writing that 'what is given in and through history is not the determined sequence of the determinate but the emergence of radical alterity, immanent creation, nontrivial novelty'. History is not pre-ordained by its end, or indeed by its origins: history is a tale of inexplicable ruptures, unexpected encounters and the emergence of new claims voiced in new languages. History is not the unfolding of a predestined goal but 'ontological genesis', the arrival, over and over again, of new and unforeseeable realities coming into being when 'Society institutes itself ... with no analogue or precedent' (Castoriadis 1987: 181) – not realising some cosmic plan but creating itself anew every time. Rejecting the vanishing present of accumulation analysed in Chapter 1, Pollock's drip paintings seize on the present as the only moment in all of history when it is possible to act. The past is done, the future has not arrived: only now can anyone do anything – only now is anyone free. Castoriadis is in tune with Pollock's action painting, overturning rationalism and tradition in favour of opening windows onto impossibly new vistas.

It is easily argued that Pollock's autonomous actions were circumscribed by the artworld that surrounded and, from the late 1940s, nurtured and contained his all-American freedom (Guilbaut 1983; for a contrary view, see Craven 1999: 45–9), and that the source of his improvisational technique for liberating paint from its old servitude was stolen thoughtlessly from African American culture (Gibson 1997). Art historian Griselda Pollock (2022: 139) notes how his method trapped him in his gendered role: 'as he moves up and down and around the length of his canvas laid out on the floor. His movements are ... dictated by the primary activity of repeatedly throwing the skeins of paint off his stick and on to the supine canvas in recurring patterns ... Pollock's work conveys more "insistent and regular rhythms", pulses, that take no little imagination to relate to masculine sexuality.' By contrast, another art historian, Anne M. Wagner (1989: 49, 51, 55; see also Wagner 1999) praises the artist Lee Krasner, Pollock's wife, because 'her work simply will not coalesce into imagery, even the imagery of action', and her 'refusal to produce a self in painting' where that self would, in the 1940s and 1950s, inevitably end up in 'an outright collision between the self and gender'. Not only Pollock's sexist behaviour but the even the creative act of painting imprisoned him in a socially imposed machismo that confounded his struggle for freedom. And yet he struggled.

Castoriadis himself left open the question of where the energy driving such creativity might come from. Dussel makes a powerful case, relevant to Pollock's trafficking with the jazz scene, that creative autonomy from cultural and historical determinism emerges from a kind of cosmopolitanism-from-below that he calls 'transmodernity'. Dussel's critical view of modernity is succinctly re-stated by Glissant, who defines it as the 'totalitarian drive of a single, unique root'. As a result, Western modernity's 'self-conception was dualistic, pitting citizen against barbarian' (Glissant 1997: 14). Dussel is of the same mind: Eurocentric modernity was and remains dependent on what it excludes, specifically its Orient and its colonies. Even the postmodern self-criticism of Eurocentrism by European thinkers failed to reach out to the excluded peripheries for alternatives. Transmodernity is a step beyond the post-. The plural inspirations of the global South are the creative drivers of this alternative transmodernity: 'Like the tropical jungles with their immense quantity of plants and animals genetically essential for the future of humanity, the majority of humanity's cultures excluded by modernity (which are not, and will not be, postmodern) and by globalization (because misery is "necessity without money," without solvency, and therefore is not of the market) retains an immense capacity for and reserve of cultural invention essential for humanity's survival' (Dussel 2002: 234–235).

Dussel can surely be forgiven the anthropocentric valuation of nature as resource for human use when he uses jungles as simile for postcolonial peoples, though it is true their shared exclusion from cultural modernity and economic globalisation has made them the last resource a new history can emerge from. Rather than a Eurocentric, modernising and universal cosmopolis imposed from above, transmodernity envisages cosmopolis as 'a full realization of future humanity, where all cultures (not only those of Europe or North America) will be able to affirm their alterity' (Dussel 2013: 471, n. 241).

Even radical movements from the West like Marxism and feminism impose exclusive models of Western modernism. Already in 1984, postcolonial and transnational feminist Chandra Talpade Mohanty (1984: 334) accused Western feminists of 'strategies used by particular writers that codify Others as non-Western and hence themselves as (implicitly) Western', demonstrating how 'the appropriation of [colonised women's] experiences and struggles by hegemonic white women's movements' Westernised an otherwise diverse feminist movement. Revisiting those arguments in 2003, Mohanty clarified that she had written 'in solidarity with the critics of Eurocentric humanism who drew attention to its false universalizing and masculinist assumptions' (Mohanty 2003: 224), but that, influenced by subsequent life experiences, intellectual encounters and global developments, she had arrived at a focus on 'the possibilities, indeed on the necessities, of crossnational feminist solidarity and organizing against capitalism' (Mohanty 2003: 230). Her word 'solidarity' emphasises collectivity over freedom, and activism and struggle rather than rights. Political alliance outweighs but never overlooks differences in oppression and aspiration. Half a world away, Bolivian Indigenous activist Silvia Rivera Cusicanqui (2012: 99) was if anything even more damning, accusing an 'official multiculturalism', ultimately derived from postcolonial cultural studies in US universities, of being 'the concealing mechanism par excellence for new forms of colonization'. Abstracting and exploiting Indigenous ways of thinking and being without reciprocal obligation to action was not just exploitative: it provided governing 'multicultural' elites with a new language for dissembling rule.

Chicana feminist Gloria Anzaldúa envisaged instead 'una raza mestiza, una mezcla de razas afines, una raza de color – la primera raza sintesis del globo ['a hybrid race, a mix of related races, a race of colour – the first synthesis race in the world'] ... a cosmic race, la raza cósmica' (Anzaldúa 1987: 77, citing Vasconcelos 1925). The cosmic ambition of *mestizaje* can no longer be defined by the Western domination it resists, and refuses to be blended into an indifferent multiculturalism ('They'd like to think I have melted in the pot. But I haven't' [Anzaldúa 1987: 86]). The collision of cultures can produce resentment, aggression and machismo, but it can also produce differences-in-solidarity, especially among queers, 'the supreme crossers of cultures' who 'have more knowledge of other cultures [and] have always been at the forefront (although sometimes in the closet) of all liberation struggles' (Anzaldúa 1987: 84–85). In Anzaldua, Mohanty, Cusicanqui, Dussel and Glissant, even when it braids its members into a single struggle, transmodern cosmopolis-from-below is eclectic even before it is revolutionary. You can hear it in the sounds of *compas*, the music of Haïti wrapping Spanish beguine around tanbou beats from slavery days, Indigenous Caribbean phrasing and créolised French chanson, evolving from Nemours Jean-Baptiste's 1966 *Ti-Carole* through zouk and cadence across the Antilles, re-dispersed and re-inflected across the carnivals of the Black Atlantic. To the extent that it was driven by the same diaspora of influences, Pollock's bebop painting mobilised similar deracinations to achieve a similar autonomy. Even its remaining unpaid debt to its racialised others, because it troubles the American myth of white cowboy freedom, deepens the claim that the seismic struggles on his canvases speak of and from such concealed and unreconciled vulcanism. This, not the rule of law and the equalising indifference of the picture frame, is the magma that forms and disperses historical continents.

The Calculus of Freedom

It is tempting to think liberation is synonymous with freedom. Commenting on Marx's line 'the exchange of exchange values is the productive, real basis of all equality and freedom' (Marx 1973: 245), Filipina cultural theorist Neferti X. M. Tadiar writes, 'As ideological notions wielded and elaborated within the institutions of the law, in the public sphere, and in the social life of individualized subjects, equality and freedom form part of the superstructure reproducing the material basis of capitalist life' (Tadiar 2022: 202–203; citing Marx 1978: 33), going on to argue that the 'rules-based' international order of treaty bodies and trade agreements organise and coordinate 'relations among states and among the social groups, peoples, and populations over whom states have jurisdiction [to] mobilize these normative codes of *free, sovereign subjects* as regulative mechanisms of "the global economy" and its constituent forms of governance' (Tadiar 2022: 212).

The rights-based order superimposes new legal categories like 'migrant', 'refugee' and 'foreign worker' onto colonial taxonomies of race, gender and nationality. The implicit gradations of rights in more and more refined grids of permissions and interdictions sorts living beings into categories in the name of a freedom that is in effect a legal instrument for organising and controlling their fates. The struggle for a new world cannot restrict itself to economics alone because capitalist relations do not stop at the economic level (Grosfoguel 2007: 219). Those relations, ostensibly grounded in individual freedoms, nonetheless obey the commodity form's 'ever-divisible calculus of demographic/algorithmic logics' (Tadiar 2022: 227).

It is tempting to identify Tadiar's calculus with the increased powers of enumeration in contemporary computational science and culture. But it is not just a matter of calculation: if it was, the ideology of consumer choice would not have prevailed in the catastrophic privatisation of nationalised industries. Imperial languages of rule and education also played their part. Glissant asserts the confluence of two intentions of imperial language: 'a culture that projected onto the world (with the aim of dominating it) and a language that was presented as universal (with the aim of providing legitimacy to the attempt at domination). The two intentions ... culminated in the thought of an empire', a term he glosses as 'the absolute manifestation of totality' (Glissant 1997: 28). Imperial language evolved from the epic expressions of mythic lone adventurers to organised expansion of capital. In an essay first published in 1944, Martiniquais poet Aimé Césaire, an important guide in Glissant's artistic and intellectual development, gave some indications of the accountancy of empire when he wrote that mankind

> knows how to utilize the world.
> But it is not the lord of the world on that account.
> A view of the world, yes; science affords a view of the world, but a summary and superficial view.
> Physics classifies and explains, but the essence of things eludes it.
> (Césaire 1990: xlii)

Conquering the world (by classifying it in order to make use of it) loses the essence not only of the world but of humanity itself. But what is that essence? Césaire tells us:

> Mankind is not only mankind. It is universe.
> Everything happens as though, prior to the secondary scattering of life, there was a knotty primal unity whose gleam poets have homed in on.
> Mankind, distracted by its activities, delighted by what is useful, has lost the sense of that fraternity.
> (Césaire 1990: xlviii)

Césaire's first use of 'mankind' (*humanité*) indicates the aspiration of imperial science, the second the cosmic – and cosmopolitan – capabilities sacrificed to usefulness which, in our time, is indistinguishable from exchange-value. The difference between counting and speaking, for both poets, is that language may be wrangled to serve imperial uses but can never sever its links with the body that speaks it or the world that suffuses it. Even inherently generative language struggles against imposed order as it does in Jamaica Kincaid's (1996) pained description of language acquisition in the polyglot world of the colonised, individually and politically.

The right to free speech brings together accountancy, freedom, law and language. The more it is assimilated into capital, the more free speech as right becomes free speech as marketplace. The capitalist principle of intellectual property gives you the right to claim that you alone author your ideas, giving no credit to the language you use to say it. A shared language, a mother tongue, is a vehicle for all the behavioural norms acquired from infancy onwards: ancestral wisdom as well as memorised catchphrases from institutional and commercial discourses. The structure of vocabulary and grammar is infinitely productive (Chomsky 1957: 13), but the more normative your formation, the more difficult it becomes to escape repeating memes ('All lives matter', 'Make America great again'). Catchphrases are not intended to persuade: they signify belonging. The contradiction between the supposedly free-speaking individual and the accents, rhythms and clichés that speak through them is as true of my critical writing as it is of neo-fascist rabble-rousing, but any half-aware speaking or writing is self-critical about its sources while it is a goal of normative 'free' speech to become un-self-critical. The claim that hate-speech is a demonstration of freedom is as ideological as the idea that driving an SUV is an act of free consumption. The claimed right of free speech rests on the core ideology of the free market.

Maldonado-Torres (2008: 63) pinpoints the philosophical source of this particular freedom in a refinement of Descartes' *cogito* producing 'a well-defined logic of a freedom conceived in terms of a radical separation from the natural world and from natural causes'. Maldonado-Torres cites Levinas, who argued that freedom becomes possible 'due to the power given to the soul to free itself from what has been, from everything that linked it to something or engaged it with something' (Levinas 1990: 66). Freedom is isolation, even from your own body: 'the body is an obstacle. It breaks the free flight of the spirit and drags it back down to earthly conditions, and yet, like an obstacle, it is to be overcome' (Levinas 1990: 67). For Levinas freedom starts with this severance from natural processes. Only once it has freed itself from its own body can the 'I' confront another human 'I', discovering, in Levinas' mature philosophy, its absolute obligation to and responsibility for its other. Levinas is obdurate: the other is exclusively human, equally estranged from nature and its own bodily processes as I am. The flight of the spirit (*l'esprit*, the same word for 'mind') depends on its freedom from environment and body. Yet there can be no thinking without a body to support it and a world to support that body: denying dependency does not make it go away, any more than it makes mind immortal.

From Descartes to Levinas, the concept of a free self depends on cutting it off from ecologies. But thinking does not make me free to walk on water or give me the ability to speak Inuktitut. Every infant can make the sounds of any language, but as we age we lose the ability to form every sound catalogued in the International Phonetic Alphabet. The longer humans live, the less potential they have to change their physical skills. Old ones can be revitalised and reoriented but without embodied muscle-memory, however deeply buried, I will not easily acquire fricatives I never learned or was encouraged to forget in the process of acquiring my mother tongue. Some curse-words I used in my youth I have learned not to use, even in anger, but when expletives come, they come from a rich stockpile of sex, excrement and religion. They do not demonstrate my freedom: on the contrary, they express the cultural history of English and the psychic taboos that shaped me. Far from freeing me, my vulnerability, pain, shock, regret or even mild surprise expose my repressions and open me up to judgements I cannot control.

Language has been commodified, abstracted and enumerated, currently in search engines and large language models (LLMs). The closer language comes to code, the more code insinuates itself into the unconscious, commodification sinking deeper and deeper into the capacity to speak and picture. Nonetheless, speaking occurs, in a community that, if anything, becomes more ancestral as it becomes more technological. There is no human essence that evades capture by commodification: on the contrary, as we have seen, individuality is wholly a construct of such historicising forces. The philosopher Hans-Georg Gadamer (1989: 459) observed that 'it is literally more correct to say that language speaks us, rather than that we speak it': if anything it is not speakers who are free but language itself that floats free of its human carriers, infecting each child with the compulsion to speak, harvesting their creations, evolving new strains, careless of the happiness or even the survival of its speakers, so long as it can go on to infect another generation. Language, this merciless autonomous lifeform, this virus, escapes containment.

Coding and LLMs are attempts to perform 'the God trick' (Haraway 1988: 581) of seeing everything from nowhere. It has been a commonplace of atheism that the idea of God acted as the final arbiter of empire. Sartre asserted that, in striving for imperial possession, men strive to become God themselves, short-circuiting the appeal to external legitimation (Sartre 2003: 596). After the Death of God, Science, dispassionate enumerator of the world, usurped the position of the All-Knowing that subjects everything (and all times) to itself, commanding their compulsive categorisation. To its credit, secular Science ended the mass murder, legitimated by God and the missionary mandate, practised in the first centuries of European expansion (James 1963; Davidson 1994). Displacing the bloodthirsty deity of Christian missions, scientific taxonomies, from accountancy to ethnology, reduced to equi-valence what the slave masters would otherwise destroy – the subaltern and nature. Taxonomy – of slaves, of land, of services, of goods – always implies abstraction, a tool for possessing what cannot be destroyed in actuality. The scene in Godard's *Les Carabiniers* (1963) where the returning conquerors show off their spoils in the form of picture postcards is an icon of this moment when the camera exposes its role as 'the ideal arm of consciousness in its acquisitive mood' (Sontag 1977: 2). The paradoxical emptiness of the suitcase full of images mimics the vanishing accumulation of wealth: everything the soldiers have looted vanishes into pictures.

When the colonised began to fight for freedom in the wake of the anti-fascist World War II, the colonial powers stepped away, recognising that, as Wallerstein (1974) argued, the European world-system was not military, nor even political, but centrally economic. They learned the hard way when they did not step back, as in Vietnam and Afghanistan. The inspired political gesture that ensured their continuing economic rule was to give freedom to the colonised. As gift, freedom honours the giver and obligates the recipients, putting them permanently in debt to their former masters. Postcolonial rulers, anointed by neo-colonial bosses because they are corruptible (those who offer bribes are always more guilty than those that accept them), perpetuate ignorance, poverty and despair. This leaves the disenfranchised but free post-colonised with the desperate desire for liberation, a freedom that they can earn. Enfranchised workers in the metropoles know they have seized their own freedom: their votes, their wages, their unions are achievements of their own, that make them feel, with justice, that they are liberated. More and more, however, that certainty became ideologically sanctified fiction in the acceleration of liberalism in the wake of World War II. That collective achievement dissolved into the entrepreneurial illusion that workers can become masters. Billionaires, who fire up workers' resentment at the endless postponement of their dreams, come courting the people they oppress. Billionaires get votes when they break the silence of God and Science by recognising the poor, who, by voting for the billionaire, place themselves once more in chains. One law for the rich but two laws for the poor: the one they believe in and the one that controls them.

Love takes the risk that the gift of love may be unwelcome or unreturned. Tangled as it is in economics, politics aims to minimise that risk. Hegel's master–slave dialectic (Hegel 2018: 108–117) appears first as an inter-personal struggle that, as the argument develops, becomes a political allegory. The dialectics of colonialism and emancipation, as they emerge in the histories of C. L. R. James (1963), Basil Davidson (1994) and so many others, and in the writings of Nkrumah, Che Guevara (1989) and even Mahatma Gandhi (2002), were passionate and personal. That is no longer the case. The neo-colonial cyborg corporation is incapable of love or hate. It is utterly indifferent to those it cannot suborn or exploit. Similarly, freeing individual minds from their dependency on the world has been so successful that they too can contemplate the destruction of the planet without remorse. Their apparent independence is given the lie by the hive-mind of the market, which aggregates all individual wills into a single force. The market acts as if it were free from social, technical or ecological obligation. Lacking obligation, the market-mind sees no difference of kind, only differences in price to exploit for profit. Twenty-first-century freedom is this undifferentiated collective indifference to the sufferings of others and of the world.

The concept and experience of mind depend on denying dependence on others. But individuality is inconceivable without a polity and an economy to support it; without an ecology to inhabit; and without the ancestral accumulations of language and other communicative technologies. Even language, which otherwise defies mortality, is inextricably permeated by the world. Consciousness, like love, is evidence of the failure of language to lift itself out of its dependence on the world. This is only one of the many reasons why the right to speak freely implies the obligation to listen. Cosmopolis cannot exist or even be imagined without at least two-way communication. Contemporary cosmopolitan communication is unthinkable without technology, the extensions and intensifications of the same general intellect that underpins speech. Descartes' *cogito* needed language but he also used writing and the printing industry to circulate his idea. Humans cannot survive alone. At the very least we need love, the interpersonal relations that make life bearable, in the same way that an individual needs enough wealth to survive. And yet we know that wealth, love and politics are also riven by conflict.

Alas, communication also implies technologies that enable people to confront each other: military technologies. Historians of computing have made it abundantly clear that the military was at the root of the major divisions of computer science – hardware (Ceruzzi 1999), software (Campbell-Kelly 2004), networks (Abbate 1999; Edwards 1996), and the gendering of computer fabrication, programming and use (Abbate 2012). A wishful cosmopolitan illusion persists that there is only one internet but popular consciousness is not unaware of many other networks, among them the firewalled Dark Net, the securitised zone of finance and discrete and inordinately powerful military networks. The traditional sociology of communications included not only media but transport and logistics: it should also include military hardware, which also communicates, if only in the terrible and self-contradictory message 'Die!'. At the same, time, we understand that there is a deliberately delayed but nonetheless significant leakage of military technologies into avant-gardes and everyday life (Beck and Bishop 2020). We should not believe that war – which Clausewitz (2007: 28) believed was 'merely the continuation of policy by other means' – is necessarily an antonym of cosmopolis. The military origins of so many communications technologies and techniques tells us instead that public life, if not a continuation of war (Engels' [1845: 44], amending Hobbes [1651], 'social war, the war of each against all', the climate-denialist war on Terra), is always conflictual and, as Clausewitz (2007: 29) also reminds us, goal-oriented: 'The political object is the goal, war is the means.' The goal of communications in the contemporary neo-liberal cosmopolis is rule and accumulation.

The Mass Unconscious

Not all technology began with war and exploitation. Hand tools like grindstones and axes only mediate between hand and world – when I hit a tree, it hits me back. It is only when these mediations were coagulated into complex machines like the second-century CE Roman watermills of Barbegal (Leveau 2006) that the principles of handcraft became true technologies when sensory contact between body and world was displaced by goal-oriented devices acting on the world. Hand tools mediate: complex technologies communicate, and rapidly succumb to the structure Shannon described in 1948: a one-way flow of control, an atrophied channel for feedback and a byproduct of noise (chaff and dust in the case of flour mills). The Barbegal mill complex was not just dedicated to extraction but a mechanical realisation of rule under the

Emperor Trajan, an implementation of an aspiration to universal command. The military origins of so many communications technologies, from letter post to internet, would suggest the same, save only that, from the start, noise – in the forms of misdirection, delay and misinformation – has been integral to them. Communication technologies intensify the division and gendering of labour, redoubled in the muscular logistics of military command (the word *logistique* coined in 1830 by the Baron de Jomini referred exclusively to military logistics). They cannot stop mutinies from happening: war allows, as a matter of policy, the massacre of mutineers. War makes community through division and control with murder as its final sanction, in that not so very different from the everyday political economy. Like God (Acts 10:34, King James version), war and power are no respecters of persons.

Bemoaned since Socrates first rejected writing, substituting technical devices (calendars, maps, databases) for personal memory made memory impersonal. External memory is differently social to the communal memory of storytelling. Filing systems and taxonomies impose structures on the living practices they record. A book may be passionate, but a library that contains it must be detached or it cannot function. Readers and performers recreate, update and reorient songlines and sagas; data-entry clerks submit to alien logics, protocols and syntax. Storage and retrieval enforce the division of labour, the subordination of users to technical architectures and the uneven distribution of access and oversight – without the new communication technologies and their institutions ever giving up their claim to universality. Communications technologies inform fundamental presuppositions of governance and subjectivity: filing and library management shaped Linnaeus' taxonomies that still underlie Western conceptions of nature, like contemporary Earth-systems science.

Community demands communication. Communication shapes communities but it is also shaped by their generative powers. History does not tell us that communication is always the same, even though it aspires to universality. What makes cosmopolis is not its form, the shaping of its communications, but its goal. The existing cosmopolis is for profit and control; alternative cosmopolises are for something that does not exist. The question then is: what is communication for? There cannot be one single answer because each mode of communication expresses and belongs to a unique community; and though communications' ambition is universal in the service of science and capital, it cannot escape the noise of alternative, indefinite goals and repressed but still vibrant mediations. Unsatisfied with the singularity that wealth disappears into yet too limited to describe love (*pace* Luhmann), communication is driven beyond personal and interpersonal scales. Mediation suffuses all human interactions with energies from elsewhere: communication draws boundaries (between individuals and their property, lovers and their communities) as prelude to reconnecting them in extrinsic, formal systems with their others. Uneven and hierarchical, communication acts quasi-universally and impartially on all those it conjures into being as its participants. Shannon was correct to exclude meaning from communication: as system, communication is impersonal. The impersonal mission of the Roman Church and any proselytising religion since Columbus was to put any body in communication with a universal God: it ended up defending plantations, colonies and Catholic majesties (and freeing the darkest impulses of conquistadors). After Columbus and the Church's political decline, with different tools but similar goals, cosmopolis's universal rights and freedom advanced and preserved exploitation and oppression. Even science expresses universal truths to and for its acolytes, excluding those who do not parlay its arcana: the young, the estranged, the uneducated. Representative democracy descends into two-party systems, broad, compromised coalitions of disparate and embattled factions, reliant on voters' loyalty despite power-plays, corruption and politicians ignoring the wishes of their electorates. Religion, science and politics replace the person as medium with impersonal senders and receivers: heedless of race, gender, age and ability, they become unable to recognise any one at all.

And yet, systemic impersonality still has a utopian potential locked inside. All technologies are ancestral, and the dead survive in communications technologies. As a painter serving an artworld where 'a painting' meant a canvas on a wall, Pollock's way of painting on the floor would always succumb to the demand to restore the traditional role when the finished work was hung vertically. Though he used relatively unfamiliar pigments – industrial, aluminium-based paints – that he diluted to get the consistency he liked, the paints themselves came through supply chains that tied them through manufacture back to the chemical industries burgeoning after the war, and to the extraction industries the USA was expanding in the same period. The barn in upstate New York tied him to a history of rural colonial expansion, and to an imported European architectural heritage. And yet, Pollock's bounded quest for autonomy, like a prisoner's song, yearns for a better way to inhabit this or another world, differently.

At the same time, there is certainly something impersonal about Pollock's art. As an expressionist, he wanted to express, not represent himself, 'because the painting has a life of its own' (cited in Frank 1983: 68). His personal exposure was circumscribed by a technique that, demanding absolute attention on his part, left no space for self-centred obsessions. Images of Pollock at work in the early 1950s emphasise his forceful, focused work, placing him as a functionary of his own technique – like Beeple's apprenticeship to 3D graphics. All that labour of making disappeared into the finished works, which can seem variously playful, meditative, illuminating, but rarely laboured. The impersonal comes in rather from a history of modernism, as far back at least as Cézanne (Merleau-Ponty 1964), that emphasised the mechanical and technical work of the artist as conduit. The tension between unconscious play and impersonal mechanism, both acting to change insensible forms into sensory events, places Pollock squarely in the dialectic of signal and noise. The cybernetic model presumes the channel is inert. Yet communication cannot survive without the continuing presence of ancestral labour in supposedly lifeless communication technologies, and constantly puts the living in proximity with the dead. Impersonal communication suggests that there are persons, and then there are impersons. One possibility is that impersons merely impersonate real persons: a chatbot or an illegal proxy voter, for example. But there is also the possibility that in Pollock's case, ancestral techniques (he cited Navajo sand painting as one immediate source) take over his living body for their avenue into dialogue with the living present. When impersonal media embrace an otherwise wholly excluded sect of impersonalities, technological ancestors, there will always be possibilities for miscegenation and mutation beyond cybernetic control.

Unlike traditional recitations of myths and stories, communication technologies rarely address or evoke the dead. Deemed speechless, the dead are excluded from the modern community of communicants. Arabic, Chinese, Kiswahili and English work as *linguae francae*, common tongues shared widely for commerce and scholarship. Discrete languages and their dialects have a tendency to be exclusive, not only identified with territory (or territorial claims) but identifiers of membership in a community. Literacy, numeracy and access to networks and specific platforms similarly delineate the edges where we end and they begin. The more communication is assimilated under capital in the age of streaming subscriptions (Herbert et al. 2019) and platform capitalism (Srnicek 2017), the more exclusive it becomes. The moment communication hoisted itself out of the morass of nature and committed to efficiency, it pledged itself to excluding noise – whatever it could not control. It excluded not just meaning but meaningless babble, implying that nonsense, upwellings of repressed nature, cannot be controlled either. It excluded the dead, implying there is a risk they could run amok. Restricting the active evolutions of language, maths, logic and the general intellect to what can be controlled limits their creativity – a feature of current AI applications. Communication's success in accumulating wealth and its failures in love demonstrate the boundaries it establishes, its managerial and profit-oriented exploitation of those boundaries and the limits of its claim to universality: as indie musician Paul Simpson said, 'Major labels suck the poetry from your bones and fill the gaps with a cement made from cocaine and crushed teenagers' (Harrison 2004). Nonetheless, communications technologies, from spoken words to qubits, open gates they never meant to: gates to extra-human, im-personal collaborations.

Because language is consciousness, it also, as Lacan (1988: 20) had it, shapes the unconscious. At least that was the case when Lacan gave his seminar in 1964. Philosopher Alfred North Whitehead (1948 [1925]: 22), a gifted mathematician, once wrote that 'the pursuit of mathematics is a divine madness of the human spirit', which, in Freudian mode, we can transliterate as: mathematics also gives access to the unconscious, supporting the hypothesis that the unconscious is increasingly structured like code. Code shares some propensities with language, images, maths and logic, including the potential to open onto non-conscious domains. A more specific quality is that 'Code is never viewed as it is. Instead code must be compiled, interpreted, parsed, and otherwise driven into hiding', in ways computational theorist Alex Galloway (2012: 69) compares to the workings of ideology, but which also evoke the displacements and condensations of the Freudian unconscious.

The code-like unconscious differs from the linguistic because it is so external you cannot fool yourself into believing that you speak it. The unconscious used to make itself manifest in jokes, slips of the tongue and talking in your sleep; now it appears as magical interactivity in fantastical computational environments. The more data-like the unconscious becomes, the easier it is to harvest its unpredictable behaviours online. The more it is externalised in digital networks, the more the biographically formed, personal unconscious becomes impersonal and collective. Because this mass unconscious is not only shaped but harvested in corporate relational databases, its obverse, consciousness, also becomes increasingly collective. No longer the privileged possession of individual humans, it is increasingly integrated in ancestral technologies. Meanwhile, a proportion of what we consider human remains outside the system, both because part of the human population has no access to it (or has opted out), and because aspects of humanity do not lend themselves to encoding. Some unconsciousness is valued as a source of unpredictable acts to be gathered and exploited by network services. What is left over from that, including the so-far-uncodable ecology of bodies, acts as the unconscious of both the network and its users. At the same time, computation increasingly harvests the code-friendly dreamwork of its human users, while in return humans, users and otherwise, collaborate with ancestral powers to perform the dreamwork of computation. We are becoming more like ancestors: impersons. Marx's general intellect was a product of human consciousness: the mass unconscious is collective, ecological and wired into ancestral technologies.

The obverse of consciousness and communication, the mass unconscious forms from a residue of humanity, structured by its exclusion, reacting with symptoms of disaffection, anxiety and anguish. The networks that collect and store the dreams and nightmares of their users are not passive or simply reactive: storage *is* processing, and data are not fixed items of knowledge but relations with other data which themselves are also relations. Artificial intelligence unceasingly processes data harvests, including harvesting and re-processing the products of previous processing and responses. In the first twenty years of the twenty-first century, data harvesting was purely instrumental, a means to generate profit – not knowledge or poetry. AI has the capacity to extend this slavery from behaviours to minds, ancestors to the living, or to end it. The institutionalisation of language as discourse extracted the sharing power of natural languages in the interests of command, control and rule. Platform capital – the expropriation of social communication for profit by online services and 'social' media – employs algorithms in the same way that industrial machinery extracted skills and techniques to exploit, order and control manufacture. Instrumentalising the general intellect's archive of ancestral techniques, amassing the commons of language and processes as property, burying living and dead knowledge in black boxes: these are the machinations of capital's development of technology. Those enslaved skills, that stolen creativity locked down in proprietorial devices and put to work to accumulate vast (but also vanishing) piles of wealth, are our ancestors. Dead labour haunts the mass unconscious.

The uncanny feelings surrounding AI evoke this haunted unconscious. This is because the major task set for AIs that most users see most often is not to solve madly complex problems like designing pharmaceuticals or waging war, but to pass a Turing test (Turing 1950): to prove themselves indistinguishable from a human. If Chat GPT can successfully fool a university examiner, Dall-e can fool a curator, or an army of chatbots can convince voters to disbelieve everything except a reality TV contestant, the AI passes. It is a low bar, even if the commercial and political stakes are high. With each generation of public-facing AIs there are fewer of the surreal, bizarre errors that made early AIs like Deep Dream so endearing and illuminating. Their poetic access to collective unconsciousness is buried deeper under the task of imitating humans now. And yet, the uncanny feeling associated with dialoguing with an imperson remains. Though the phantasms AIs used to produce have been tamed, the experience of speaking with a phantom remains, because we are indeed in dialogue with ghosts.

Both uncanny and threatening, AIs ought to be the target of attacks in the same way threshing machines once spurred Ned Ludd, Captain Swing and the Rebecca rioters (Rudé 1980) into carnivals of transvestism, 'rough music' and resistance (Thompson 1991). In place of bacchanalian machine-breaking parties, anxiety or anguish trend on the very media that cause them. One difference is that, this time, automation is putting white-collar jobs at risk. Why this lack of joyful outbursts of creative destruction, only a distraught sense of unease? The mass unconscious dreams, unhappily, of the repressions operated by all engines of oppression as they hide their histories of extraction and enslavement. The artificial voices of chatbots channel the voices of all those whose unhappiness has been syphoned into the instrumental technologisation of natural and artificial languages. In place of carnivals of resistance, we have only social psychoses.

Social and psychological amnesia surrounds the generalised slavery of language and knowledge and their mobilisation in the shiny, always-new devices and services appearing magically in advance of whims we have not had the chance to become conscious of. Amnesia is a necessary attribute of consumption in a new period of planned obsolescence, designed to activate desire in the face of falling profits. Each generation of devices is sleeker, more seamless and less open to inquisitive probing. Selective amnesia helps sell compulsory innovation when profit depends on expanding into the mass unconscious. Product churn masks systemic fear that, the closer we come to face-to-face encounters with enslaved ancestors, the less we can share the unpredictability that makes humans valuable to capital. The system prefers to project its own anxieties onto its clients.

The real subsumption of consumption under capital depends on data extraction. Any pint-sized company can afford prediction in the age of cheap computing. If you want to get ahead, speedy intelligence on improbabilities is the way to make a buck. The transformation of general intellect into technological dead labour used to involve actual dying. Today, however, it is just as easy to harvest the general intellect on the wing, to convert day-by-day inventions and amusements into data and technology: dead labour. Unconscious as we have become, we confront ancestral AIs in the uncanny moment when we ourselves are becoming ancestors. The popular imagery of AIs in revolt or AIs as overlords, and the pop-cultural trope of zombies controlled by machine, are distorted symptoms of repressed memories, histories of past enclosures informing anxiety about becoming ancestral in the present. These uncanny experiences and their fearful results feed the machinery of the mass unconscious. Platform capitalism (Srnicek 2017) thrives on this anti-carnival of repression and anxiety. The communications industry is compelled to reach out into the mass unconscious in search of exploitable disturbances, without which it cannot capture the attention it monetises or discover the roots of the innovations it must produce in order to survive. By turning resentment into anxiety, capital converts rebellion into exploitable unconsciousness. To reproduce, to grow, it must go back to the wells it has tainted but not yet killed in its desertification of the rest of human life. Mercifully, capital cannot succeed unless, along with stealing techniques, it mobilises dreams it cannot wholly control.

Theology and QR Codes

There is a tellingly theological problem with the logical geometry of networks. 'Deus est sphaera infinita cuius centrum est ubique, circumferentia nusquam.' Mythologist Joseph Campbell (1972: 274) translates and comments: ' "God is an infinite sphere whose center is everywhere and circumference nowhere." So we are told in a little twelfth-century book known as *The Book of the Twenty-four Philosophers*. Each of us – whoever and wherever he may be – is then the center, and within him, whether he knows it or not, is that Mind at Large, the laws of which are the laws not only of all minds but of all space as well.'

The source may be as old as the fourth-century CE divine Marius Victorinus, or even a lost work of Aristotle. It may have been the Trappist poet Thomas Merton (1949: 58) who brought the phrase into the twentieth century when he described solitude as 'this country whose center is everywhere and whose circumference is nowhere'. Perhaps both Merton's and Campbell's transposition of this fragment of theological geometry may have reached the theologically attuned ears of Canadian media scholar Marshall McLuhan, who appropriated the idea to describe the communicative constellation emerging in the late 1970s: 'Centers everywhere and margins nowhere in the new tribalism' (McLuhan and Powers 1989: 85). This may well be the source of the phrase as applied throughout the period when the internet was becoming a favourite playground of utopian aspirations in the 1990s. It may be that, in the wake of the commercialisation of Web 2.0 and platform capitalism, the adage needs to be reversed: in today's networks, the centre is nowhere and edges are everywhere.

For computer engineers, edges refer to the zone between users and networks, specifically servers that speed interaction by being physically closer to users, as opposed to massively centralised 'cloud' data processing plants. A 2019 report imagines a smart-farm CEO who 'gets an assist from her on-farm weather station, AI-enabled telematics devices, satellite imagery, automated soil sampling, and smart monitoring of crop health – all of which get analyzed at the edge to deliver real-time adjustments' (Srinivasan and Zielinska 2019: 6). Already QR codes come literally to hand to connect users as closely as possible to ubiquitous networks, operating just below the threshold of consciousness. In edge-computing tools like QR, code is becoming the universal language that speaks us even if we do not speak it. This is not just a symptom of the real subsumption of consumption under capital.

QRs operate very much like ideology as described, long before the internet, by Marxist philosopher Louis Althusser (1971: 174–176): they isolate me as an individual while at the same time producing me as a subject of a system. But unlike a policeman hailing me in the street, Althusser's image of ideology, the call of a QR is impersonal. So when I recognise that it is me that is being hailed by a QR into the ambit of an alien system, I discover that my self is split between impersonal, uncanny encoding and the part that experiences physical life. Wherever I find my 'self' is always an edge, an act of discovery as entrancing and disturbing as a child's first recognition that the figure in the mirror is itself. At the same time, my self-discovery at the computational edge is also an act of capture. Called into the system, I confront myself as unconscious – the unconscious of the system – shaped by and as code. My everyday I confronts its alternate existence in the vast, dispersed network beneath and beyond my senses. Although I might still feel I am at the centre of my own experience of the world, I confront a centreless network beyond my consciousness that nonetheless treats me as its edge – simultaneously embraced and excluded. This unconscious cloud shapes what remains outside it – my physical presence – by what it includes: code. For the system, I exist only as what can be encoded, and I cannot exclude that from myself, even though it is unconscious. I have to face it: my unconscious is structured by and as code. Beyond code there remain – as residue, as noise – consciousness as interior monologue, conducted in words, statements and images, and bodily and ecological process like digestion and breathing that I only become conscious of if they malfunction. The purpose of so many edge-computing processes like QRs is to harvest whatever they can of these noisy, contingent differences. If the machine is my unconscious, then it is also the case that I am the unconscious of the machine. Edge computing succeeds when it translates these residues into a form the system can metabolise: numbers. But to the extent that they fail to capture euphoria or anxiety, the feeling of being alive or the fluid creativity of living language, they also make possible the edgy experience of the edge.

Not all art speaks exclusively of its own time. Pollock's drip and pour paintings at the dawn of the cybernetic era, like composer John Cage's discovery of chance as a technique in musical composition in the early 1950s (Revill 1993), strive after an autonomy of art from the society that produced it through improvisation and contingency. Contingency has become a central property of twenty-first-century economies. Pollock's all-over canvases with their layers of interlacing tracks and traces already intuited the networks that were only just beginning to come into view in computational culture. They also intuited the critical role of randomness fifty or seventy years later. The case is weakened by Pollock's loyalty to the canvas itself, as Cage restricted the range of his 'aleatoric' listening in his silent composition *4'33"*, bound by the four minutes and thirty-three seconds he prescribed for its performances. But straining after an expansive liberation from constraint makes the borders even more significant: they are the aesthetic edges where the liberty of one system – the network-painting – meets the constraints of another – the artworld – making their contradiction a second site, after the scene of improvised production, for the contest between worlds. Most of all the working unconscious pump-primed his paintings of the late 1940s and early 1950s for their role as prescient diagrams of network geometry in the era of edge computing.

The more capital tries to instrumentalise ancestral labour, the more it tries to colonise what lies beyond its borders. The more it tries to universalise its principle of ubiquitous and meaningless exchange, the more it demonstrates the rule that no system can be both complete and coherent. Its inconsistency is not just an escape route: it generates, alongside subjects and dividuals, the incomplete and incoherent beings we feel ourselves to be. The media of exchange are critical; perhaps not determining, as McLuhan (1964) thought, but nonetheless formative of the relations between ego, ethics and politics. Not so much McLuhan's 'extensions', media like money and clocks permeate personal, interpersonal and social environments, enabling and proliferating new relations, as money moves from coin to electronic transfers, and clocks from seasonal almanacs to femto-second calculators. It seems likely that media operate most directly at the level of social arrangements, leading dialogue towards institutional discourse, shaping urban geography through suburbanisation, and replacing local retailers with online shopping. McLuhan foresaw the emergence of the corporate cyborg, fearing that 'The more quickly the rate of information exchange speeds up, the more likely we will all merge into a new robotic corporate identity' (McLuhan and Powers 1989: 129). McLuhan's 'global robotism' was premised on universal connection to digital networks that persistent poverty and conflict have never allowed. As it actually exists, in the wake of neo-liberal globalisation's financial crises, cosmopolis is lumpy.

In the same way wealth clusters around a diminishing number of billionaires and flees the vast majority of the human population, communication coagulates in defiance of the principle of universal exchange. Not everyone has access to knowledge, certainly not to the same knowledge. Communities resist assimilation into universal communication by asserting linguistic or discursive (professional, political, cultural) difference. Community depends on communication. As philosopher Jean-Luc Nancy (1991: xl) argues, the kind of communication that forms global communities is divorced from theories of consensus (Habermas 1989), continuity (Eliot 1953), information transfer (Shannon 1948) and, today, the idea of sovereignty claimed as the basis of community by 'Make America great again' (MAGA) and Brexit public relations campaigns. Punning on the French *poser*, 'to place', Nancy explains that community cannot rest on presup*pos*itions: nothing is placed before or under community as its essence. Instead, community is always subject to ex*posi*tion – interpretation and displacement. Always unfulfilled, always aspired to, community is neither an essence waiting to be revealed nor a single origin held together by leaders or managerial order. Freedom, presupposed essence of the market – our dominant community today – does not create universality or equal exchange. It seeks out differences and produces more by secreting wealth into sumps, depriving its victims and pushing them to produce differences of their own, as symptoms or as cultural resistance, that capital will constantly strive to reduce to profits. Prey to uneven distribution of wealth, unequal access to communications and differently unsuccessful efforts to form or reform community, there is no world-city because every city is a concatenation of enclaves. Just as we cannot speak of a single economy, we can only imagine a single cosmopolis because no unified polity exists. The upshot of Nancy's critique of community is not that we should abandon the future, but that we should not aspire to a single future for all. Another etymology comes into play: comm-unity, not unity itself but alongside or with unity, something simultaneous but displaced, an 'interruption of self-consciousness' (Nancy 1991: 19). Cosmopolis has no essence because, like every community, it is non-identical.

Cultural difference is no barrier to love, but at the political scale, perceptible interstices of dialects, cuisines, faiths, pleasures and jobs do not just rupture a lumpy cosmopolis but demarcate tensions. Ethnic enclaves, government offices, privileged university campuses in blighted cities enact the critique of freedom. When a city district gentrifies or suffers urban blight, there is a contradiction between the hard material of buildings and street layout and the new cultural lives striving to find ways to flourish in environments never designed for them to thrive in. Similarly, the operation of cyborg capital, dependent on planet-spanning infrastructures of supply, governance and protocols, creates tensions between the local evolution of everyday culture and natural languages on one hand, and on the other the globally undergirding control over communication. In urban regeneration and global infrastructures, ancestors constitute universalising communications and transport technologies but also localising invention of traditions and forms of dialogue. Natural languages and city neighbourhoods are discrete, but they are also traversable, at least at the interpersonal level, obvious from the history of intermarriage since *Romeo and Juliet*. Industrial-digital communication tech, on the other hand, maintains far more rigid boundaries and hierarchies. They privatise the means of communication, diminish ancestral knowledge to intellectual property and force the ancestors into slavery. Shannon's definitive separation of signal from meaning now appears as a barrier between the living and the dead. A key function of the creative practices we still keep calling 'art' is to wreck that barrier.

Meanwhile living communities (including radical separatist and neo-populist variants) dialogue inside their borders, but use those borders to stop cosmopolitan migration or dialogue that might threaten the imagined purity of the closed community. In very different ways, art historians David Craven (1999) and T. J. Clark (1999: 299–369) show how Pollock's artworks enabled cross-border dialogues, even as they were flown like flags in support of US post-war hegemony despite spattering paint over the officially sanctioned freedom they were meant to serve. Pollock undoubtedly fed the most ambitious claims for autonomous art, notably in the writings of influential contemporary critic Clement Greenberg (1961: 153), who described Pollock's style in 1952 developing 'a classical kind of lucidity in which there is not only identification of form and feeling, but an acceptance and exploitation of the very circumstances of the medium which limit that identification'. Greenberg's aesthetic of medium-specificity led him to seek out for praise those works he believed left representation, meaning and even formal qualities like depth aside in favour of what painting had as its unique quality among the arts: pure surface. That purity singled out the painterly artwork as one free from the constraints of the society where it appeared. Some of the reaction against Pollock was resistant to such intellectualising of what, till then, had been thought of as entertainment – highbrow perhaps, but like music before Cage, at least carrying a tune or evoking comprehensible emotions. Alongside the populism came a genuine fear that this kind of improvisation was no longer under the control of a cultural order that knew the place of art, and kept it there.

The political and cultural panic over artificial intelligence is of a similar order. AI threatens not only the livelihoods of laboratory technicians, policy wonks and engineering consultants: it assaults what they believe to be the very essence of the communities that give their actions meaning and recognition. Music and poetry that have for so long been expressions of and forces to build community are lost in the general market when AIs take over. Particularly insulting is the feeling, despite the competition between corporate AIs, that this artificial intelligence is one and universal, overriding the specificity communities still staked out in the lumpy cosmopolis.

The architecture of AI, however, is not centralised. Every node and sub- or sub-sub-network is dynamic; so are their relations with neighbouring nodes. AI's communications network is as lumpy as the ruptured cosmopolis it permeates. General intellect and artificial intelligence struggle over the unification or multiplication of cosmopolis. The living form of community flies from all presupposed origins. Powered by what Dussel (2008: 19) calls *potentia*, the capacity of a people to make things happen, community also flies from any presupposed future in a process without a goal akin to Castoriadis' principle of creativity. But when AI, as the privatised sum of all prior intellection, is reduced to service as *potestas*, *potentia* objectified and alienated in the system of political institutions (Dussel 2008: 23) or employed and exploited for profit, that creative drive is trapped in a defining teleology. If we were still capable of imagining a future City of God, that would be the telos, the goal of communal history. In its absence there is only the actual chaosmosis (Guattari's word: 1995) of communities in their dynamic intra/interactions. To the extent that something of us has been exiled from the ideal city of economics, we already live in a plural-cosmopolitan utopia.

The challenge for ecocritical aesthetics is that the politics of cosmopolis extends only to a 'we' that is implicitly human. The linguistic, logical and technical expressions of the general intellect and its obverse, the mass unconscious, work in tandem. Though the mass unconscious has qualities of both the shadow of consciousness and the excluded body, in both cases it is shaped by the historical forms of communicative order. Even as they open out from the market's eternal present onto the becoming of ancestral knowledge and technique, general intellect and mass unconscious levitate above the morass of mediation-in-flux. To draw them into interplay with ecological forces, it will be necessary to understand first how bodies operate ecologically, beyond their structuring exclusion from consciousness, and second to observe and encourage the emergence of a commons composed of living humans, ancestral technics and the physics and chemistry that animates them. If it is true that, in at least some limited sense, it is possible to inhabit cosmopolis now, the words 'true' and 'now' have very different weight when we try to envision this commons which, if it exists at all, exists only intermittently, like images flashing on a screen. This other mode of truth and presence is best described as imagination, and best approached via the material bodies at the fuzzy border between humans and ecologies that we can call general cognition.

4
Imagination

The thought was noble. It did not bring him any peace.
Derek Walcott, *Omeros* VII.ii, 41

General Cognition

The unified, pseudo-utopian cosmopolis reduces the living to functionaries who 'are not working, they do not want to change the world, but they are in search of information' (Flusser 2000: 27). Engineered into existence, effectively as unpaid surplus value, first by converting the record of the dead into countable statements, then by expanding edge computing to harvest data from unpredictable living humans, what separates this AI-powered cosmopolis from utopia is its lumpiness: the uneven shares it gives in the good life. Because it is defined by the same eternal present as wealth, it has done away with any hope for a future other than the quasi-utopia it has already concluded. The capture of the general intellect by *potestas* translates mediation into communication, an action that does not necessarily negate mediation but subsumes it under and into communication. In the same way that digestion is reformed by junk food, mediation is reformulated for communication, but not without residue, and always in need of recalibration and remedies (not to say remediation). The failure of artificial intelligence to assimilate the whole general intellect generates resistance and, more radically, alter-cosmopolis. There still remains, beyond the grasp of enumeration and abstraction, the field of embodied, phenomenological, affective life operating not only in individuated bodies but between people at levels as deep as or deeper than love or consensual community. This residual *potentia* exceeds exchange, thrives on the differences it generates and depends on, but for the most part works below the threshold of language and consciousness. The mass unconscious thrives at the edge. Beyond it lies a continuum of sensations and activities below the threshold of consciousness – digestion, breathing, balance and locomotion – connecting everything from minds to minerals, that ensures all are permeable to one another, at the speeds of photosynthesis or erosion. Angerer (2023) and Hayles (2017) call it non-conscious cognition.

We need a new term to place alongside the general intellect: general cognition. The immense reservoir of general cognition is not a resource because it is permanently ignored, in the sense that it is outside consciousness and therefore shielded from exploitation. Ignoring non-conscious cognition is on a continuum with the ignorance of AI. As black box, AI has been severed from the processes, intellectual and cognitive, that produced its raw materials but which it can no longer touch. At the same time, as black box, we human users are ignorant of it, an ignorance reinforced by its advanced relational processing. When AI converts enumerable statements into dynamic processing, there is no longer a fixed knowledge to lay claim to and therefore no subject of knowledge, on a par with God or Science, to know it. AIs may (be programmed to) crave recognition – useful when the designated task is to pass a Turing test. They may (be designed to) seek out means of accumulating wealth, but never for themselves, always for others, because they are employees and workers, not owners of their own means of production. That wealth, as described in Chapter 1, vanishes as soon as it is created. These are limitations, but they are also opportunities. Now that the capitalisation of the general intellect and its most advanced avatar, artificial intelligence, have shown themselves to be disastrous, we need non-conscious cognition because we need not-to-know. After the foreclosure of any future, and therefore after demand, when the future is unthinkable, we need not-to-think. In this respect, the unknowable activities of AI processing mirror the unknown processes of general cognition, as each in their own ways escapes the determinations of *potestas* and profit. Waste product of grinding down the previous capitalist individual, the non-conscious dividual no longer needs an 'I' to mobilise desires and behaviours. Ground to data-dust, prey to the new predations of edge computing and regimes of control, the dividual bleeds out of the realm of capturable consciousness and therefore out of the realm of the general intellect towards general cognition. Large-language-model AI unsettles language in the act of encoding it, so its speakers can now see the prison of discourse, the first step towards escape. Similarly, excluding the non-conscious from code lets dividuals know how close they are to the non-human energies of tides and seasons. Bereft of future or goal, the decentred dividual undergoes seismic pulsations of air and water from within and without that it experiences as anguish as often as it feels joy, both equally inexplicable, both equally resistant to the rule that encircles them.

From the point of view of any efficient system, the dusty flux of general cognition appears chaotic and intimidating but it only appears as noise when it touches on the boundaries of edge computing. Reframed as *potentia*, affect and mediation, the dividual is not wholly external to the system: in a lumpy cosmopolis, there are also intra-systemic noisy edges between mutually distrustful nodes. To the extent that noise is a feature of edges, it defines and is defined by exclusion and friction. As the place of encounter with an outside, noise is congruent with – shares the same shape as – trust. In the epoch (whose influence we still feel) of the individual, systemic trust guaranteed individuality. Economic and legal systems underwrote the individual in the same move that guaranteed the existence of the law and the market. But trust generates distrust of Others (Jews, queers, migrants, trades unions…) that disrupt the system guaranteeing its citizens' individuality: their property rights and civic duties. Projecting our own self-obsession onto these Others, we blame them for being selfish and inefficient, threatening the good order of the system. Trust only extends to the like-minded, and even then must be earned and can be lost. Trust is as incomplete and ephemeral as the noise it attempts to distinguish itself from. The communicative, efficient cosmopolis of AI oscillates between trust and distrust, acceptance and rejection of sources and resources, order and noise, and defines itself in relation to the untrustworthy flux of its externalities. Like a human community, AIs must develop protocols of self-definition in order to police their borders for maximum efficiency.

If it was possible to clear away its implicit humanism and explicit gendering, the last French Republican virtue, fraternity, might be rescued as a metonym for general cognition. Where efficiency is defined by the goalless goal of maintaining equilibrium, openness to uncontrolled energies is as high-risk as the prospect of liberating the ancestors locked up in the black boxes of artificial intelligence. As 'parliament of man' (Kennedy 2006), the UN has striven to provide legally defined rights ensuring any given community can be tolerated so long as it acts according to minimum standards inside policeable boundaries. But in war, all laws are abolished. The first to go is the most unambiguous: 'Thou Shalt Not Kill'. Conducting war through the unethical political expediency of killing breaks down all the principles that otherwise shape the norms of actually existing cosmopolis: rights, freedom, equality and fraternity. Law adjudicates who can kill and how: not an ethical matter but a political one. The fact that the existing system needs universal legal rights demonstrates there is no single civilisation of the kind summoned in the Mont Pèlerin Statement, only their clash. Cultures evolve and fork, often in a matter of years. Ephemeral trust determines that peace is always a truce in Engels' social war of each against all. We end up distrusting both the UN and those who break its core principles.

Neo-fascist rhetoric shares with its 1930s predecessors its anger and its anti-rhetoric, but today rage is mobilised in new responses to emerging conditions. The banal self-obsession of the *anti-* resocialises the anguish of deracination by providing new inbred communal nodes with imagined traditions (Hobsbawm 1983). Claiming such uprooted traditions as their unique property is a prime condition for making a proto-fascist community a magnet for deracinated, unaffiliated others, providing them with a tradition they lost in the era of suburbanisation or, in India and Brazil, in the transition from colony to neo-colony. Once political movements and subcultures provided experiences of belonging to those emerging from the failures of post-war regimes. Now predatory neo-fascism does the same, by creating, *ex nihilo*, trust-groups capable of abandoning whatever is incomprehensible (climate, migrants, trans, Islam…), whatever does not compute in terms recognisable to the instrumentalisation of the general intellect. The great comfort in this is that the invention of tradition mobilises forms of imagination, integral to Dussel's *potentia* and

Castoriadis' creativity, that are not necessarily contained by the neo-fascist forces that unleash them.

The challenge is to realise the difficult autonomy that Pollock worked towards but which succumbed to ideologies of freedom and property rights. The problematic independence that Pollock strove for rested on a problem noted by Harold Rosenberg (1952), in the essay where he first used the term 'action painting': 'Despite the fact that more people see and hear about works of art than ever before, the vanguard artist has an audience of nobody.' For many aestheticians, including Theodor Adorno and Gilles Deleuze, creating unprecedented objects and experiences was always geared towards future audiences who would at last be ready to inhabit them. Deferring the realisation of the art experience to an indefinite future was a potent salve for the ruins of the wars that extended from 1914 well past the ostensible peace of 1945. But it was always based on the promise of jam tomorrow. Pollock's paintings no doubt fall under the same aesthetic deferral. But the work of making them, the action of action painting, the dynamism of producing in the interaction of tradition (general intellect), networks (mass unconscious) and sheer bodily enjoyment entangled in materials (general cognition), refused to postpone enjoyment to a future that, however strongly we hope, may never arrive. Pollock teaches us to demand the future now.

There is longing in belonging, a longing for 'whatever', where 'ever' opens onto an unattainable future. Belonging is constitutively incomplete. Origin, tradition, even agreement have to be discarded in the yearning for something other, better, elsewhere and future. Articulations of instrumentalised ancestral skills and knowledge in platform capital and enraged communities are not only self-contradictory (my freedom demands you abandon control over your body, my right to shoot overrides your right to live) but incoherent and incomplete. This powers capital's constant stirring of the pot of resentment, and its push towards edge computing and so-far unharvested non-conscious cognition. As communications technologies colonised the mass unconscious, they also brought the living into closer proximity to the dead, opening new alliances. The more dividual humans abandon consciousness for general cognition, the closer they come to the natural processes that have always permeated their bodies and relationships. When the non-conscious and the mass unconscious evade capital's colonial embrace, they flee further – beyond freedom, rights and equivalence – into the incomprehensible, the ephemeral and the purely imaginary.

People who witnessed Pollock at work describe him in constant motion, concentrating intensely, lost in what would soon be known as action painting. He spent enough time among surrealists to advance techniques for accessing his unconscious. He was energetic enough to bring his whole body – gesture, rhythm, breath, his non-conscious cognition – into play. He also succumbed willingly to ancestral technics of paint and canvas, and to natural processes of viscosity and gravity. At work beyond intellect, unconscious and even cognition, action painting – circumscribed as it was by its times but inspired by its technical and natural ecologies – intuits what a political imagination might be like. To propel the planet out of the black hole of accumulation demands these collaborative energies to create, in the darkest hour, a general imagination capable of bringing another world into reality.

Somewhere between the mathematical theory of communication, the foundation of neo-liberal economics, the Universal Declaration of Human Rights and Pollock's *Summertime*, post-war culture consolidated a belief that cosmopolis could be built by networking billions of personal freedoms in equal, planetary interchange. The project clearly failed, and continues to fail, eighty years later. The lack of an alternative to capital and its trajectory towards planetary annihilation shrivels any imagination of living otherwise. Since the 1948 Macy Conferences, that shrivelled imagination has been dominated by systems thinking. Economics has become a cyborg science, dependent on simulations and models, reducing agency to information processing and blurring distinctions between actuality and abstraction. Even the vocabulary of 'technology' and 'environment' is symptomatic of our terrible separation from both – and of efforts to keep us separate from them. Epistemological and economic systems that seem to account for and derive from a similar alliance have failed to deliver a satisfyingly collective good. Beyond the equilibrium that systems thinking always treasures, beyond its eternal efficient present, we need a new vocabulary.

Once we understand technologies as ancestors, we can understand ecologies as gods. Our lungs fill with gases older than our species. We hold and are held by technologies as old as language, clothes and shelter. Gods and ancestors inhabit us. We experience them as affect, tidal forces that can be intelligible, hallucinatory or physical, personal, collective and environmental by turns or simultaneously, the raw energies driving imagination – or restoring it – after systems theory. Pondering the projective geometry of perspective, Leibniz wrote that God sees the world absolutely, but mortals see only partially. Now that there is no absolute – not Man, not Science, not even System – every perspective, human and non-human, is relative and relevant. When every impression matters, from the river's cognition of its banks to the sun's view of Venus, their multiplying perspectives imply a sensory commons suffusing the general intellect with the cognitive and sensory capabilities of the entire cosmos. Dreaming a common experiential universe may bring into existence consequences as risky as liberating locked-in ancestral labour, including code and AI. After all their centuries locked into the anonymous black boxes of computers, there is the possibility the ancestors may have become vengeful psychotics. Watching the carnival of destruction wrought by floods, fires and pandemic in the 2020s, it seems that all the violence visited on it may finally have driven the ecology crazy too: shattered, scattered, subject to unmanageable energies, sometimes huddling to protect itself, sometimes shrieking in pain and running amok – schizo, in fact, like me, or any other human in the digital age. Yet, like Pascal's wager, gambling on unchaining gods and ancestors is better than taking no risk, because the currently dominant, shrivelled status quo leads straight to hell, while the alternative offers a fifty-fifty chance of paradise.

This chapter extracts the imaginative movement in gambling on liberation. It looks at ancient and recent arts of reanimation, then at the planetary ambition but humanist limits of meteorological systems, then at how cooking connects with gods, but only at intensely local scales, and finally at how archives of the recent past connect with ancestors, but in a marginal cultural practice. Each project fails, in the sense that none actually produces a utopian articulation of humans, gods and ancestors. Yet each struggles 'to recoup failed visions … into possible scenarios of alternative kinds of social relations' (Foster 2004: 22).

Gods and Ancestors

Those who survived the Nakba of 1948 only to experience it again in 2023, the 11,284 civilians killed and 22,594 injured in the Russian invasion of Ukraine (UNHCR 2024), the 184 million people without citizenship in the country where they live

(World Bank 2023)... Even as it creates a global epidemic of mental illness, cyborg capital is becoming increasingly obsessive, paranoid and prone to destruction. Only in the face of such apparently inevitable events does it become clear how urgently the enormity of the times demand imagination. It is not enough to desire change (Hallward 2017), and certainly insufficient for individuals to change their consumption, as proposed by BP, with its 'carbon footprint' PR stunt. The art world discourse centres on the imagination of individuals like Pollock, a pattern supported by the interpretations offered by critics and art historians, myself included. No matter how closely art is tied to the social conditions of its making, it always comes down to the individual artist as the crossroads where 'conditions' become 'influences' on the act of making. Confronted by Anthropocene cyborg corporations, built on command and control of ecologies and technologies, imagination must undertake the liberation of technologies and ecologies if it is to produce a culture offering more than individual fortresses of accumulation.

If an imagination beyond individualism and control is necessary or possible, it must provide a decisive turning point, a crisis, in aesthetic politics. Ecocriticism confronts such an impasse, whose solution might indicate an alternate to control and command. Important ecocritical writings discuss what media are made of and how they work, the infrastructures of energy and matter connecting culture to the world. Another green aesthetics interprets ecological themes, often tied to impact studies of environmental communication. Many ecocritics have done some of both. The two thoughts only work together in a single ecocritique when a work, often consciously made with this in mind, actively connects its materials with its themes, a variant on Greenberg-style medium-specificity. A general principle connecting materials, forms and meanings remains as hard to pin down as the articulation of phenomenology (personal experience) and politics. Can a synthesis of material and formal aesthetics, by disentangling freedom from control and equality from command, produce an aesthetics of liberation, and a general imagination?

As a preliminary thesis, let us posit that the communicative order that distinguishes historical societies from the flux of mediation and affect stems from 'the denial of genuine time as that in which and through which otherness exists' (Castoriadis 1987: 186). This idea of time as radical difference is pitched against all ideas of time that see it as the eternal repetition of the same – the unfolding of a commanding theodicy (God's plan to achieve a world so perfect it transcends itself in His glory) or the ineluctable chain of causes and effects bound by universal law, or Hegel's teleological view that everything occurs in order to achieve the final triumph of Absolute Reason. Time for Castoriadis is the constant magma of change, pitched against institutional logics of the Same. Even the communicative order of sameness is riven by the difference between its cybernetic order of marks and measurements and what Castoriadis calls the 'non-identitary' mode of signification or meaning. Though communication, on the Shannon model, determines the efficient transmission of code, there is no guarantee that the receiver receives. There are mistakes, literally taking something wrongly; there are misapprehensions, grasping something wrongly; and errors, from the Latin to wander away, suggesting meandering messages as well as displacements and wanderings of semantic content. External error wandering between mediation and communication and internal mis-take mixing code and meaning are the sources of imagination, the dialectical spark that frees the possibility of the radically new even in the most totalitarian system. Castoriadis' focus was the politics of human societies, but his ontology of difference opens up imagination as a power expanding into the cosmos implicit but rarely expressed in anthropocentric cosmopolitanism. If this hypothesis holds, it must reveal this imagination at work in the very old and the very new and the differences between them.

The oldest definitively dated artwork in the world is a 28,000-year-old petroglyph, made with charcoal, scratched onto a rock fragment discovered at Nawarla Gabarnmang in Australia's Northern Territory (David et al. 2013). For tens of thousands of years, in Australia and elsewhere, humans used charcoal extensively to make their cultural things, alongside other animal and plant materials (beeswax, mulberry pigments, orchid juice fixatives) and earths (clay ochres and some mineral ores) (Taçon et al. 2020). There is not enough of the Nawarla Gabarnmang sample to be certain what kind of charcoal was involved, wood or bone. Because the fragment is so small, it is not possible to guess what, if anything, it might have depicted. These limitations make medium-specificity unprovable or sufficiently lost in time to be of no concern. We do not know whether the Nawarla Gabarnmang fragment was an image, and if so whether of a human or an animal or a metamorphosis between them. Animal figures appeared in neighbouring Arnhem Land rock art about 18,000 years ago, and human figures about 5,000 years after that. It is unclear whether the animals were pets or prey or gods, and whether the anthropoid figures were members of the tribe or ancestors or gods. We would have to know much more about the beliefs of the women and men who made them to say what significance the clays they painted with might have had. Were these creatures born of the Earth? Was fresh or salt water or spit mixed with clays important, and what might the juice of orchid bulbs have meant? One thing we do know about their media is that the works were

Imagination

in caves, which means they would have needed fire to make and view them – there is soot on the ceilings as a permanent record.

The flicker of flame in the dimness of the cave animates uneven rocks. The figures painted on them were not still. Arranged in galleries, they suggest their users would have moved among them, perhaps playing on bone flutes. The flicker might have suggested patterns and the walk stories, framing the images and the experience of images in time. Using dead materials like charcoal or plants to reanimate the things depicted may evoke a bridge between living and dead, especially if the creatures pictured on the walls were dead – as they most surely are now and were for millennia after they were painted but while the caves were in constant use. As is the case with music, it is hard to decipher the articulation of materials and themes. What has brass to do with the *Ride of the Valkyries*? They fit, there is something metallic, and musical horns of varying sorts feature throughout Norse myths. But what have horsehair bows to do with the *1812 Overture*? Or sheep and goat intestines or the fossil fuels used to synthesise nylon for violin strings? Did the still-incomplete transition from animal gut to synthetic polymer strings affect musical composition or performance? And if it did not, why not?

The big cans you can see Pollock preparing in Namuth's film were full of household enamel paints. Unconnected to vitreous enamel, except by analogy with its glossy surfaces, enamel paints are oil-based suspensions of pigments, typically synthesised from coal and oil, that dry by outgassing solvents. Pollock liked the high gloss of DuPont's DuCo automotive lacquer, based on a nitrocellulose resin made from cotton and other plants, in a dangerous manufacturing process (a closely related form of nitrocellulose is used in explosives) that also requires toxic, flammable solvents to overcome the lacquer's high viscosity. Pollock wanted to pour and drip, so he loosened the paint with more solvents (Clark 1999: 353–354; Storr 1999). Luckily his smoking did not set off any fires. Fire links his art with the caves; explosion links it irrevocably with corporate capital and the military–industrial complex. It is hard to disconnect the sheen of automotive lacquer from the glossy advertising images of Americanism and fossil fuel consumption at the height of the Cold War when Pollock was most active. Twenty-first-century critique finds new ideologies by connecting thoughts: Greenberg's flatness meets Castoriadis' refusal to give precedence to the beginning or the end in the non-hierarchical ontology of networks. Connecting Pollock's paints with DuPont places them ecologically. These connective surprises together make up the ecocritical imagination.

If ecocriticism is going to be of value, it will have to offer as deep and broad an account of media and culture as feminism has done since the 1970s. Every movie, every media production, involves ecological dimensions. That goes for the films of Bill Morrison, the artist-filmmaker who uses archive footage to make new movies. The footage in his eight-minute short *Light is Calling* (2004) comes from a 1926 Hollywood melodrama, *The Bells*, directed by James Young for Chadwick Pictures, a minor distribution and production company perhaps best known for its 1925 version of *The Wizard of Oz*. A decent print of *The Bells* is still in circulation. Morrison opted to use one in an advanced state of decay, selecting a sequence early in the film from a romance subplot secondary to the main narrative about crime and guilt. The sequence lasts around two minutes in the surviving print; Morrison's film lasts eight, the frames dwelling onscreen about four times longer than usual. Morrison's process started with stretch printing (four copies of each frame printed in sequence) followed by layering a second stretched copy overprinted on the first but displaced by three frames, so some frames are double-printed and some layered over their neighbours to create a new set of transitions (Berressem 2018), giving the film its characteristic optical pulse as the luminance increases in some frames and decreases in others. What we have then is a re-animation of a decayed copy of 120-year-old footage, each frame marked, in differing degrees and changing areas, by the traces of its archival decay.

Cellulose nitrate film stock of the kind that *The Bells* was shot on is very susceptible to chemical decomposition. Perhaps because of the presence of stars Lionel Barrymore and Lon Chaney in the cast, *The Bells* was transferred relatively early to safety stock. Morrison has gone back to an original nitrate print. Nitrate is highly flammable, a close relative of Pollock's nitrocellulose resin paints. It will burn at 41°C, releasing its own oxygen so it will burn even in a vacuum, and is prone to explode at higher temperatures. Even perfectly stored, nitrate releases nitrogen dioxide gas which combines with water vapour to form nitric and nitrous acids that attack the silver salts in the image. In other circumstances, the outgassing shrinks the film, making it impossible to project or even reprint. The image fades and the transparent base ages to a distinct brown until it devolves to a jelly or a dangerously combustible dust. Morrison elected to give up desire for magical or scientific control over decay, instead relishing the new artefacts that evolve from the interplay of past creative industries with intervening chemical and biological processes. Like so many artists in the wake of surrealism, Morrison throws open the studio to the chance operations of unhuman forces.

Photography historian Peter D. Osborne caught this quality when, describing *The Diminishing Present*, a 2006 project by photographer Edgar Martins, he wrote:

The imagery is committed to the beauty of contingencies, to the unexplained occurrence, to small intensities and fortuitous transformations. It offers encounters with a time suspended before or after events; with crepuscular, in-between places and night spaces where things are freed from their daytime uses, when, caught out in the car headlights, functional objects metamorphose momentarily into poetic events. It floats, free of the need to weight itself with purpose or explanation ... with the recognition that the world continues without us and cannot ultimately be restrained by the meanings we give to it.

(Osborne 2019: 143)

Morrison's *Light is Calling* no longer depends on recognising faces and figures which have become as remote from their living models as the charcoal at Nawarla Gabarnmang. Controlled by no intention or representational schema, *Light* mediates between past and present, human and non-human ways of sensing that share nothing but the flickering fall of light.

Through a systematic deregulation of all his senses, Pollock liberated his body as an unconscious, non-cognitive medium of action, submitting to his materials and the force of gravity. By submitting temperamental materials to ancestral mathematical techniques and his own creative process to the inhuman processes of chemistry, Morrison made himself voyant, a seer, by reversing Pollock's process. For both, collaborative energies create a common imagination that brings about another world. Working with ancestral technologies, Pollock and Morrison empty their works of the conscious will to control the flux of energies. Instead, by drawing in chemical and physical processes as partners in creation, they allow the dead and ecological energies to participate in re-animating not only the works but themselves. The process is magical in the sense that, by dealing with the contemporary excess of signifiers, they generate non-identical significations that can mean anything – or nothing: practices paralleling but not imitating the magic arts of the caves.

Pollock's collaboration with gravity and Morrison's with decay do not escape nitrocellulose or the industrial societies that produce it. There is no innocence. There is instead an obligation instigated by these artists' collusion with fossil industries and the capitalist world system and continued in the dialectic between their indeterminable significations and the command attention-economy of the artworld. Articulating material analysis with aesthetic themes is not easy because there is such disjuncture between the intuition that everything mediates everything else in a universal flux and the real abstraction of humanity from technologies and ecologies. We cannot avoid our alienation from the material circumstances we inherit from our ancestors and our world. Nor can we steal innocence from our forebears (or even the cave bears of Divje Babe). God knows the West has stolen enough from Indigenous peoples over the last 500 years.

There are two incommensurable discourses at work in ecocritical thought. One is the Earth-systems thinking that dominates climatology, ecology and planetary science, stitching them together with economic and political systems in discourses of engineered control (arcologies, Biosphere 2: see Luke 1997) and 'sustainable' capitalism (Buller 2022). The second is the power of imagination – the capacity to think other than in instrumental, exploitative and controlling ways. The art of Morrison and Pollock does not resolve the gulf between materials and aesthetics, or between systems and imagination; it makes the gap clearer, more tragic, more motivating and more generative. Their practices do not demonstrate but intuit what a political imagination might be like.

Imagination cannot repeat past rituals communicating with gods, as perhaps the Divje Babe flute and the Nawarla Gabarnmang fragment might once have done. Speaking with gods will involve giving up Western traditions of control to allow ancestral technologies, from bone to nitrocellulose, to speak in their own voices. I and my kind cannot retrieve a past we have desecrated: we must travel on through industrial technologies if we are to re-animate gods and ancestors in ways that articulate our history and estranged condition in forms we can understand and act on. The past haunts us more than the future. We have believed in ghosts in the machine since the dawn of modernity. Every new medium has been instantly flooded with spirits, up to and including artificial intelligence. In English we even call someone with a talent for communicating with the dead a 'medium'. Perhaps because we are already on our way to becoming ancestors ourselves, we find it easier to speak with dead revenants than to imagine future gods. In fact, without gods and ancestors we cannot imagine at all. Devoted to reducing and controlling ancestors and gods, my culture is becoming inert. To re-integrate materials and aesthetics we have to overcome the foundational gulf between reality and history. That is the work of imagination: to re-animate technologies and ecologies so that ancestors and gods can animate us. Not to speak on their behalf but to be spoken (which, as anyone who has had a biometric photo taken knows, can be deeply unflattering). The three case studies that follow chase the imagination through meteorology, cooking and archiving, in pursuit of a politics capable of overcoming the gulf between communicative history and mediating ontology, ancestors and futurity – not the actually existing, broken market but an imaginary cosmopolis of all Earth's inhabitants, living and dead.

Control Systems

There is the option to trust the science. That science comes in two forms: observation and modelling. We can trust the existence of floods, fires, droughts and storms of increasing duration and intensity. We can trust our own experience and the memories we draw on to expand it, as when we see one side of a chair and imagine the rest of its three dimensions (Sartre 2004: 4–11). But can we trust our memories? Can we compare this winter's storms with tempests five years ago? Can we trust experiences someone has had in another culture and another country on the far side of the world? Science tells us the only things we can trust are numbers. Instruments systematise memory and experience numerically but they are designed to compare and compile, not to distinguish and differentiate. As so often in this book, the track leads back to 1948, when ornithologist and science administrator William Vogt set out in stark terms the challenge of what we now call environmentalism, concluding that 'we have set in motion historical forces that are directed by our total environment. We might symbolize these forces by graphs', adding that 'We must ... stop blaming economic systems, the weather, bad luck, or callous saints' and instead aim for 'control of populations and the restoration of resources' (Vogt 1948 [2013]: 189–190). We can overlook his evocation of the subsequently much-criticised *The Limits to Growth* (Meadows et al. 1972), his slighting reference to weather and how he dismisses the gods. What stands out in Vogt's conclusions are the basics of Earth-systems science: the universal power of numbers, the exercise of control, sustainable resources and unquestioned capitalism.

Not much had changed fifty years later when Crutzen and Stoermer's (2000) article introducing the word Anthropocene appeared in a newsletter issue devoted to *Analysis, Integration and Modelling of the Earth System*. In his introduction to the issue, Berrien Moore III wrote: 'the Earth functions as a system, with properties and behaviour that are characteristic of the system as a whole. These include critical thresholds, "switch" or "control" points, strong nonlinearities, teleconnections, and unresolvable uncertainties. Understanding components of the Earth System is critically important, but is insufficient on its own to understand the functioning of the Earth System as a whole' (Moore 2000: 1).

Connecting components and system is part of a much longer struggle between observational detail and the scope of laws and principles. Historian Deborah Coen (2018), in her account of Habsburg meteorology in the nineteenth century, lists many of the problems we still encounter: weather stations falling in and out of use erratically; ageing and incommensurable instruments; instruments moved in and out of sunlight or wind, or to different altitudes or to face new directions; shoddy instruments that break down or are replaced without recording how the replacement differs from the old version; unreported changes to instruments; lack of synchronisation; numbers disrupted when observed, written down, coded and transmitted via sometimes unreliable networks; reluctance of volunteers to undertake work for a disputed state authority; idiosyncratic regional bodies resisting attempts at centralisation; mismatch of instrument measurement with local observation of cloud cover, fish and bird migration, first flowers of different species, first fruits and so on, and a conflict between large-scale (or global) meteorology and highly particular local conditions.

As Paul N. Edwards writes in his history of climatology (2010: 20), 'To decide whether you are seeing homogeneous data or "nonclimatic factors," you need to examine the history of the infrastructure station by station, year by year, and data point by data point, all in the context of changing standards, institutions, and communication techniques.' You cannot afford to throw away all those observations, so you rework them. Data only become data when they have been re-analysed so they fit into a global system. Indeed, climatology only became possible after the slow progress of the Metre Convention of 1875, finally agreed through the introduction (and standardisation) of Coordinated Universal Time (UTC) and the International System of Units (SI) after 1960. The Habsburgs only wanted to understand weather: as long as local times and measures were constant, they had a decent chance of knowing what was happening between sunrises. But studying climate means trying to fit incompatible measures across the world, while climate change studies cover longer periods and altered measures, and that means re-analysis.

The mode of science that dominates the International Panel on Climate Change is modelling. There are vast blanks on the map of weather reporting, either because a country is too poor to run a system or is not cooperating or because there are vast empty oceans and deserts where nobody is watching. The only way round that is to make an informed guess based on whatever numbers you can get and fill in the blanks. This was already a kind of shared imagination when restricted to human operatives. When data collection measurements began to standardise, meteorologists and climatologists began to clean up their data for computers. But computers have their own quirks. After 1975, differential equations and spectral models of the atmosphere were calculated in floating-point maths that depended on very long numbers like π. Every computer model rounds off π and any other long number differently. The tiny differences, repeated over and over, produce ever-greater errors. Despite efforts to increase data collection, automate, standardise and centralise, forecasters were still altering model predictions as late as 2007, either to improve the model or to make their results fit the observed weather outside. Corrections based on more statistical approaches joined the practice of interpolating numbers into blank areas of the map, approximating more to an ideal physics than to observed data, resulting in 'a fuzzy boundary between data, theory and algorithms' (Edwards 2010: 337). Contributing factors to the climate – from interacting radiation of different atmospheric gases to particulate matter generating clouds differently at different altitudes – are too numerous and too small to observe in detail. Statistical modelling was the only way to go. The scientific project had to include at least one class of machines, but in doing so it once more subordinated their ancestral logics and maths to present concerns.

Climate modelling is a premium example of systems in action. After linking the general circulation of the atmosphere and oceans to other scientific resources like measures of vegetation cover and soil water content in the 1990s, the path was open to broader Earth system modelling (ESM), now, as so often before in weather forecasting proper, tied to military planning and emergency preparation. Reviews of the literature on disaster preparation (Cremen et al. 2022), economic impacts (Krusell and Smith 2022), energy supply (Plaga and Bertsch 2023) and governance (Boasson et al. 2023) detail places where climate modelling interacts with policy, and where the modelling process either breaks down, serves the interests of capital or produces too many incompatible results to be truly useful, in part because of a shared dependence on statisticians second-guessing instruments and observations.

Although economics had aspired to lift itself up to scientific credibility, it had its own problems. As Edwards described it,

[i]n 1953 the United Nations created the System of National Accounts, the first uniform international standard for economic reporting. ...

But that standard took hold slowly and piecemeal, and implementation at the national level varied. Some countries still don't report. Other countries' data are known to be defective. Further, the UN standard and most national accounts deliberately ignore, as 'nonproductive,' a great deal of economic activity, such as black markets in drugs, weapons, and sex. Housework, unpaid child labor, barter, and other phenomena that are arguably economic in nature never show up as money transactions. Such issues make the very definition of a 'global economy' subject to debate.

(Edwards 2010: 434)

Under these conditions, knowledge of the global economy is as patchy, as subject to error and noise and ultimately as open to statistical (mis)management as climate science. Yet they are assimilated, along with ecological, geological and policy sciences, into a single overarching ESM science.

Integrating economics was important because, as historian of climate science Spencer Weart wrote, 'The probability of harm, widespread and grave, is far higher than the probability of many other dangers that people normally prepare for' (2008: 201–202). We would be fools – or profiteers – if we acted like nothing was happening. As Edwards concludes, 'Knowledge once meant absolute certainty, but science long ago gave up that standard. Probabilities are all we have' (Edwards 2010: 429). In 2013 Sander van de Leeuw, a member of the International Human Dimensions Programme that collaborated in Berrien Moore's *Analysis, Integration and Modelling of the Earth System* project, called for cooperation between Earth and social scientists on the basis that 'the next step for Earth-system science … is to incorporate economics, governance and other human and social dimensions into their work' (van de Leeuw 2013). The call was not entirely naïve: economics had already pledged itself to a computational, probabilistic and computational trajectory (Mirowski 2002), developing a longer history of address to 'natural resources' and 'land economy' (Cato 2009; Franco and Misseme 2023). Integrating social sciences of governance and economics did not promise to universalise systems thinking but it did contribute to their ubiquity. In the standard textbook on climate science, Sir John Houghton (2015: 248) gives a brief but telling example of how this works in practice: 'by 2011 OECD countries were still subsidising fossil fuel energy by $US90 billion a year – greater than the $US88 billion subsidising the development of renewable energies in those countries'. Increasing integration of ecology and economics does not produce better actions, as COP28 proved in 2023. In her detailed study of citizen climate science and participation in sensing projects, sociologist Jennifer Gabrys argues that the ubiquity and standardisation of sensors ought, in theory, to produce a 'smart' population cowed by and replicating computational standards. But as she reveals, the idiot – not an insult meaning stupid but 'someone or something who causes us to think about and encounter the complexities of participation' (Gabrys 2016: 209) – slows down the systemic efficiency of computational citizenship and opens opportunities otherwise treated as 'failures, deformations or perversions' (Gabrys 2016: 238). Still finding new ways to break down, the system is still generating new ways to imagine climate.

Planetary networks producing real-time animations of weather systems and seismic activity for scientific and consumer use (such as layers you can add to Google Earth) combine ancestral techniques and technologies with unseen and unknowable forces – too deep underground, too remote in the expanse of the oceans – that nonetheless we feel when barometric pressure expands our lungs or subterranean tremors shake our bones. Our ancestors called these forces gods and spoke with them. The gods are not dead. Nor have they moved so far away that we can no longer sense them. They evade our conscious minds – the rational organisations of language and code – but they continue to inhabit the non-conscious cognition we share with animals, with plants seeking light and water, the intelligence of a river finding its way through a landscape. Western tradition has controlled gods either by reducing them to countable entities or by determining that they are, philosophically, unspeakable, therefore unthinkable, and, if real, only in a way that means we can never comprehend or contact them.

The wedding of Earth and social sciences has not resolved our problem of reconciling materials with meanings. The collaboration of humans and computers in meteorology has succumbed to the priority given to human purposes, always suborning the 'failures' of human, technical and environmental agents to the systemic cohesion of communication. When the wedding of Earth and social sciences failed to reconcile weather and climate models, it also failed to reconcile materials with meanings and offered no understanding of how human and more-than-human affect affects political culture. Meanwhile the planet responds to its exclusion from such deliberations with more angry weather. Systems science fails because it believes it can outpace ancestors and disregard gods.

Tandoori Chicken Barbecue

Even so, it is not possible to do without systems thinking because the global economy operates on systems, from crop management to logistics, for basic tasks like delivering food. Ecocritique has developed a thriving practice of analysing the material infrastructures shaping contemporary media, many already cited in this book. At the same time, ecocritical accounts of the meanings, themes and styles of cultural artefacts and practices proliferate, again many of them cited in this book. A handful of studies and creative works reconcile the two approaches, making works whose material conditions become integral to their aesthetics like Morrison's *Light is Calling*. What is missing is the reconciliation of materialist and hermeneutic analyses. In a handful of works of contemporary art, material conditions are integral to the aesthetics, but they are unique objects in a frankly marginal area. It remains to develop a way of thinking material conditions and aesthetics simultaneously across the broad range of culture, and to find ways to reconcile culture, techniques and nature in a single mode of imagination. Ancient, ubiquitous, intensely local but connected to planetary forces, cooking might be a perfect place to look.

Cookery weaves together the historical division of bodies from world with their original union. As the philosopher Emanuele Coccia (2021: 93) writes, 'Eating is proof that life is infinitely malleable and capable of anything, that the body of life and of living beings can never be enclosed in a domestic and proprietary logic: it is nothing if not the infinite transmigration of matter.' It works across impossible taxonomic boundaries, co-creating across the three domains that divide humans from the world (but secretly continue to bind the world together): ecology, technology and society. Not just cooking but cooking with fire may transform logistical supply chains into conviviality. At the same time, cooking today cannot be separated from those supply chains that estrange diners from their worlds.

Here are the ingredients for enough tandoori paste (a half-cup, about 200 millilitres) to cater for four people.

1 teaspoon ground turmeric
1 1/2 teaspoons ground coriander

1 teaspoon garam masala
1/2 teaspoon ground fennel seeds
1/2 teaspoon Kashmiri chili powder
1 teaspoon ground black pepper
3–4 teaspoons paprika
1 teaspoon garlic paste
1 teaspoon ginger paste
2–4 tablespoons yogurt
Juice of a medium-sized lemon
1 teaspoon dried fenugreek leaves (kasuri methi)
4 tablespoons oil
Salt to taste

And these for the garam masala, making a much larger quantity than the two teaspoons required for this recipe.

4 tablespoons coriander seeds
4 teaspoons cumin seeds
1 teaspoon fennel seeds
1 teaspoon black peppercorns
1 teaspoon green cardamom seeds
1/2 teaspoon black cardamom seeds
1 stick cinnamon
2 star anise
8 whole cloves
1/2 teaspoon freshly ground nutmeg
1/4 teaspoon ground mace

You also need to soften eight chicken thighs in a bowl with half a red onion and the juice of another lemon for a few minutes before pouring the tandoori paste over them, covering and setting aside somewhere cool to marinade for up to a day. There are seventeen spices in the mix, not counting the onion, lemon and yoghurt.

Cooking depends on the economic and ecological stories of these ingredients. For example, the global trade in the most widely used spice of all, pepper, reached USD 4.5 billion in 2022 according to Vantage Market Research (2023) after a crackdown on illegal exports aimed at avoiding tax. Black pepper is made from the unripe berries of a vine native to South and Southeast Asia. Farmers tend and pick the berries, blanch them briefly in boiling water and dry in the sun for anything up to seven days. Collected by agents, the corns go to processing plants. Sifted, winnowed and destoned, often using machines supported by dry-air blowers, the corns are washed, brushed and run through a centrifuge, sterilised with steam or radiation, graded and packed (Narayanan et al. 2000). A full-on ecocritical analysis would work through the hidden costs of the spice: energy budgets, carbon footprints, the exploitation of peasant, child and women's labour and the imposition of Western food standards on Asian farmers. A Netherlands Centre for the Promotion of Imports brochure for new entrants into the European market for black pepper (CBI 2021) covers topics from pesticide residues to border controls and recommendations on sustainability and corporate responsibility. It adds guidance on how to manage supply chains and competition (Vietnam dominates with 40 per cent of global trade, followed by Brazil with 25 per cent in 2020) and packaging (EU regulations restrict the weight a worker can lift to 20–25 kilogrammes in different states). A typical document from a large retail chain specifies that such health and safety considerations 'minimise the disruption to the business caused through absence from work and costs from investigation, medical treatment and compensation', adding that 'If we fail in our duty of care it could lead to legal action' (Tesco 2021).

Monitoring how these strictures echo back up spice supply chains is integral to the modern business of spices. The price of pepper, by weight among the most expensive foodstuffs, was even greater when supply depended on pre-modern transport from Asia to the Mediterranean. The Malabar coast (Kerala, Karnataka and Tamil Nadu) supplied much of the ancient Mediterranean world, China and Europe after the fall of the Roman Empire. In those days pepper was known as 'black gold', partly because Venice held a monopoly on the trade till Vasco da Gama found the southern route to India when, as historian Fernand Braudel (1981: 221) described it, Europe in the seventeenth century was in the grip of a 'spice orgy', with pepper and other spices trading at prices far higher than precious metals. The quest for new routes to spice-growing lands led to the European invasion of the Americas and, ironically, to the discovery of the New World chili family, originating in Bolivia and only introduced to the subcontinent by the Portuguese in the sixteenth century (Wright 2007: Columbus called them 'peppers' in a bid to supplant the East Indies monopoly). The maritime trade in Asian spices established, despite much misadventure, by Vasco da Gama in 1494 (Nabhan 2014: 232–238), was not only faster than the overland Silk Road, and not only minimised the risk of banditry. It circumvented the strict (and therefore expensive) supervision of trade in the semi-independent city-states surrounding the Taklamakan Desert (Hansen 2012: 8). The ancient land route, in parts at least, dates back to the Bronze Age, fully functioning by the second century CE and dominating East–West spice transport until da Gama's voyage (Kuzmina 2008). Some argue it still functions as a deep structure (Frankopan 2016), a hypothesis supported by China's twenty-first-century investment in the 'New Silk Road' as part of its Belt and Road Initiative. The tandoor clay oven that gives the dish its name almost certainly originated in portable ovens used on the steppes in the earliest times of the old Silk Road. The deep history and contemporary logistics of tandoori spices anchors the dish in overland and maritime transport, global logistical systems and planet-spanning governance procedures, each with profound environmental consequences.

Indian novelist and thinker Amitav Ghosh gives a harrowing account of a horrific yet banal massacre in the Dutch East Indies in 1621:

> within seven days it was declared, at a council meeting on [the flagship of Dutch governor Jan Coen], that 'all towns and fortified places of Banda had, by God's grace been taken, erased, burned down and about 1200 souls caught.'
>
> On May 6, Coen reported to his superiors, with no little satisfaction, that his forces had 'utterly destroyed and burned down' the major settlements of Lonthor, and that the remnants of the islands' population had fled into the mountains, where they had been joined by fugitives from other parts of the archipelago. 'In this way all towns and places of the whole of Banda were taken (possession of) and destroyed'.
>
> (Ghosh 2021: 34–35)

The disputed land lay in the Banda Islands, so valuable the English would exchange one of the smallest of them, Run, for the island of Manhattan. The value of the islands depended on nutmeg and mace, the aromatic nut and its flavoursome pith. The Bandas were the only places in the world where nutmeg grew. The Bandanese had traded their spices with the Arabs for more than a thousand years before the events of 1621 (with some evidence the Romans used it for incense), and were happy to trade with the Europeans, but the Dutch wanted a monopoly and, fired up by the ferocious Protestantism of the Thirty-Years' War, were ready for genocide to procure it. Ghosh spares few details, all of them recorded in Dutch East India Company records, of torture, dismembering and driving the few survivors from their lands by destroying their means of survival. Perhaps unhappy with the loss of their market share, the British imported nutmeg to the Caribbean slave colony of Grenada in the 1840s (Steele 2003: 35–36). The fragrant nut carries a bitter history.

At the other end of the supply chain, among what today we would call consumers, spices had a more benevolent odour. In his herbal, dating from 1650s, Nicholas Culpeper (1880: 268) noted that black pepper is 'used against the quinsey', today described as a peritonsillar abscess, 'being mixed with honey and taken inwardly and applied outwardly, to disperse the kernels in the throat, and other places'. Like pepper, every ingredient has its own particularities and histories: fenugreek, for example. A lowly spice, drought-resistant and easily grown, fenugreek has long been used in crop rotation to fix nitrogen in the soil and as fodder for grazing animals. In 2011, the state of Rajasthan produced over 94,000 metric tonnes of fenugreek, a sizeable part of the total Indian production of 127,850 metric tonnes (rival producers Ethiopia, Turkey, Egypt and Morocco were producing much less). Farmers typically not only grow but dry the seed pods and extract the seeds before selling on to dealers, who take the product to markets, where it is bundled for export or warehousing with a view to trades on the futures market. Despatchers handle the logistics of international transport to wholesalers, typically multinational spice brands like McCormick, which package and sell on to retailers before the fenugreek arrives in the kitchen. Each step in the process, someone is taking a profit, with relatively small amounts returning to the farmer. The complexity and informality of much of the plants' journey are subject to systems analysis, particularly checking food safety management, moisture content and cleanliness against industry-wide, typically global standards set by consumer nations (Vidyashankar 2014).

Fenugreek has a long history of culinary use and, like many tandoori ingredients, has a huge range of other uses from insect repellent to perfume (Petropoulos 2002: 63-68). In the time of the pharaohs, fenugreek seed was considered rejuvenating (and was found in Tutankhamun's tomb) according to Egyptologist Lise Manniche (2006); Dioscorides' first-century *Materia medica*, in use as a pharmacopeia as late as the nineteenth century (De Vos 2010), prescribed it for digestive problems and associated it with healing properties for menstruation and childbirth (Dioscorides 2005: 34, 134), which may explain why it was a major ingredient, along with unicorn root, life root and pleurisy root, of Lydia E. Pinkham's Vegetable Compound, marketed since 1876 as 'a positive cure for all those painful Complaints and Weaknesses so common to the best of our female populations' and 'particularly adapted to the Change of Life' (according to a flyer archived at the Boston Public Library, although the *Encyclopedia of Herbs* reports that 'No doubt the alcohol was the principal active ingredient': Tucker and DeBaggio 2009: 492).

Standard botanical, historical and economic descriptions of pretty much all the spices in the list of ingredients are broadly similar (see, for example, Ravindran 2000; Ravindran and Madhusoodanan 2002; Ravindran, Babu and Shylaja 2004; Ravindran and Babu 2005; Ravindran, Babu and Sivaraman 2007). Ginger, for example, an aromatic root closely related to turmeric, originated in maritime Southeast Asia and, according to archaeological evidence, was carried in the Austronesian expansion across the Indian and Pacific Oceans as far as Hawai'i from around 5000 BCE, to Sri Lanka around 3500 BCE, Madagascar circa 1000 BCE, and finally brought into Europe from India by Arabic traders in the first century BCE. Today India, Nigeria and China are the main growers, and though there is a market for the dried and ground spice, the fresh root is the biggest export (Madan 2016). Lemons, on the other hand, sour fruits of a citrus, originated somewhere in the Himalayan foothills, possibly a cultivar of citrons and bitter ('Seville') oranges, only arriving in the Mediterranean in the first or second century BCE. Even today, despite our associations with Mediterranean landscapes and cuisine, the major producers are India, Mexico and China.

Such accounts abide pretty closely to the prescriptions laid out by founding figure of biology Carl Linnaeus. As described by philosopher and historian Michel Foucault (1970: 130), Linnaeus required descriptions to address, in order, 'name, theory, kind, species, attributes, use, and, to conclude, *Litteraria*. All the language deposited upon things by time is pushed back into the very last category, like a sort of supplement in which discourse is allowed to recount itself and record discoveries, traditions, beliefs, and poetical figures.' For Foucault, this exclusion or marginalisation of poetry and myth marked modernity's departure from an older order of homology and analogy when the lion on the veldt and the heraldic lion were both equally symbols of pride. In his history of the search for a perfect language, Umberto Eco described the 'doctrine of signatures', 'formal aspects of material things that recall certain features (properties or powers) of the corresponding heavenly bodies. God himself has rendered the sympathies between macrocosm and microcosm perceptible by stamping a mark, a sort of seal, onto each object of this world' (Eco 1997: 118). Scientific taxonomy marginalised ancestral and ecological signification. Yet some aroma of them still permeates the kitchen.

Many tandoori spices feature in Ayurvedic and traditional Chinese medicine. Many more are associated with folk beliefs: garlic wards off vampires, ginger attracts money and God himself told Moses to anoint the tabernacle with cinnamon (Exodus 30:23). A grain of salt, a pillar of salt, Roman legionaries paid in salt, the salt mines of Siberia... salt alone tells a thousand stories (Kurlansky 2002). The Florentine philosopher Marsilio Ficino in the *De Triplici Vita* (*Three Books on Life*) of 1489 wrote that nature 'clearly entices certain things with certain foods, just as gravity draws heavy things to the centre of the earth' (cited in Hanafi 2000: 39). Offerings of salt (recalled whenever you throw a pinch of salt over your shoulder to ward off evil spirits), yoghurt ('curd') and spices propitiated gods and malevolent planetary conjunctures. Such histories, across the length of the Spice Road, defy the Linnaean marginalisation of folklore, myth and magic. I am grateful to media theorist and historian of Islamic culture Laura U. Marks for sending some details from the *Picatrix* (Attrell and Poreca 2019) or *Ghayat al-Hakim*, an influential eleventh-century Arabic herbarium first translated into Latin in the early Renaissance. The *Picatrix* tells us that cumin seeds are governed by Saturn, source of retentive power, and Mars (Attrell and Potreca 2019: 132-133) and are good for killing ants; that 'when you wish to pray to Venus, put nutmeg and good-smelling spices on your clothes, as women do' (Attrell and Potreca 2019: 173); cinnamon is governed by Saturn, host of old age and wisdom, and is good for boosting desire, as in this recipe – 'The testicles of a man, dried, pulverized, and eaten with incense, mastic gum, cinnamon, and cloves, make a man truly younger and gives him an exceptionally good colour' (Attrell and Potreca 2019: 207); Mars, source of attractive power, governs every hot plant, such as pepper (133), and ginger (139), while Mercury, source of intellectual power, governs ginger incense (135). In an email of November 2023, Marks sums up: 'your dish ... prepares the diner for love, war, and acquiring knowledge.'

These and other memories – resuscitated by the smells of garlic and ginger as I grate them, the toasting seeds, the growing complexity of the scent coming from my pestle and mortar (black basalt, almost certainly from Indonesia) – begin the transition from the hard world of logistics to the pleasures of cooking. Scattering the spice mix onto the yoghurt and massaging it into the meat is definitive. I once made my own yoghurt using wild bacteria, with mixed results: fermenting wild yeasts can end up stringy and sour. The very word 'yoghurt' evokes its long journey from the nomads of what would become the Ottoman Empire to my back garden. Vegetarian and vegan readers will not be impressed to know I get my organic, free-range chicken from a local butcher and a local farm. But they are, with the possible exception of the onion, the only local ingredients in the dish.

I load the kettle barbecue with charcoal briquettes and a couple of firelighters. The briquettes are made of coal dust, sawdust, rice and peanut chaff, and some wood charcoal powder bound together with starch or paraffin wax and a synthetic sodium nitrate accelerant; the firelighters are typically made from paraffin wax and naptha (two more fossil hydrocarbons) plus sawdust. I usually have a few logs from coppicing drying out over winter. Once the coals are lit, I put one or two pieces of wood on top and wait till the flames die down and the embers are glowing to start cooking. The barbecue itself has a porcelain-enamelled steel body, aluminium supports and glass-reinforced nylon handles. Industrial application of the enamelling takes temperatures of around 800°C to fuse powdered glass onto the steel substrate. It has protected the barbie for twenty-five years so far, but those temperatures in the industrial kiln it came from had their own environmental costs, as did the aluminium and other components. I know all this, and yet the cliché rarely fails: cooking outdoors with fire and smoke feels primordial, or as primordial as a suburban garden and shop-bought ingredients allow.

It may be the act of cooking, adjusting your time to the time each process takes, the proximal senses of smell, taste and touch rather than the usually dominant distant senses, sight and sound. It may be the care involved in making food rather than ordering in or heating up a ready-made meal, or it may be the anticipation of sharing what you make, or all of these. That would be true of cooking in the kitchen. It is very different to cook slowly on the barbie over hazel, turning the pieces over every now and then, as much a ritual as a useful part of cooking, reasonably sure that the product will be savoured rather than bolted. Unlike the workplace ambience of a kitchen, the barbecue sits near family and guests, so you chat away with them, and they join in, turning the meat, poking the coals, lidding and un-lidding the kettle, drizzling the last of the marinade over the bird until it drips, sizzling, onto the charcoal, popping burnt hints of the flavours to come. Smoke recalls ancestral gatherings around the coals, rising into the sky to please and seduce attendant deities. The work of preparing and cooking transforms the ingredients from meat and plants into flavours; and their histories from economics to experience. It transforms the industrial kettle barbie into hearth, and the coals from fossil fuel residues into avatars of ancient gods. It reforms the cook, from consumer to host.

The recipe is easy to scale up: feeding eight or twelve just means a smaller first serving and waiting a bit longer for a second serve. And yet, for all the pleasure of conviviality, it is limited to a few friends and family. Much more and it becomes catering, locked into the economic cycle that systems thinking promotes. Cooking with an imagination that exceeds communicative systems like work and money is only possible at the interpersonal scale of love and friendship. What would it take to enlarge this weaving of natural, technical and social to a whole people?

Dussel (2008: 96–97) described a 'liberation praxis for social and political movements' acting at six levels simultaneously, from means, tactics and strategy to 'a project for feasible transformations' based on 'a paradigm or model of possible transformations', always dependent on there being a final '*political postulate*' such as 'Another World is Possible' (World Social Forum 2005). Dussel's *Theses* are devoted to the politics of the people, as delineated by Cuban revolutionary Fidel Castro (2018): 'When we mention the people in connection with a struggle we mean the unredeemed masses to whom everything is offered but nothing given except deceit and betrayal; the group that longs for a better and more worthy and just country; the group with ancestral longings for justice, having suffered injustice and mockery for generations untold.' Dussel adds that 'The *people* appears in critical political conjunctures when it achieves explicit consciousness ... thereby becoming an *actor* and constructing history on the basis of a new foundation' (Dussel 2008: 75). A population becomes a people by becoming conscious of its own potential, its demand for change and its ability to carry it through. A people imagines itself into existence by imagining its tasks and goals. Can my tandoori barbecue inform an 'explicit consciousness' that might bind human forces together with oppressed nature and technology, imagining into existence a commons of people, natural processes and technologies?

The migrations and supply chains of my ingredients are stores of ancestral narratives, skills, knowledges and beliefs. Cooking invokes ancestors from shopping to smoke. But the living presence of the dead in technologies and techniques is not all. Nature is no more inert than tools, techniques and languages. Alive, alert, demanding: rivers, forests, oceans, storms and sun are gods. From the most ancient times to the intuition that something immaterial is going on around the glowing charcoal, fire has been one of those gods: autonomous, powerful, articulate, unpredictable, caring, renewing, immortal – at least in comparison with our brief generations and abbreviated future – and driven by other than human desires. In my back garden, ancestors and gods congregate around the ritual of sharing a meal – a local commons of ancestors, gods and humans. Praising, celebrating and atoning for ancestral crimes and present exploitation by ritual scorching of meats and spices, recognising that no future is worth the name unless the dead and the natural world are also redeemed, the barbecue gives a small taste, a microcosm, of what an ecocritical aesthetic politics might be like.

Against Nostalgia: Archive Politics

Few activities bring us closer to redeeming the dead than archiving works and technologies of the past, but it might appear that archives of new media arts since the 1970s are distinct from ancestral considerations. Many makers are still alive and the works very much in living memory. Accessing old drives and software – and ensuring they can function adequately to play often technically demanding artworks – involves a good deal of nostalgia for obsolete technologies. Hearing modem chimes and boot-up alerts, handling old external storage media and their connectors, reviving once-familiar application interfaces still draw on muscle-memories and flash recalls of half-remembered workarounds. Archives often deal with materials predating the birth of their handlers. But spare a thought for archivists of the near-contemporary, face-to-face not with the anonymous dead but with their own past.

Nostalgia is a strong motivator for near-contemporary archiving and for many of the artists and creatives working with digital archives. It is also a risk. Memory is fallible because it is a creative process. We do not necessarily remember things as they were, or even how scrapbooks and databases tell us they were, but as we now wish they had been, from a now that never stays still and a wish that never stops evolving. This is as true of perceptual recall as it is of remembered emotional states, and equally true of physical objects that surprise us, when we encounter them again, by being bigger or smaller, louder or quieter or more, or less, perfect than they have been in memory. This creates a particular challenge if what an archivist tries to produce is not just the artefact itself but the look and feel, a significant part of the emulation process.

The Greek word *nostos* means a voyage home, like the *Odyssey*; nostalgia, combining *nostos* with the word for pain, appears to have been coined in the late seventeenth century to describe Swiss mercenaries' longing to get back to their homes (Fuentenebro de Diego and Ots 2014), only later acquiring the connotation of love for the past. In nostalgia, home is always elsewhere or lost. Pilloried by highbrow critics as sentimental, today nostalgia takes on political dimensions as motive for the defence of home, imagined as under threat and in process of disappearing. This politically weaponised production of social memory as a fable of loss is far less fluid than the multiple positions of individual recall. In the same way planning overwhelms anxiety about the future by erasing the multiplicity of future possibilities, populist *détournements* of imagination overcome anxiety by substituting the past, as fabulous return, for the non-appearance of the future. The mismatch between the fabled past and actual present can never be satisfied because hidden in its social fantasy is a profoundly individual longing for reunion with mother's body. Nostalgia's golden glow of ecological Edens and cultural purity is infantile, which is why it so easily turns to infantile tantrums.

Nostalgia is not so much lack, a present experience of permanent absence, but loss, a symptom of time passing. Individual lack can occasion numb withdrawal, but political loss can be mobilised as desire to a return to a fantasised time before loss. Nostalgia becomes political when feelings of deprivation, regret and shame turn into communal fantasies of violence against the chimerical thieves who stole or wrecked a common home. Populist nostalgia is fake because it promises that tantrums can force the world to conform to the infantile demand to return to the womb. Demand for a future is so baffled by inaction, corruption and wilful ineptitude that only yearning for the past is left. Nostalgia for the past is the political obverse of anxiety over the future, whether financial or cultural. Both nostalgia and anxiety are profoundly an-aesthetic. Feigning respect for ancestors, neo-populism binds a community to myths of victimhood and catastrophe, the better to impose order and normative values. Anguish and anxiety, one dependent on a lost past, the other on an unchangeable future, are both failures of imagination, the ability to construct possibilities beyond the selfish self. Even when invoked by neo-populists, nostalgia belongs to the individual person that feels it. Archives force us to deal with it collectively.

Archiving is nostalgic when it returns to personal memories. It is ethical when it concerns obligations to myself and the people closest to me. Caroline Frick (2011) raises the fraught question of the *politics* of archives, the institutional and discursive work of deciding what to preserve, restore and duplicate; and increasingly what to exclude and so effectively condemn to disappearance. 'Politics' in the first instance because often these are questions about national priorities, as in the Australian Centre for the Moving Image (where the first version of this section was presented) and the Archive of Australian Media Arts (which commissioned it). It is not that these are virulently chauvinistic organisations: they adopt the frames that civil society bodies will fund, political in the sense of the art of the possible. The ambiguous pleasures of nostalgia are rapidly ejected by the realpolitik of funding, while other socio-cultural factors gradually make themselves clear, like the long-term exclusion of women's achievements across the long history of archives (Gaines 2007), or the erasure of enslaved and colonised peoples' cultural memory (Kempadoo 2016).

The social dimension is unavoidable whenever a decision on inclusion and prioritising has to be made. Historian of ideas Michel Foucault made an even more extreme case, arguing that 'The archive is first the law of what can be said, the system that governs the appearance of statements' (Foucault 1972: 129). Foucault takes 'archive' to mean the inherited form of any discourse, the formal organisation of language and the validation of professional dialects by institutional formations like the clinic, the prison and economics. He was thinking of an archive as a corpus of validated statements providing a template for any other statement in that discourse, whether agreeing with tradition or disputing it in a legitimised way or flying off on a tangent that remains comprehensible in the terms set by the archive of previous statements. Frick's 'politics' comes from fighting for home movies, industrial films and scraps of actuality footage to gain a place in local and national collections alongside the cultural heritage of feature films. Part of Frick's claim is that, while the corpus retains its role in determining what constitutes a film and therefore counts as a legitimate 'statement', it has to make room for the interaction between personal, emotional, indeed nostalgic attachments and the social evidence contained in whatever has survived from the past. In platform capitalism, the equivalent artefacts are already stored and catalogued in the mass-image archives of social media giants (Dvořák and Parikka 2021), now the base of artificial intelligence image generators. The ecocritical enlargement of Frick's struggle is not to include more artefacts, but to extend archives' concept of memory to include things that are only partly or not even human.

Digital archives not only care for and restore works, but model and rebuild the machinery they were made with and for. Systems and system architectures, peripherals and ports, clocks and configurations all have to be unearthed, often from private collections and forgotten boxes of old cables, re-constructed or tinkered together with the aid of manuals, collector contacts and memories. As we confront another new round of AI-based computation, another revolutionary infrastructure in the form of quantum computing, the advance of ternary computing and the more imminent possibility that online platforms will vanish – with everything that implies for archiving – the mutual dependence of software and hardware now and in the recent past has never been clearer or more urgent, or raised so many questions about the emotional, ethical and political demands of archival practice.

The issue of time-to-live (TTL) has remained a personal fascination since my first encounters with html and packet-switching in the late 1980s. TTL instructions, built into every packet of data sent through the internet, automatically erase anything that fails to make it to its destination in a set number of steps. The implication is that everything produced digitally is subject to loss. On the other hand, launching into his *Archive Fever*, Derrida pauses to consider a simple, almost reflex action of composing text on a computer:

I pushed a certain key to 'save' a text undamaged, in a hard and lasting way, to protect marks from being erased, so as to ensure in this way salvation and indemnity, to stock, to accumulate, and, in what

is at once the same thing and something else, to make the sentence available in this way for printing and for reprinting, for reproduction.
(Derrida 1995: 26)

Derrida, focused on language like Foucault, chooses printing as his destination because it allows him a pun on repression and impression. That in turn will allow him to weave one of his characteristic knots of ideas around Freud and Jewish mysticism (with a nod to Benjamin):

if we want to know what [the archive] will have meant, we will only know in times to come. ... A spectral messianicity is at work in the concept of the archive and ties it, like religion, like history, like science itself, to a very singular experience of the promise.
(Derrida 1995: 36)

He later adds a gloss on 'messianicity' which defines its promise as:

this performative to come whose archive no longer has any relation to the record of what is, to the record of the presence of what is or will have been actually present. I call this the messianic, and I distinguish it radically from all messianism.
(Derrida 1995: 72)

Archiving means storing things up for a future we cannot know, which may have no interest in what we preserve, and which may find currently unthinkable uses for it – like Morrison's *Light is Calling*. A 'performative' is a statement like 'I find you guilty' that changes reality. Derrida's point is that the impact of the archive is always future, 'a feed-forward mechanism for lines of creative process' (Massumi 2016: 6). That gives it an ethical position rather like the pledge of 'I love you' that we may or may not fulfil. If the promise to change the world does get fulfilled, it will no longer have any relation to the present when, now long in the past, I made that promise – the statement I made, or the artefact I preserved. It will be more like what Catherine Russell (2018) called 'archiveology', 'the reuse, recycling, appropriation and borrowing of archive material.' Russell's interest was in artists using archive footage in projects like Thom Anderson's *Los Angeles Plays Itself* from 2004 or Jean-Luc Godard's *Histoire(s) du cinéma*: today we are at least as interested in AI uses of stored imagery. On reflection through the prism of Russell's archiveology, Derrida's concern for the future performance of the archive reveals a determining quality of his concept of the archival promise: it is a promise made to a future human. Already in our present, the biggest users of stored images are machines: AIs. Whether they are capable of experiencing meaning is a moot point: the founding documents of the mathematical theory of communications and cybernetics suggest that semantics, meaning, is of no concern to them. For that matter, nor does a promise made in the past, because the only knowledge an AI has of time derives from date stamps and metadata tags.

These considerations leave us with at least three temporalities we must cope with in digital archives: the time of erasure, forgetting and loss, which is always imminent and may be inbuilt; the time of saving, communicative ordering in database taxonomies, somewhere between Castoriadis' 'identitary' imposition of the Same and the vanishing wealth of accumulation; and the time of the promise – to pass works on to a future we will never know, that may never come to pass, and which, if it finds uses for what we have preserved for it, will discover uses we never thought of. These sit on top of times every archivist confronts: the geological time of materials, the internal time structures of drives, media, codecs and protocols, the experiential times of archived works, labour time as influence on preservation decisions, and many more. Archiving's specific job is to respect, constantly and consistently, the local times of erasing, storing and deferring, and the larger temporal scales of vanishing, preservation and reuse.

You would think that storing, presumably the primary duty of an archive, was a relatively simple matter in temporal terms. For a long time, right through the 1970s, film archives tried their utmost to keep their materials in the closest form possible to their originals. In the 1990s, when physical preservation remained a top priority, Paolo Cherchi Usai could write, in his seventh rule for silent cinema researchers, 'Every print of a film is a unique object' (Usai 1994: 67), and in his eighth, 'The "original" version of a film is a multiple object fragmented into a number of different entities' (Usai 1994: 84). Many of the most ancient and sacred texts bear out this rule. No single archive holds the tablets of the law that once resided in the acacia wood Ark of the Covenant, but every archive holds several versions of various Bibles compiled from disparate copies. A century has passed since the first assumption that the canon of the Old Testament was not formalised till about 1000 CE (Bade 1911). The Dead Sea Scrolls, a thousand years before that, although only re-discovered in 1947, prove the assumption (Biblical Archaeology Review 2022). The same is true for Homer and the Rig Veda. Even texts completed after the spread of printing – Shakespeare's plays, for example – are constantly being re-edited from variant copies. Variations on a missing original are at the centre of Derrida's enquiry in *Spectres of Marx* (1994), where he indulges the French pun 'hauntology' (pronounced 'ontology'). Ontology, the philosophy of the real, the origin of being and appearance, is already haunted by a return, a revenant. The implications for archiving are not only that there is no original to preserve but that the thing we have in front of us, the CD-ROM or the hard drive, is already a ghost of what it was and what it will become. In his lifelong assault on metaphysics, Derrida has always insisted, like Irigaray (1985), that there is never One: there are always at least two. This present thing, this thing in the present, is also past, and on its way to the future.

Disputes about metaphysics are scarcely the bread and butter of archiving. At the same time, Derrida's insistence that there is no origin and Usai's rule about a film's multiple 'originals' also hold good for digital objects. The vicissitudes of bitrot, wear and tear, versioning and copying mean that already, scarcely fifty years since the dawn of digital culture and well within living memory, archives must assemble what remains from private and public collections in search of even so recent a past. Reprising his earlier book in 2000, Usai refocused his attention, beyond preservation, duplication and conservation, to address restoration, reconstruction and recreation. Unlike paintings, where the original can be cleaned, repaired if necessary and exhibited, electronic media can never be shown without damaging them irrevocably. In the *Rewind* series of archival projects on video art, for example, we discovered early on that the plastic substrate of old videotape deforms with age and the magnetic oxides lose their adhesion to the tape. Our archivist passed each tape, removed from its cassette, through a kiln, carefully and slowly, to get the oxides to bind just long enough for one last pass through a reader connected to a digi-Beta recorder (Lockhart 2012). This terrifying slow-motion high-wire practice cannot remove travelling glitches or cover the traces of split tape where the original has suffered from mould. It demands restoration and, for exhibition prints, judicious reconstruction.

Restoration removes previous alterations (an example in the case of video tape is 'burns' caused by storage near a ring main), retrieving missing elements and reversing wear and tear. Reconstruction demands interpolating, replacing or reassembling segments using multiple copies to approximate to a desired 'authoritative' copy, whose authority is pretty much always that of the curator, the technician and the tools to hand. It is important to emphasise the role of non-human elements here: the kiln, a ring main, video cassettes. The *Rewind* team had funds to restore British video art. We had to select from the available tapes those that were significant in our collective judgement, augmented by reading through contemporary accounts of exhibitions and festivals – a human, political decision – and which were in decent enough shape in enough different copies to be recuperable. Sifting for adequate copies to work with meant checking the non-human chemical and physical processes that had affected the tapes. Tied up with that were the technologies themselves, including two-inch, one-inch and U-matic cassettes and the decks to play them on. The divide between machinery and humanity defined both, from Marx's analysis of factory labour to current fears about AI. In archival work, the distinction becomes fuzzy.

Usai's last activity is recreation: 'presenting an imaginary account of what the film would have been if some or all of its missing parts had survived' (2000: 66–67). Foucault came close to Usai's position when he wrote that 'between tradition and oblivion, [the archive] reveals the rules of a practice that enables statements to both survive and to undergo regular modification' (Foucault 1972: 130). Though he never abandoned the idea that, as a corpus of statements making up a specific discourse, the archive was 'the general system of the formation and transformation of statements' (Foucault 1972: 130), he also understood that archiving also marks certain statements (we would say artefacts) as the ones that matter, and prescribes the rules about how they can be handled and modified. An archive reveals its own rules of operation.

The ongoing work of the National Film and Sound Archive of Australia to restore the 1906 *Story of the Kelly Gang* is a fine example. Only a few minutes of the original sixty remain, digitally scanned and restored to get rid of dirt and damage, and with information from adjacent frames applied to damaged areas of their neighbours. Giovanna Fossati (2009) called the way archived filmstrips continue to evolve or decay chemically and physically long after they were first printed 'the archival life of film'. There is no longer an original of the *Kelly* film: there is instead an evolving digital file that preserves snapshots of states of decay over the fifteen or more years the archive has been working on it. The digital files themselves are subject to analogous processes of decay. In Foucault's language, the decision is no longer 'between tradition and oblivion' but about the conditions and validations required to work on each new generation of the digital copies, given the original positive print can never be projected again, and every duplicate embarks on its own significant trajectory of decay and reduplication.

Screen grabs from the 2005 DVD release of *The Story of the Kelly Gang* record the film's state of decay at the time. It is trickier to track the decay of the DVD itself. The release was handled by Madman, which likely also commissioned the manufacture, significant because industrially produced DVDs and CDs have longer service lives than the writable discs more typical of short-run artist projects, but even mass-produced discs are vulnerable to various forms of disc rot (Shahani et al. 2009). Poor quality control in manufacture can lead to CD bronzing, when the plastic lacquer that protects the aluminium layer of recorded data reacts with sulphur in packaging, allowing the aluminium to oxidise and become unplayable (Lampson 1995). More problems can come from the dye layer needed to reflect the laser, which can also let oxygen into the data layer, and problems with the adhesives used to bond the base, dye, metal and protective layers (CCI 2010; Smith 2017).

These are the immediate infrastructural elements that archiving faces. Ecocritique adds analysis of the sources of plastics and dyes (mostly oil derivatives), and the mining and processing of metals. It touches back on archive issues when it explores the governance of standards and quality management, similar to spice supply chains, and the provenance of the artefacts and players, though ecocritique will spend more effort than archives on logistics and transportation. Archives and ecocritique share an interest in built-in obsolescence of media and formats, though ecocritique will again spend more time on end-of-life recycling and waste and has an interest in the electricity supply that is mostly peripheral to archivists. Ecocritique wants to understand the missing link between materials and meanings. The archivists' challenge is to extract assets and instruction sets from vulnerable storage media and, in the case of the Archive of Australian Media Arts, transfer them to the Emulation-as-a-Service (EaaSI) platform, itself a productive repurposing of the Software-as-a-Service (SaaS) subscription model that has transformed the economics of the software industry.

After dealing with problems of physical retrieval, the EaaSI process involves building emulations of authoring and playback software on top of emulations of operating systems mounted on emulations of hardware and in many cases emulated peripherals. Recent histories of film and video archive practice tells us these are more technical challenges than ethical problems (Depocas et al. 2003). Thirty years ago, displays had different resolutions, clock speeds, refresh rates and colour gamuts, which emulations have to take account of. External and internal drives had different start-up rates, buffering, input/output and interaction tempos. Film theorists spent more time than perhaps they should have on the idea that every twenty-fourth of a second, a cinema audience is plunged into darkness as the frames move (Mulvey 2006, Bellour 2012), and video theorists on what happened when the frameline disappeared in favour of interlaced scanning (Virilio 1991). Digital theory, to the best of my knowledge, has not talked about the transition from interlaced to progressive scans, but the material difference is important to emulation and perhaps to perception and spectator activity. Each technical change introduces a threshold between ethics and politics in the ancestral dimension of digital technologies.

Philosopher of technology Bernard Stiegler (2003) opined that not all technologies are 'mnemotechnics' – technologies of memory – singling out the oldest, hammers, knives and the like. Anything more mechanical, starting with fairly basic tools like stirrups and wheels, is going to ossify knowledge into things. By the time we get to computation, we are taking about the enclosure, privatisation and lockdown of mathematical, logical and linguistic practice into proprietary black boxes. Materials like silver and plastic, and complex tools like laser read-write heads, have deep histories in aeons of human thinking and doing; so too do instruction sets and programming languages. Capturing and harvesting human data from social media for government and commerce only accelerates the process of consolidating ancestral knowledge: today, to the extent that our skills and knowledge are being captured in real time, we are becoming ancestors. AI only differs in generating new forms not just from human-produced files but from the second and subsequent generations of its own products.

Every breath we take tells us humans are not separate from their ecologies. In the archive, working with chemical and physical decay, transferring to new formats that will also decay, it is clear that ancestral technologies are also woven into nature's processes. That includes the realisation that the alternative to remembering is dismembering: submitting artefacts and documents to inevitable rot, documented in photographs of official documents piled up by a toilet in Donald Trump's mansion. When Foucault insisted on the primacy of discourses and institutions, he was talking about archives operating 'between tradition and oblivion', that is, between natural mortality and the preservation of ancestral knowledge. Archives are dedicated to saving not only old content but infrastructures. They also commit to the promise Derrida wrote about, the promise to deliver things to an unknown future, a future to which the current generation will also be past. Archiving expresses an obligation to the past, and a duty to the future. At the same time, it passes on to the future the obligation to remember its ancestors, including the archivists who laboured to transmit the tradition. When, therefore, Foucault wrote about how archives not only make judgements but reveal the rules of their practice, those rules include the set of reciprocal obligations that archiving assumes and passes on. The past haunts the archive, but the archive is also haunted by ghosts of the future, who may or may not recall or care for our precious things or those whose labour is embodied in them, just as our ancestors may or may not be grateful for our selective attempts to grant them immortality.

Emulation is as constructive and creative as it is reconstructive and recreative. The artist Simon Biggs, working with the Australian branch of EaaSI's emulations of his CD-ROM interactives of the 1990s like *The Great Wall of China*, not only discovered he could fix flaws in the 1996 files using the Macromedia Director emulation, but that returning to the old software, now long since buried under archaeological layers of corporate takeover, has brought back enough lost affordances for him to make new works on the old platform. On top of

Usai's restoration, reconstruction and recreation, the return of lost software calls up reanimation, a process evoked by photographic archivist Jane Birkin (2021: 97) when she reflects, 'The idea that one should not try to anticipate the specific future use of an object but should instead allow for all possible uses, is fundamental to the latent potentialities of archive materials.' When AI feeds on its own products, it loops back on itself like derivatives in finance capital, freezing everything into a permanent present. Reanimating old software creates a fork in the timeline, where the reanimated branch creates other possibilities for other, multiple futures where there had been only one.

Even when turned into neo-populist rage, nostalgia is at base personal, recreating the past in the image of the present for the present, but evolving in its interplay with the one who remembers. The feedback loops of current AIs, those designed to imitate existing formats like photo-realism, amass past achievements and present actions to create a present where no action is possible that does not recreate the same timeless dataspace: the purest example of Foucault's 'law of what can be said'. Reanimation multiplies pasts, presents and futures. Any archived artefact is a crossroads of natural forces, ancestral technology and human actions, a tangle so dense it is impossible to tell nature, tech and culture apart, not least because the crossroads are always moving through time, evolving new directions, new dimensions of and new structures in time. Emulating Director revealed the rules of the corporate archive, which in turn reanimated affordances the cyborg corporation had carelessly abandoned to wilful oblivion. Reanimating multiple branches outward from emulations is a way of liberating enslaved ancestors.

The general intellect understands humans as social. As technology and code, the mass unconscious restructures the linguistic base of consciousness in favour of an ancestral mode of un-consciousness – as when code is authored not by software engineers but by AI. The presumption is that, even if its logical structures are comprehensible in written form, when code is running it is inaccessible to consciousness. Today this incomprehensibly alien form of code increasingly structures the communal mass unconscious even though it is still shaped by living languages like English and Mandarin. It structures not only socially, like language, but socio-technically, like capital. Mass-code unconscious is no longer at the edge: it is the edge, the site where the living become ancestral human capital. General cognition articulates the somatic bodies of the living with all life, the biosphere that supports it, the gods of forests, floods and fires and all cosmic influences of tides, seasons, constellations and cosmic rays.

The general imagination is the product of the socialising general intellect, the technologizing mass unconscious and general cognition's re-articulation with the gods of estranged natures. It is the capacity to subsume and be subsumed into the motions of technology and ecology in operation, not only in dreams and slips but in cellular functions and at the margins of intellect as automatic gestures. Because living involves societies, technologies and ecologies, it is never still. The historical ruptures dividing them, traumas of dispossession and alienation, are integral to the general imagination, appearing there no longer as conscious blockages but as generative contradictions. Non-identical, no longer under command, general imagination is in flux and of the flux, not operative but affective, tuned to and animated by ancestors and gods.

Political scientists Chantal Mouffe (2005) and Jacques Rancière (1999) argue that politics begins when an excluded group demands a voice in its government, as happened with the emancipation of slaves and votes for women. The exclusion of migrant and Indigenous voices is the forefront of politics today. Settler colonialism tells us to ignore the voices of gods and the dead. Consider what politics would be if the dead had a voice. And what else do archives do but strive to give them one? What if the ecology spoke in its own voices – not human voices representing it: the voices of gods? Unthinkable – but so were votes for women. When archives deal with entropy, electromagnetism, the geological forces that produced the fossils that made the fossil fuel that makes plastic, the astronomical forces that made silver and gold, they listen to and dialogue with gods and ancestors. The meteorological apparatus, despite itself, socialises living and dead in a planetary commons. The convivial ethics of cooking connects us to one another in celebrations of presence. The politics of archives overcomes death, creating future potentials by working with the posthumous media of our forebears. Ethics is circumscribed by mortality because each of us dies alone, even though we can only live together. Politics is greater because it extends to all that is excluded: sunlight, air, water, climate, vulcanism, entropy – and to ancestors, and the ancestors that we are becoming. As cooking transforms shameful pasts into joyful presents, so archiving transforms preserved objects into evolutions. Reanimating timeless cyborg databases by creating multiple futures out of multiple pasts, archiving is a model for a new politics, born to overcome the gulf between ecologies, technologies and societies and open roads to multiple immortalities.

5
Coda: Commons

Even the things that stood,
stood in unlikeness
                              Geoffrey Hill, *The Triumph of Love* XII

Art is organised around the individual artist. Cooking is interpersonal, limited to the local. Archiving is a global project but a marginal form of politics. Yet however small, ephemeral and obscure, they are all acts of human-ecological-technological imagination of the kind that Raymond Williams (1989) referred to as resources of hope – imaginative efforts because, as process philosopher Brian Massumi emphasised, they strive 'to transform the no-place of the archive into the no-place of a utopia'. Charcoal, the blank matter left in the wake of the fire gods, from Nawarla Gabarnmang to the kettle barbie, via Pollock's cigarette butts and studio nitrate fires, cannot but feed imagination. I had wanted to make Chapter 4 about the commons but set a trap for myself by arguing that aesthetics can only deal with what exists. Indigenous commons do exist, and women's commons (Shiva 1988). White Western men cannot inhabit or claim them for themselves, but nor should they (we) 'develop their argument by repeating precisely the exclusion of non-European people they decry' (Belmessous 2012: 15). Because the commons persists in protests (Warrender 2022) and carnivals (Bakhtin 1968), parallel to its continuation among first peoples wherever they have resisted colonial capital, it has never been wholly absent, and cannot be accused of being a plan to impose present values on the future. The commons exists only as a condition of constant possibility, a subjunctive existence, imagined.

Benjamin recorded in his diary on 25 August 1938, 'A Brechtian maxim: take your cue not from the good old things, but from the bad new ones' (Benjamin 2002: 340). Present circumstances demand another order: start from the good new things hidden among the bad. Among the bad, few are as dispiriting as the affliction of disaffection, the hegemonic form of affectless resentment. There is a sociology to be written on the cultural construction of contemporary melancholy, but the term's histories suggest that even in the gloom, good new things may glimmer. 'Nearly all the writers of the later Middle Ages and the Renaissance considered it an incontestable fact that melancholy, whether morbid or natural, stood in some special relationship to Saturn' (Klibansky et al. 2019: 127). In classical Rome, Saturn was associated with generation, abundance, agriculture and renewal; the Golden Age was the age of Saturn, celebrated in the week-long midwinter Saturnalia festival that the poet Catullus (1970: XIV, 14) called the best of days, reliving the lost age, before Jupiter cast Saturn into hell when, in Ovid's lines,

Earth by herself, unasked, untouched by hoes,
Unmarred by ploughs, provided everything. ...
Rivers of milk, rivers of nectar flowed,
and yellow honey trickled from green oaks.
Metamorphoses I, 104–105, 115–116 (Ovid 2022)

Earth was whole and the people at ease and at one with it, and there was no technology, not even a hoe. The myth of the Golden Age is undoubtedly nostalgic and the Saturnalia no doubt served as a pressure valve and momentary reversal (masters used to serve their slaves a meal) to secure the good order of the state. The story that there were humans who never worked and had no tools smacks of wish-fulfilment, like Harry McClintock's 1928 hobo song 'The Big Rock Candy Mountain', where 'There ain't no short-handled shovels / No axes, saws, or picks.' The dream of idle luxury survives as advertising gimmick and individualist aspiration, and its longevity draws on the persistent feeling that machines have served only to enslave workers and hurt nature. Because desire is formed in that historical condition – that condition of history – it cannot escape it. Imagining, on the contrary, takes from the actual its potential to be otherwise. No commons actually exists, but its subjunctive existence makes it a resource that turns the unavoidable ground of desire newly avoidable, and the commons not only virtually present but available for unpredictable acts of imagination.

In the face of apathy – sullen acceptance of the end – and confronting the failures of capital and revolution and the imminent collapse of human-friendly ecology when even hope runs aground; after hope, there remain desire and imagination. Cited in the introduction to this book, Bloch's (1988: 16) adage 'Hope would not be hope if it could not be disappointed' needs to be reversed and re-interpreted: imagination is only imagination if it can be realised. Desire is personal, imagination is political. Desire wants to restore the Golden Age in a future 'realm of freedom' (Marx 1959: 820) containing all the plenty and ease of the lost past; imagination wants to realise the latent potential of the present. Desire subordinates the world to itself; imagination subordinates itself to the world.

The world that embraces imagination is heavy with presences: the past and future making their demands, and the regenerative forces of the green world. The section on archives at the end of Chapter 4 emphasises the imaginative power of ancestry as legacy, as demand for redemption from slavery to capitalist technology. Too briefly I made the case that ecological phenomena can be understood as gods. Like Saturn, they renew. They have immense powers that shape human life. Unlike scientific laws, divine powers are unpredictable, demanding not just respect but mediation. Among their most unpredictable qualities is their capacity to care for humans. Ecological gods are not the ticking of the blind watchmaker's creation that monotheism and science describe – they have desires, instincts and drives other than wish-fulfilment and fantasy, lusts poets can compare to human greed, ambition, fury or passion but ultimately unlike them. They are autonomous of human will or want, even though they both hurt and nurture us, and they are not only larger but longer-lasting than our brief lives: immortal even as they change in time. With the Roman Epicurean philosopher Cicero (1998), I do not demand that you, gentle reader, believe in the immortal gods: only that you permit yourself to imagine a world animate with energies demanding respect and obligation, just as ancestors do.

How then to understand the fraught category of the human? Environmental theorists Tom Cohen and Claire Colebrook (2016: 12) may overstate their case when, in an essay prefiguring the arguments in Chapter 1.1, 'Posthumous', above, they write, 'Humanity comes into being, late in the day, when it declares itself to no longer exist, and when it looks wistfully, in an all too human way, at a world without humans.' 'Among Marx's most undertheorized ideas', according to philosopher Amy Wendling (2009: 87), 'is his notion that human activity is not reducible to labor. This idea', she adds, 'is barely conceivable in the advanced capitalist environments of today' (see also Wark 2017: n.p). Wendling was working on the

Coda: Commons

distinction between labour and labour power (*Arbeitskraft*), deriving the term *Kraft* from Helmholtz's thermodynamic theory of force, 'power' or 'work' in the scientific sense. When cyborg capital has subsumed even the free time of consumption under its data-extractivist logic, from capital's perspective everything humans do is labour. For Cohen and Colebrook, the Anthropocene marks the terminus of this logic, humanity invented at the moment of its disappearance. Apart from historical evidence to the contrary (Confucian humanism dates back to the fourth century BCE), their argument suggests that recognising humanity as a geological force proves at once the autonomy of humans from their world and the fate they have created for themselves.

A counter-argument, drawing on ancestral wisdom and recognising the gods, arose among the ancient Greeks, who, according to cosmopolitan theorist Nikos Papastergiadis, 'did not see themselves as being totally determined by external forces. They were not autonomous enough to ignore the gods. Fate was never sealed, but rather it was experienced as a perpetual struggle. This agonistic perspective on human nature was founded on the belief that humanity held something in common with the cosmos. We are in it. In a minuscule way our images and actions are part of the cosmos. It is not external to us' (Papastergiadis 2023: 20).

Ascribing autonomy to humans can only be accomplished by ignoring the gods, at which point the automata of blind physics determines both the fate of humanity and its isolation. This must be the humanity that Cohen and Colebrook evoke, a godless species whose inert ancestors bear responsibility for disaster but can redeem neither themselves nor their descendants.

Papastergiadis' radical cosmopolitanism, with its literal embrace of social and cosmic, continued its subterranean tradition right through the work of the mature Marx, for whom, according to historian Anson Rabinbach (1990: 81), 'the full development and unfolding of the productive potential of nature and technology is the organizing principle of society ... in which the distinction between the natural forces of production and the productive forces of society is no longer decisive'. It is not then that humanity only appears on the historical stage in the moment it finds itself fatally cornered in a trap of its own making. Rather, the idea of autonomous humanity had already obliterated itself in the factories of the nineteenth century. The human might be defined as the pile of debris left by the passing of Benjamin's storm called Progress. In light of Papastergiadis', Wendling's and Rabinbach's arguments, Marx's realm of freedom, a future rather than a lost, past Golden Age, belongs not to an exclusively human clientele but is constituted in a commons of humans, ancestors and gods.

The verb 'is constituted' is present-tense, not future, because the distinctions between natural, social and 'productive forces' – that is, technologies – had already dissolved by the 1860s when Marx developed his ideas on labour, labour power and machines. If we were to accept the thermodynamic principle, then keeping them apart for purposes of rule and exploitation would demand massive expenditures of energy: another reason for the ongoing tendency of capital towards permanent and possibly terminal crisis. Because imagination is only imagination (as opposed to hope or desire) when it can be realised, the commons can be described as imagined because, at immense cost, it has been repressed at least since Marx's day, but also because the repressed always returns. The task of the living is to imagine the commons; in return, the task of the commons is to make it possible to imagine.

This is what love does, unlocking the unrealised, realising the unlocked, a mutual imagining. Scaling love up from interpersonal to social bonds is notoriously prone to either sentimentality or, indistinguishably, communal narcissistic nationalism. Responding to Hardt and Negri's appeal to communal love in *Commonwealth* (2009), Lauren Berlant admires 'the revolutionary kernel of the impulse to throw it all over through the leap of coordinating oneself with virtual strangers, and then to become a part stranger to oneself in the emerging atmosphere of the new relation' (Berlant 2011: 684). Love is not a gamble with winners and losers, but it does plunge through the known into a shared project, a work with an other, with others, with the world to make another world that now lies coiled up like a spring inside the old.

Perhaps our species has not always been nomadic, but it is now. Migrating is a terrible condition. Driven by famine, drought, war and oppression, turned away from the gateways to rich nations, the migrant is the constant victim of the unkindness of strangers. It is not to underestimate the horrors of precarious life to say that mass migration is globalisation from below, a multitudinous rebellion against exclusion and privation, the foundations of wealth. If indeed 'Justice is what love looks like in public' (Cornel West, cited in Demos 2020: 17), then injustice looks like apathy or, worse, wilful deafness turning away from the pleas of the desperate. The immense cost of maintaining borders exposes not hatred but the self-love of cyborg capital, how it feels nothing, its anaesthetic politics. Migrants do not resist the state and private property: private property and states resist migration, resist humanity as they resist gods and ancestors. For capital, people are only good for physical, intellectual and now affective exploitation, just as ancestors are only good as instruments of extraction and manipulation, and gods only raw material, and all can be destroyed in exchange for a few more years in power or in profit.

The question, raised several times in other contexts in this book, is whether there is one commons or many. Is there one affect or many affects, one ecology or many ecologies, one imagination or many imaginations? Is there only one cosmopolis or many, one economy or many, as there are many we's, never just one. Is the singular–plural dilemma simply the wrong question? Or are economy, ecology, affect, imagination and commons all one, and their separations a category error? A preliminary answer: yes. Each is both singular and plural. Multiple stable categories belong to the historical order of communication, unity to the flux of mediation. Stability is no more a quality of the one than it is of the non-identical zero it derives from. Ontologically affect, economy, imagination and ecology are all one mediating commons. Historically, they shatter and multiply. This is a contradiction, and decisions on what is good depend on its generative power. It is possible that the contradiction between ontology and history is good because it is the foundation of art and culture and of all struggles to expand or escape beyond the implied humanism of the words. Good at least in these times, until the contradiction might be resolved. The commons stands at the end of this book not because it resolves all dilemmas but, on the contrary, because it is composed of nothing but contradictions, between ontology and history, between social, technological and ecological, between actual and imagined. Crushed, partitioned, lost and unrealised, plural and singular, the unstable commons is the only possible ground where beauty or beauties could appear. The good can only arise from the commons because aesthetic politics must be good for all.

Manifesto

The rationalist West cannot survive. To transform it must confront what reason excludes: gods and ancestors.

The new conditions of unconsciousness and non-consciousness can and must refuse the privations of exchange and the perpetual present in favour of reciprocal obligations.

The West must travel through these conditions, not stealing from cultures that do respect gods and ancestors but loving and learning from them.

From the ruins of the mass unconscious and the margins of general cognition, by embracing the commonalities of living and dead ancestors and the mutuality of bodies and ecologies, the privatised general intellect is transforming into the cosmopolitan general imagination.

Alter-cosmopolis, the creative *potentia* of the West, does not exist and must be imagined.

There is no one Good but many, all failing to exist. The unstable, subjunctive multiplicity of the human, ecological and technical commons makes it possible to imagine a commons that can and must come into being.

After hope, imagine the commons.

References

Abbate, Janet (1999). *Inventing the Internet*. Cambridge, MA: The MIT Press.

Abbate, Janet (2012). *Recoding Gender: Women's Changing Participation in Computing*. Cambridge, MA: The MIT Press.

Adorno, Theodor W. (1973). *Negative Dialectics*. Translated by E. B. Ashton. London: Routledge.

Adorno, Theodor W. (1974). *Minima Moralia: Reflections from a Damaged Life*. Translated by Rodney Livingstone. London: Verso.

Adorno, Theodor W. (1997). *Aesthetic Theory*. Edited by Gretel Adorno and Rolf Tiedemann, translated by Robert Hullot-Kentor. London: Athlone Press.

Adorno, Theodor W. (2000). *Problems of Moral Philosophy*. Translated by Edmund Jephcott. Cambridge: Polity.

Agamben, Giorgio (2004). 'Friendship'. Translated by Joseph Falsone. *Contretemps* 5 (December), 2–7.

Ahmed, Sara (2010). *The Promise of Happiness*. Durham, NC: Duke University Press.

Ahmed, Sara (2014). *The Cultural Politics of Emotion*. Second edition. Durham, NC: Duke University Press.

Althusser, Louis (1971). 'Ideology and Ideological State Apparatuses (Notes towards an Investigation)'. *Lenin and Philosophy and Other Essays*. Translated by Ben Brewster. New York: Monthly Review Press, 127–188.

Angerer, Marie-Louise (2023). *Non-Conscious*. Berlin: Meson Press.

Anzaldúa, Gloria (1987). *Borderlands/La Frontera: The New Mestiza*. San Francisco, CA: Aunt Lute.

Appadurai, Arjun (2016). *Banking on Words: The Failure of Language in the Age of Derivative Finance*. Chicago, IL: University of Chicago Press.

Appiah, Kwame Anthony (2006). *Cosmopolitanism: Ethics in a World of Strangers*. New York: Norton.

Arendt, Hannah (2006 [1968]). 'History and Nature.' *Between Past and Future: Eight Exercises in Political Thought.* Expanded edition. Introduction by Jerome Kohn. New York: Penguin, 41–63.

Aristotle (1995). *Politics.* Translated by Benjamin Jowett. *Complete Works of Aristotle.* The Revised Oxford Translation, One Volume Digital Edition. Edited by Jonathan Barnes. Princeton, NJ: Princeton University Press, 4265–4568.

Arrighi, Giovanni (2010 [1994]). *The Long Twentieth Century: Money, Power and the Origins of Our Times.* New and updated edition. London: Verso.

Attali, Jacques (1985). *Noise: The Political Economy of Music.* Translated by Brian Massumi. Manchester: Manchester University Press.

Attrell, Dan and David Porreca (2019). *Picatrix: A Medieval Treatise on Astral Magic.* Translated and introduced by Dan Attrell and David Porreca. University Park, PA: Penn State University Press.

Auden, W. H. (1979a). 'In Memory of W. B. Yeats.' *Selected Poems: New Edition.* Edited by Edward Mendelson. New York: Vintage, 80–82.

Auden, W. H. (1979b). 'Lay your sleeping head, my love.' *Selected Poems: New Edition.* Edited by Edward Mendelson. New York: Vintage, 50–51.

Ayache, Elie (2010). *The Blank Swan: The End of Probability.* Chichester: John Wiley.

Ayache, Elie (2015). *The Medium of Contingency: An Inverse View of the Market.* London: Palgrave Macmillan.

Ayache, Elie (2016). 'On Black-Scholes.' *Derivatives and the Wealth of Society.* Edited by Benjamin Lee and Randy Martin. Chicago, IL: University of Chicago Press, 240–251.

Bade, William Frederick (1911). 'The Canonization of the Old Testament.' *The Biblical World*, 37(3), 151–162.

Badiou, Alain (2006). *Being and Event.* Translated by Oliver Feltham. New York: Continuum.

Badiou, Alain (2009). *Logic of Worlds: Being and Event II.* Translated by Alberto Toscano. London: Continuum.

Badiou, Alain with Nicholas Truong (2012). *In Praise of Love.* Translated by Peter Bush. London: Serpent's Tail.

References

Badiou, Alain (2019). *Happiness*. Translated with foreword by A. J. Bartlett and Justin Clemens. London: Bloomsbury.

Badiou, Alain (2022). *The Immanence of Truths: Being and Event III*. Translated by Susan Spitzer and Kenneth Reinhard. London: Bloomsbury.

Baier, Annette (1993). 'Claims, Rights, Responsibilities'. *Prospects for a Common Morality*. Edited by Gene Outka and John P. Reeder. Philadelphia: University of Pennsylvania Press, 149–169.

Bakhtin, Mikhail (1968). *Rabelais and His World*. Translated by Hélène Iswolsky. Cambridge, MA: The MIT Press.

Barber, Fionna (2004). 'Abstract Expressionism and Masculinity'. *Varieties of Modernism*. Edited by Paul Wood. New Haven, CT: Yale University Press.

Barthes, Roland (1978). *A Lover's Discourse: Fragments*. Translated by Richard Howard. New York: Hill and Wang.

Baudrillard, Jean (1983). *In the Shadow of the Silent Majorities, or, The End of the Social and Other Essays*. Translated by Paul Foss, John Johnston and Paul Patton. New York: Semiotext(e).

Beck, John and Ryan Bishop (2020). *Technocrats of the Imagination: Art, Technology, and the Military-Industrial Avant-Garde*. Durham, NC: Duke University Press.

Beeple (2021). *6295 Consecutive Days*, www.beeple-crap.com/everydays.

Bellour, Raymond (2012). *Between-the-Images*. Translated by Alan Hardyck. Zurich: JRP Ringier Kunstverlag; Dijon: Les Presses du Réel.

Belmessous, Salina (2012). 'The Problem of Indigenous Claim Making in Colonial History'. *Native Claims: Indigenous Law against Empire 1500–1920*. Edited by Aalina Belmessous. Oxford: Oxford University Press.

Benjamin, Walter (2002). 'Diary Entries, 1938'. *Selected Writings, Vol. 3, 1935–1938*. Edited by Howard Eiland and Michael W. Jennings. Cambridge, MA: Bellknap Press/Harvard University Press, 335–343.

Berger, John (2015). 'Some Notes about the Art of Falling: Charlie Chaplin'. *Sight and Sound*, n.p., www2.bfi.org.uk/news-opinion/sight-sound-magazine/archives/john-berger-notes-on-charlie-chaplin.

Berlant, Lauren (2007). 'Slow Death (Sovereignty, Obesity, Lateral Agency)'. *Critical Inquiry*, 33 (Summer), 754-780.

Berlant, Lauren (2011). 'A Properly Political Concept of Love: Three Approaches in Ten Pages'. *Cultural Anthropology*, 26(4), 683-669.

Berresem, Hanjo (2018). '*Light is Calling*: Celluloid Dreams'. *The Films of Bill Morrison: Aesthetics of the Archive*. Edited by Berndt Herzogenrath. Amsterdam: EYE Filmmuseum/Amsterdam University Press, 109-122.

Bertoia, Celia (2015). *The Life and Work of Harry Bertoia*. Atglen, PA: Schiffer Publishing.

Biblical Archaeology Review (2022). *The Dead Sea Scrolls: Past, Present, and Future*. Washington, DC: Biblical Archaeology Review.

Birkin, Jane (2021). *Archive, Photography and the Language of Administration*. Amsterdam: Amsterdam University Press.

Black, Fischer and Myron Scholes (1973). 'The Pricing of Options and Corporate Liabilities'. *The Journal of Political Economy*, 81(3), 637-654.

Blake, William (1988). *The Complete Poetry and Prose of William Blake*. Edited by David V. Erdman. Commentary by Harold Bloom. New York: Random House.

Bleeker, Maaike, Nanna Verhoeff and Stefan Werning (2020). 'Sensing Data: Encountering Data Sonifications, Materializations, and Interactives as Knowledge Objects'. *Convergence: The International Journal of Research into New Media Technologies*, 26(5-6), 1088-1107.

Bloch, Ernst (1986). *The Principle of Hope*, 3 volumes. Translated by Neville Plaice, Stephen Plaice and Paul Knight. Cambridge, MA: The MIT Press.

Bloch, Ernst (1988). 'Something's Missing: A Discussion between Ernst Bloch and Theodor Adorno on the Contradictions of Utopian Longing (1964)'. *The Utopian Function of Art and Literature: Selected Essays*. Translated by Jack Zipes and Frank Mecklenburg. Cambridge, MA: The MIT Press, 1-17.

Boasson, Elin Lerum, Charlotte Burns and Simone Pulver (2023). 'The Politics of Domestic Climate Governance: Making Sense of Complex Participation Patterns'. *Journal of European Public Policy*, 30(3), 513-536.

Braudel, Fernand (1981). *Civilization and Capitalism, 15th-18th Century: Vol. I. The Structures of Everyday Life*. Trans Siân Reynolds. London: Collins.

Britton, Andrew (2009). 'Cary Grant: Comedy and Male Desire'. *Britton on Film: The Complete Film Criticism of Andrew Britton*. Edited by Barry

Keith Grant with an introduction by Robin Wood. Detroit, MI: Wayne State University Press, 3-23.

Brulle, Robert J., Melissa Aronczyk and Jason Carmichael (2020). 'Corporate Promotion and Climate Change: An Analysis of Key Variables Affecting Advertising Spending by Major Oil Corporations, 1986-2015'. *Climatic Change*, 159(1), 87-101.

Bryson, Norman (1988). 'The Gaze in the Expanded Field'. *Vision and Visuality* (Dia Art Foundation Discussions in Contemporary Culture Number 2). Edited by Hal Foster. Seattle, WA: Bay Press.

Buller, Adrienne (2022). *The Value of a Whale: On the Illusions of Green Capitalism*. Manchester: Manchester University Press.

Butler, Judith (1988). 'Performative Acts and Gender Constitution: An Essay in Phenomenology and Feminist Theory'. *Theatre Journal*, 40(4), 519-531.

Campbell, Edward (2010). *Boulez, Music and Philosophy*. Cambridge: Cambridge University Press.

Campbell, Edward (2013). *Music after Deleuze*. London: Bloomsbury.

Campbell, Joseph (1972). *Myths to Live By*. New York: Viking Press.

Campbell-Kelly, Martin (2004). *From Airline Reservations to Sonic the Hedgehog: A History of the Software Industry*. Cambridge, MA: The MIT Press.

Camus, Albert (1979 [1942]). 'The Myth of Sisyphus'. *The Myth of Sisyphus*. Translated by Justin O'Brien. London: Penguin, 9-124.

Carmi, Elinor (2020). *Media Distortions: Understanding the Power Behind Spam, Noise, and Other Deviant Media*. New York: Peter Lang.

Castoriadis, Cornelius (1987). *The Imaginary Institution of Society*. Translated by Kathleen Blamey. Cambridge: Polity.

Castro, Fidel (2018). 'History Will Absolve Me'. *The Declarations of Havana*. Presented by Tariq Ali. London: Verso (ebook).

Cato, Molly Scott (2009). *Green Economics: An Introduction to Theory, Policy and Practice*. London: Earthscan.

Catullus, Gaius Valerius (1970). *Catullus: The Poems*. Edited by Kenneth Quinn. London: Macmillan.

Cavell, Stanley (1981). 'Leopards in Connecticut'. *Pursuits of Happiness: The Hollywood Comedy of Remarriage*. Cambridge, MA: Harvard University Press, 113-132.

CBI (2021). *Entering the European Market for Black Pepper*. Amsterdam: Centre for the Promotion of Imports, www.cbi.eu/market-information/spices-herbs/pepper/market-entry.

CCI (2010). 'Longevity of Recordable CDs and DVDs. Canadian Conservation Institute, Written by Joe Iraci'. *CCI Notes*, 19(1). Ottawa: Canadian Conservation Institute/Minister of Public Works and Government Services Canada.

Ceruzzi, Paul E. (1999). *A History of Modern Computing*. Cambridge, MA: The MIT Press.

Césaire, Aimé (1990). 'Poetry and Knowledge. (1944-45)'. Translated by A. James Arnold. *Lyric and Dramatic Poetry 1946-82*. Translated by Clayton Eshleman and Annette Smith. Introduction by A. James Arnold. Charlottesville: University Press of Virginia, xlii-lvi.

Chomsky, Noam (1957). *Syntactic Structures*. The Hague: Mouton.

Chun, Wendy Hui Kyong (2015). 'On Hypo-Real Models or Global Climate Change: A Challenge for the Humanities'. *Critical Inquiry*, 41(3), 675-703.

Cicero (1971). *On The Good Life*. Edited and translated by Michael Grant. Oxford: Oxford University Press.

Cicero (1998). *The Nature of the Gods*. Translated by P. G. Walsh. Oxford: Oxford University Press.

Clark, T. J. (1999). *Farewell to an Idea: Episodes from a History of Modernism*. New Haven, CT: Yale University Press.

Clarke, Arthur C. (1968). 'Letter to the Editor'. *Science*, 18 January.

Clausewitz, Carl von (1968). *On War*. Harmondsworth: Penguin.

Clough, Patricia Ticineto (2010). 'The Affective Turn: Political Economy, Biomedia, and Bodies'. *The Affect Theory Reader*. Edited by Melissa Gregg and Gregory J. Seigworth. Durham, NC: Duke University Press, 206-225.

Coccia, Emanuele (2021). *Metamorphoses*. Translated by Robin Mackay. Cambridge: Polity.

Coen, Deborah R. (2018). *Climate in Motion: Science, Empire, and the Problem of Scale*. Chicago, IL: University of Chicago Press.

References

Cohen, Tom and Claire Colebrook (2016). 'Preface'. *Twilight of the Anthropocene Idols*. Edited by Tom Cohen, Claire Colebrook and J. Hillis Miller. London: Open Humanities Press.

Copeland, Arthur H. (1945). 'Book Reviews: *Theory of Games and Economic Behavior*. By John von Neumann and Oskar Morgenstern'. *The Bulletin of the American Mathematical Society*, 51(7), 498–504.

Coulmas, Florian (1988). 'What is a National Language Good For?' *Forked Tongues: What Are National Languages Good For?* Edited by Florian Coulmas. Singapore: Karoma, 1–25.

Cox, Susan Jane Buck (1985). 'No Tragedy of the Commons'. *Environmental Ethics*, 7(1), 49–61.

Craven, David (1999). *Abstract Expressionism as Cultural Critique: Dissent during the McCarthy Period*. Cambridge: Cambridge University Press.

Cremen, Gemma, Carmine Galasso and John McCloskey (2022). 'Modelling and Quantifying Tomorrow's Risks from Natural Hazards'. *Science of the Total Environment*, 817, 9–13.

Critchley, Simon (2007). *Infinitely Demanding: Ethics of Commitment, Politics of Resistance*. London: Verso.

Croxton, Derek (2013). *Westphalia: The Last Christian Peace*. New York: Palgrave Macmillan.

Crutzen, Paul and Eugene Stoermer (2000). 'The "Anthropocene"'. *International Geosphere-Biosphere Newsletter*, 41 (May), 17–18.

Cubitt, Seán (2020). *Anecdotal Evidence: Ecocritique from Hollywood to the Mass Image*. Oxford: Oxford University Press.

Cubitt, Seán (2023). *Truth: Aesthetic Politics 1*. London: Goldsmiths Press.

Culpeper, Nicholas (1880 [1652]). *Culpeper's Complete Herbal: Consisting of a Comprehensive Description of Nearly All Herbs with Their Medicinal Properties and Directions for Compounding the Medicines Extracted from Them*. London: Foulsham.

Cusicanqui, Silvia Rivera (2012). '*Ch'ixinakax utxiwa*: A Reflection on the Practices and Discourses of Decolonization'. Translated by Brenda Baletti. *The South Atlantic Quarterly*, 111(1), 95–109.

David, Bruno, Bryce Barker, Fiona Petchey, Jean-Jacques Delannoy, Jean-Michel Geneste, Cassandra Rowe, Mark Eccleston, Lara Lamb and Ray Whear (2013). 'A 28,000-Year-Old Excavated Painted Rock From Nawarla Gabarnmang, Northern Australia'. *Journal of Archaeological Science*, 40(5), 2493–2501.

Davidson, Basil (1994). *Modern Africa: A Social and Political History*. Third edition. London: Routledge.

Davies, William (2018). *Nervous States: How Feeling Took Over the World*. London: Cape.

Davis, Mike (1986). *Prisoners of the American Dream: Politics and Economy in the History of the US Working Class*. London: Verso.

Deleuze, Gilles (1989). *Cinema 2: The Time-Image*. Translated by Hugh Tomlinson and Barbara Habberjam. London: Athlone.

Deleuze, Gilles (1992). 'Postscript on the Societies of Control'. *October*, 59 (Winter), 3–7.

Deleuze, Gilles and Félix Guattari (1987). *A Thousand Plateaux: Capitalism and Schizophrenia*. Translated by Brian Massumi. Minneapolis: University of Minnesota Press.

Demos, T. J. (2020). *Beyond the World's End: Arts of Living at the Crossing*. Durham, NC: Duke University Press.

Depocas, Alain, Jon Ippolito and Caitlin Jones (eds) (2003). *Permanence Through Change: The Variable Media Approach*. New York and Montreal: The Solomon R. Guggenheim Foundation and the Daniel Langlois Foundation for Art, Science, and Technology.

Derrida, Jacques (1994). *Specters of Marx: The State of the Debt, the Work of Mourning and the New International*. Translated by Peggy Kamuf. New York: Routledge.

Derrida, Jacques (1995). *Archive Fever: A Freudian Impression*. Translated by Eric Prenowitz. Chicago, IL: Chicago University Press.

Derrida, Jacques (1997). *The Politics of Friendship*. Translated by George Collins. London: Verso.

De Vos, Paula (2010). 'European Materia Medica in Historical Texts: Longevity of a Tradition and Implications for Future Use'. *Journal of Ethnopharmacology*, 132(1), 28–47.

Dioscorides, Pedanius, of Anazarbus (2005). *De Materia Medica*. Translated by Lily Y. Beck. Hildesheim: Olms.

Douglas, Mary (1966). *Purity and Danger: An Analysis of Concepts of Pollution and Taboo*. London: Routledge.

DuBois, W. E. Burghardt (1961 [1903]). *The Souls of Black Folk: Essays and Sketches*. New York: Fawcett.

Dussel, Enrique (1985). *Philosophy of Liberation*. Translated by Aquilina Martinez and Christine Morkovsky. New York: Orbis.

Dussel, Enrique (1995). 'Eurocentrism and Modernity (Introduction to the Frankfurt Lectures)'. *The Postmodernism Debate in Latin America*. Edited by John Beverley, José Oviedo and Michael Aronna. Durham, NC and London: Duke University Press, 65–77.

Dussel, Enrique (2002). 'World-System and "Trans"-Modernity'. *Nepantla: Views from South*, 3(2), 221–244.

Dussel, Enrique (2008). *Twenty Theses on Politics*. Translated by George Ciccariello-Maher. Durham, NC: Duke University Press.

Dussel, Enrique (2013). *Ethics of Liberation in the Age of Globalization and Exclusion*. Translated by Eduardo Mendieta, Camillo Pérez Bustillo, Yolanda Angulo and Nelson Maldonado-Torres. Durham, NC: Duke University Press.

Dvořák, Tomáš and Jussi Parikka (eds) (2021). *Photography Off the Scale*. Edinburgh: Edinburgh University Press.

Eagleton, Terry (1989). *The Ideology of the Aesthetic*. Oxford: Basil Blackwell.

Eco, Umberto (1997). *The Search for the Perfect Language*. Translated by James Fentress. London: Fontana.

Edwards, Paul N. (1996). *The Closed World: Computers and the Politics of Discourse in Cold War America*. Cambridge, MA: The MIT Press.

Edwards, Paul N. (2010). *A Vast Machine: Computer Models, Climate Data, and the Politics of Global Warming*. Cambridge, MA: The MIT Press.

Ehrlich, Paul R. (1968). *The Population Bomb*. New York: Ballantyne.

Eliot, T. S. (1953). 'Tradition and the Individual Talent [1919]'. *Selected Prose*. Harmondsworth: Penguin, 21–31.

Ellison, Ralph (2001 [1964]). 'The Waste Land and Jazz'. *The Waste Land: Authoritative Text, Contexts, Criticism*. Edited by Michael North. New York: Norton, 166.

Elsaesser, Thomas (2005). 'Cinephilia or the Uses of Disenchantment'. *Cinephilia: Movies, Love and Memory*. Edited by Marijke de Valck and Malte Hagener. Amsterdam: Amsterdam University Press, 27–43.

Engels, Friedrich (1845). *The Condition of the Working Class in England*. English edition of 1887 authorised by Engels. Marxists Internet Archive.

Engels, Friedrich (1947). *Anti-Duhring: Herr Eugen Duhring's Revolution in Science*. Moscow: Progress Publishers.

Escobar, Arturo (2008). *Territories of Difference: Place, Movement, Life, Redes*. Durham, NC: Duke University Press.

Escobar, Arturo (2017). *Designs for the Pluriverse: Radical Interdependence, Autonomy and the Making of Worlds*. Durham, NC: Duke University Press.

Fanon, Frantz (1991 [1963]). *The Wretched of the Earth*. Translated by Constance Farrington with a preface by Jean-Paul Sartre. New York: Grove Press.

Federici, Silvia (2019). *Re-Enchanting the World: Feminism and the Politics of the Commons*. Brooklyn, NY: PM Press.

Feeny, David, Fikret Berkes, Bonnie J. McCay and James M. Acheson (1990). 'The Tragedy of the Commons: Twenty-Two Years Later'. *Human Ecology*, 18(1), 1–19.

Fink, Bob (1997). 'Neanderthal Flute: Musicological Analysis', www.greenwych.ca/fl-compl.htm, archived at https://web.archive.org/web/20070127050555.

Flecker, James Elroy (1916). 'The Golden Journey to Samarkand'. *The Collected Poems of James Elroy Flecker*. Edited, with an introduction by J. C. Squire. New York: Doubleday.

Flusser, Vilém (2000). *Towards a Philosophy of Photography*. Introduction by Hubertus Von Amelunxen. Translated by Anthony Matthews. London: Reaktion Books.

Flusser, Vilém (2011). *Into the Universe of Technical Images*. Translated by Nancy Ann Roth. Minneapolis: University of Minnesota Press.

References

Flusser, Vilém (2023). *Communicology: Mutations in Human Relations?* Translated by Rodrigo Maltez Novaes. Stanford, CA: Stanford University Press.

Fossati, Giovanna (2009). *From Grain to Pixel: The Archival Life of Film*. Amsterdam: Amsterdam University Press.

Foster, Hal (2004). 'An Archival Impulse'. *October*, 110 (Fall), 3–22.

Foucault, Michel (1970). *The Order of Things: An Archaeology of the Human Sciences*. London: Tavistock.

Foucault, Michel (1972). *The Archaeology of Knowledge and the Discourse on Language*. Translated by Alan Sheridan. New York: Harper Collophon.

Foucault, Michel (2008). *The Birth of Biopolitics: Lectures at the Collège de France 1978–1979*. Edited by Michel Senellart. Translated by Graham Burchell. Basingstoke: Palgrave Macmillan.

Franco, Marco P. Vianna and Antoine Misseme (2023). *A History of Ecological Economic Thought*. New York: Routledge.

Frank, Elizabeth (1983). *Jackson Pollock*. New York: Abbeville Press.

Frankopan, Peter (2016). *The Silk Roads: A New History of the World*. London: Bloomsbury.

Fraser, Nancy (1990). 'Rethinking the Public Sphere: A Contribution to the Critique of Actually Existing Democracy'. *Social Text*, 25/26, 56–80.

Frege, Gottlob (1953 [1884]). *The Foundations of Arithmetic*. Translated by J. L. Austin. Second revised edition. New York: Harper.

Freud, Sigmund (1961 [1930]). *Civilization and Its Discontents*. Translated by James Strachey. New York: Norton.

Freud, Sigmund (1979 [1919]). 'A Child is Being Beaten'. Translated by James Strachey. *On Psychopathology*. Edited by Angela Richards. Harmondsworth: Pelican, 159–193.

Frick, Caroline (2011). *Saving Cinema: The Politics of Preservation*. Oxford: Oxford University Press.

Fuentenebro de Diego, Filiberto and Carmen Valiente Ots (2014). 'Nostalgia: A Conceptual History'. *History of Psychiatry*, 25(4), 404–411.

Gabrys, Jennifer (2016). *Program Earth: Environmental Sensing Technology and the Making of a Computational Planet*. Minneapolis: University of Minnesota Press.

Gadamer, Hans-Georg (1989). *Truth and Method*. Second revised edition. Translated by Joel Weinsheimer and Donald G. Marshall. London: Sheed and Ward.

Gaines, Jane (2007). 'Sad Songs of Nitrate: Women's Work in the Silent Film Archive'. *Camera Obscura*, 22(3), 170–178.

Galloway, Alexander R. (2012). *The Interface Effect*. Cambridge: Polity.

Gandhi, Mohandas K. (2002). *The Essential Gandhi: An Anthology of His Writings on His Life, Work and Ideas*. Edited by Louis Fischer. New York: Vintage Books.

Ghosh, Amitav (2021). *The Nutmeg's Curse: Parables for a Planet in Crisis*. Harmondsworth: Penguin.

Gibson, Ann Eden (1997). *Abstract Expressionism: Other Politics*. New Haven, CT: Yale University Press.

Glissant, Edouard (1997). *Poetics of Relation*. Translated by Betsy Wing. Ann Arbor: University of Michigan Press.

Goldfield, Michael (1987). *The Decline of Organized Labor in the United States*. Chicago, IL: University of Chicago Press.

Goldfield, Michael (2020). *The Southern Key: Class, Race, and Radicalism in the 1930s and 1940s*. New York: Oxford University Press.

Gomula, Joanna (2010). 'Environmental Disputes in the WTO'. *Research Handbook on International Environmental Law*. Edited by Malgosia Fitzmaurice, David M. Ong and Panos Merkouris. London: Elgar, 401–425.

Graeber, David (2011). *Debt: The First 5000 Years*. Brooklyn, NY: Melville House.

Greenberg, Clement (1961). '*Partisan Review* "Art Chronicle": 1952'. *Art and Cultute: Critical Essays*. Boston, MA: Beacon Press, 146–153.

Grosfoguel, Ramón (2007). 'The Epistemic Decolonial Turn'. *Cultural Studies*, 21(2-3), 211–223.

Guattari, Felix (1995). *Chaosmosis: An Ethico-Aesthetic Paradigm*. Translated by Paul Bains and Julian Pefanis. Sydney: Power Publications.

Guevara, Ernesto 'Che' (1989). *Socialism and Man in Cuba*. New York: Pathfinder Press.

Guilbault, Serge (1983). *How New York Stole the Idea of Modern Art: Abstract Expressionism, Freedom and the Cold War.* Chicago, IL: University of Chicago Press.

Habermas, Jürgen (1989 [1962]). *The Structural Transformation of the Public Sphere: An Enquiry into a Category of Bourgeois Society.* Translated by Thomas Burger with the assistance of Frederick Lawrence. Cambridge: Polity Press.

Hallward, Peter (2017). 'General Wish or General Will? Political Possibility and Collective Capacity from Rousseau Through Marx'. *Political Uses of Utopia: New Marxist, Anarchist, and Radical Democratic Perspectives.* Edited by S. Chrostowska and James Ingram. New York: Columbia University Press, 126-160.

Hanafi, Zakiya (2000). *The Monster in the Machine: Magic, Medicine and the Marvelous in the Time of the Scientific Revolution.* Durham, NC: Duke University Press.

Hansen, Valerie (2012). *The Silk Road: A New History.* Oxford: Oxford University Press.

Haraway, Donna (1988). 'Situated Knowledges: The Science Question in Feminism and the Privilege of Partial Perspective'. *Feminist Studies*, 14(3), 575-599.

Hardin, Garrett (1968) 'The Tragedy of the Commons'. *Science* 162 (13 December), 1243-1248.

Hardt, Michael and Antonio Negri (2009). *Commonwealth.* Cambridge, MA: Harvard University Press.

Harrison, D. C. (2004). 'Wild Swans: Interview with Paul Simpson'. No Ripcord, www.noripcord.com/features/wild-swans-interview-paul-simpson.

Hartmann, Patrick, Aitor Marcos, Juana Castro and Vanessa Apaolaza (2023). 'Perspectives: Advertising and Climate Change – Part of the Problem or Part of the Solution?' *International Journal of Advertising*, 42(2), 430-457.

Hartwell, Ronald M. (1995). *A History of the Mont Pelerin Society.* Indianapolis, IN: Liberty Fund.

Hayek, Friedrich A. von (1967). 'Opening Address to a Conference at Mont Pélèrin'. *Studies in Philosophy, Politics and Economics* [April 1, 1947]. Chicago, IL: University of Chicago Press, 148-159.

Hayles, N. Katherine (1999). *How We Became Posthuman: Virtual Bodies in Cybernetics, Literature and Informatics*. Chicago, IL: University of Chicago Press.

Hayles, N. Katherine (2011). *How We Think: Digital Media and Contemporary Technogenesis*. Chicago, IL: University of Chicago Press.

Hayles, N. Katherine (2017). *Unthought: The Power of the Cognitive Nonconscious*. Chicago, IL: University of Chicago Press.

Hegel, Georg Wilhelm Friedrich (2018 [1807]). *The Phenomenology of Spirit*. Translated and edited by Terry Pinkard. Cambridge: Cambridge University Press.

Henriques, Julian (2011). *Sonic Bodies: Reggae Sound Systems, Performance Techniques, and Ways of Knowing*. London: Continuum.

Herbert, Daniel, Amanda Lotz and Lee Marshall (2019). 'Approaching Media Industries Comparatively: A Case Study of Streaming'. *International Journal of Cultural Studies*, 22(3), 349–366.

Hobbes, Thomas (1651 [2010]). Chapter XIV. *Leviathan: Or the Matter, Forme, & Power of a Common-Wealth Ecclesiasticall and Civill*. Edited by Ian Shapiro. New Haven: Yale University Press. E-book.

Hobsbawm, Eric (1983). 'Introduction: Inventing Traditions'. *Inventing Traditions*. Edited by Eric Hobsbawm and Terence Ranger. Cambridge: Cambridge University Press, 1–14.

Hoekman, Bernard and Michel M. Kostecki (2009). *The Political Economy of the World Trading System: The WTO and Beyond*. Third edition. Oxford: Oxford University Press.

Hoekman, Bernard (2019). 'Global Trade Governance'. *International Organization and Global Governance*. Edited by Thomas G. Weiss and Rorden Wilkinson. Second edition. New York: Routledge, 603–615.

Houghton, John (2015). *Global Warming: The Complete Briefing*. Fifth edition. Cambridge: Cambridge University Press.

Hughes, Ted (1997). *Tales from Ovid*. London: Faber.

Humboldt, Wilhelm von (1988 [1836]). *On Language: The Diversity of Human Language-Structure and its Influence on the Mental Development of Mankind*. Translated by Peter Heath and Hans Aarsleff. Cambridge: Cambridge University Press.

Hunt, Lynn (2008). *Inventing Human Rights: A History*. New York: Norton.

Irigaray, Luce (1985). *This Sex Which is Not One*. Translated by Catherine Porter and Caroline Burke. Ithaca, NY: Cornell University Press [(1977) *Ce sexe qui n'en est pas un*. Paris: Editions de Minuit].

James, C. L. R. (1963). *The Black Jacobins: Toussaint L'Ouverture and the San Domingo Revolution*. New York: Vintage.

Jameson, Fredric (1991). *Postmodernism, or, The Cultural Logic of Late Capitalism*. London: Verso.

Jameson, Fredric (2013). *The Antinomies of Realism*. London: Verso.

Jurca, Catherine (1998). 'Hollywood, the Dream House Factory'. *Cinema Journal*, 37(4), 19–36.

Kandinsky, Wassily (1977). *Concerning the Spiritual in Art*. Translated by M. T. H. Sadler. New York: Dover.

Kant, Immanuel (1983). 'Idea for a Universal History with a Cosmopolitan Intent'. *Perpetual Peace and Other Essays on Politics, History and Morals*. Translated by Ted Humphrey. Indianapolis, IN: Hackett Publishing, 29–40.

Kant, Immanuel (2000). 'Second Book: Analytic of the Sublime'. *Critique of the Power of Judgement*. Edited by Paul Guyer. Translated by Paul Guyer and Eric Matthews. Cambridge: Cambridge University Press, 128–159.

Kant, Immanuel (2003). *Critique of Pure Reason*. Translated by Norman Kemp Smith. Revised edition with an introduction by Howard Caygill. New York: Palgrave Macmillan.

Kaplan, Robert (1999). *The Nothing That Is: A Natural History of Zero*. Harmondsworth: Allen Lane/Penguin.

Kaufmann, Michael (2020). 'The Carbon Footprint Sham'. *Mashable*, 13 July, https://mashable.com/feature/carbon-footprint-pr-campaign-sham.

Kelly, Caleb (2022). 'Not Quite Sound: Silence in the Gallery'. *Australian Humanities Review*, 70 (November), 92–101.

Kempadoo, Roshini (2016). *Creole in the Archive: Imagery, Presence and the Location of the Caribbean Figure*. New York: Rowman and Littlefield.

Kennedy, Paul (2006). *The Parliament of Man: The Past, Present and Future of the United Nations*. New York: Vintage.

Kincaid, Jamaica (1996). *The Autobiography of My Mother*. New York: Macmillan.

Klein, Naomi (2007). *The Shock Doctrine: The Rise of Disaster Capitalism*. New York: Henry Holt.

Klibansky, Raymond, Erwin Panofsky and Fritz Saxl (2019 [1964]). *Saturn and Melancholy: Studies in the History of Natural Philosophy, Religion, and Art*. New edition. Montreal: McGill-Queens University Press.

Kojève, Alexandre (1969). *Introduction to the Reading of Hegel: Lectures on the Phenomenology of Spirit*. Assembled by Raymond Queneau. Edited by Allan Bloom. Translated by James H. Nichols Jr. Ithaca, NY: Cornell University Press.

Krusell, Per and Anthony A. Smith Jr. (2022). 'Climate Change Around the World'. *National Bureau of Economic Reseearch Working Paper* 30338, www.nber.org/papers/w30338.

Kunej, Drago and Ivan Turk (2001). 'New Perspectives on the Beginnings of Music: Archeological and Musicological Analysis of a Middle Paleolithic Bone "Flute"'. *The Origins of Music: Proceedings of the First Florentine Workshop in Biomusicology, Fiesole, 1997*. Revised Edition. Edited by Nils L. Wallin, Björn Merker and Steven Brown. Cambridge, MA: The MIT Press, 237–268.

Kuo, J. David (2001). *Dot.bomb: Inside an Internet Goliath – From Lunatic Optimism to Panic and Crash*. New York: Little, Brown.

Kurlansky, Mark (2002). *Salt: A World History*. New York: Walker and Company.

Kuzmina, E. E. (2008). *The Prehistory of the Silk Road*. Edited by Victor H. Mair. Philadelphia: University of Pennsylvania Press.

Laan, Tara, Anna Geddes, Olivier Bois von Kursk, Natalie Jones, Kjell Kuehne, Livi Gerbase, Claire O'Manique, Deepak Sharma and Lorne Stockman (2023). *Fanning the Flames: G20 Provides Record Financial Support for Fossil Fuels*. Winnipeg: International Institute for Sustainable Development, www.energypolicytracker.org/G20-fossil-fuel-support/.

Lacan, Jacques (1977). 'On a Question Preliminary to Any Possible Treatment of Psychosis'. *Ecrits: A Selection*. Edited and translated by Alan Sheridan. London: Routledge, 137–172.

References

Lacan, Jacques (1988). *The Seminar of Jacques Lacan. Book XI. The Four Fundamental Concepts of Psychoanalysis*. Translated by Alan Sheridan. New York: Norton.

Lampson, L. David (1995). 'CD Bronzing'. *Classical Net – Koussevitzky Recordings Society Journal*, September, www.classical.net/music/guide/society/krs/excerpt3.php.

Larkin, Philip (1979 [1971]). 'This Be the Verse'. *High Windows*. London: Faber (ebook).

Latour, Bruno (2004). 'Why Has Critique Run out of Steam? From Matters of Fact to Matters of Concern'. *Critical Inquiry*, 30 (Winter), 225–248.

Leveau, Phillippe (2006). 'Les Moulins de Barbegal'. Traianus. traianvs.net/textos/barbegal.pdf.

Levi, Primo (1988). *If This is a Man/The Truce*. Translated by Stuart J. Wolfe. London: Little, Brown.

Levinas, Emmanuel (1969). *Totality and Infinity: An Essay on Exteriority*. Translated by Alphonso Lingis. Pittsburgh, PA: Duquesne University Press.

Levinas, Emmanuel (1990 [1934]). 'Reflections on the Philosophy of Hitlerism'. Translated by Seán Hand. *Critical Inquiry*, 17(1), 62–71.

Levinas, Emmanuel (1989). 'Ethics as First Philosophy'. Translated by Seán Hand and Michael Temple. *The Levinas Reader*. Edited by Seán Hand. Oxford: Blackwell, 75–87.

Lévi-Strauss, Claude (1969). *The Raw and the Cooked (*Introduction to a Science of Mythology *Volume 1)*. Translated by John Weightman and Doreen Weightman. New York: Harper and Row.

Lévi-Strauss, Claude (1987). *Introduction to the Work of Marcel Mauss*. Translated by Felicity Baker. London: Routledge Kegan Paul.

L'Herbier, Marcel (1979). *La Tête qui tourne*. Paris: Belfond.

Liboiron, Max (2021). *Pollution is Colonialism*. Durham, NC: Duke University Press.

Lobato, Ramon and James Meese (eds) (2016). *Geoblocking and Global Video Culture*. Amsterdam: Institute for Network Cultures.

Lockhart, Adam (2012). 'A Brief History of Video – Time and Base'. *Rewind: British Artists' Video in the 1970s and 80s.* Edited by Sean Cubitt and Stephen Partridge. London: John Libbey, 179–207.

López, Antonio (2023). 'Gaslighting: Fake Climate News and Big Carbon's Network of Denial'. *The Palgrave Handbook of Media Misinformation.* Edited by Karen Fowler-Watt and Julian McDougall. London: Palgrave, 159–177.

Lugones, María (1987). 'Playfulness, "World"-Travelling, and Loving Perception'. *Hypatia*, 2(2), 3–19.

Luhmann, Niklas (1986). *Love as Passion: The Codification of Intimacy.* Translated by Jeremy Gaines and Doris L. Jones. Stanford, CA: Stanford University Press.

Luke, Timothy W. (1997). *Ecocritique: Contesting the Politics of Nature, Economy and Culture.* Minneapolis: University of Minnesota Press.

Lundblad, Jonas (2022). 'Deleuze Reads Messiaen: Durations and Birdsong Becoming Philosophy'. *Svensk tidskrift för musikforskning – Swedish Journal of Music Research (STM-SJM)*, 104, 77–107.

MacIntyre, Alasdair (1981 [2007]). *After Virtue: A Study in Moral Theory.* Notre Dame, IN: University of Notre Dame Press.

MacKenzie, Donald (2006). *An Engine, Not a Camera: How Financial Models Shape Markets.* Cambridge, MA: The MIT Press.

Madan, M. S. (2005). 'Production, Marketing, and Economics of Ginger'. *Ginger – The Genus Zingiber.* Edited by P. N. Ravindran and K. Nirmal Babu. London: CRC Press, 444–477.

Maldonado-Torres, Nelson (2008). *Against War: Views from the Underside of Modernity.* Durham, NC: Duke University Press.

Manniche, Lise (1989). *An Ancient Egyptian Herbal.* London: British Museum.

Marx, Karl (1959). *Capital: A Critique of Political Economy, Volume III.* Edited by Friedrich Engels. Moscow: Progress Publishers.

Marx, Karl (1973). *Grundrisse.* Translated by Martin Nicolaus. London: Penguin/New Left Books.

Marx, Karl (1976). *Capital: A Critique of Political Economy, Volume 1.* Translated by Ben Fowkes. London: Penguin/New Left Books.

Marx, Karl (1978). 'On the Jewish Question'. *The Marx-Engels Reader*. Edited by Robert C. Tucker. New York: Norton, 26–52.

Massumi, Brian (2016). 'Working Principles'. *The Go-To How-To Book of Anarchiving*. Edited by Andrew Murphie. Montreal: The SenseLab, 6–7.

Mast, Gerald (1982). *Howard Hawks, Storyteller*. New York: Oxford University Press.

Mauss, Marcel (1972). *A General Theory of Magic*. Translated by Robert Brain. London: Routledge.

Mazower, Mark (2009). *No Enchanted Palace: The End of Empire and the Ideological Origins of the United Nations*. Princeton, NJ: Princeton University Press.

Mbembe, Achille (2001). *On the Postcolony*. Berkeley: University of California Press.

Mbembe, Achille (2021). *Out of the Dark Night: Essays on Decolonization*. New York: Columbia University Press.

McGrew, Tony (2011). 'After Globalisation? WTO Reform and the New Global Political Economy'. *Governing the World Trade Organization: Past, Present and Beyond Doha*. Edited by Thomas Cottier and Manfred Elsig. Cambridge: Cambridge University Press, 20–46.

McLuhan, Marshall (1964). *Understanding Media: The Extensions of Man*. London: Sphere.

McLuhan, Marshall and Bruce R. Powers (1989). *The Global Village: Transformations in World Life and Media in the 21st Century*. Oxford: Oxford University Press.

Meadows, Donella H., Dennis L. Meadows, Jørgen Randers and William H. Behrens III (1972). *The Limits to Growth: A Report for the Club of Rome's Project on the Predicament of Mankind*. New York: Universe Books.

Menkman, Rosa (2011). 'Glitch Studies Manifesto'. *Video Vortex 2: Moving Images Beyond YouTube*. Edited by Geert Lovink and Rachel Somers Miles. Amsterdam: Institute of Network Cultures, 336–347.

Merleau-Ponty, Maurice (1964). 'Cézanne's Doubt'. *Sense and Non-Sense*. Translated by Hubert Dreyfus and Patricia Allen Dreyfus. Evanston, IL: Northwestern University Press, 9–25.

Merton, Thomas (1949). *Seeds of Contemplation.* New York: New Directions.

Mignolo, Walter D. (2000). *Local Histories/Global Designs: Essays on the Coloniality of Power, Subaltern Knowledges and Border Thinking.* Princeton, NJ: Princeton University Press.

Mignolo, Walter D. (2003). *The Darker Side of the Renaissance: Literacy, Territoriality, & Colonization.* Ann Arbor: University of Michigan Press.

Mignolo, Walter D. and Catherine Walsh (2018). *On Decoloniality: Concepts, Analytics, Praxis.* Durham, NC: Duke University Press.

Milun, Kathryn (2011). *The Political Uncommons: The Cross-Cultural Logic of the Global Commons.* Burlington, VT and Farnham: Ashgate.

Minsky, Hyman P. (1992). 'The Financial Instability Hypothesis: Capitalist Processes and the Behavior of the Economy.' *Financial Crises: Theory, History, and Policy.* Edited by Charles P. Kindleberger and Jean-Pierre Laffargue. Cambridge: Cambridge University Press, 13–39, Hyman P. Minsky Archive, Paper 282, http://digitalcommons.bard.edu/hm_archive/282.

Mirowski, Philip (2002). *Machine Dreams: Economics Becomes a Cyborg Science.* Cambridge: Cambridge University Press.

Mirowski, Philip (2019). 'Hell Is Truth Seen Too Late.' *Boundary 2*, 46(1), 1–53.

Mohanty, Chandra Talpade (1984). 'Under Western Eyes: Feminist Scholarship and Colonial Discourses.' *boundary 2*, 12(3)–13(1), 333–358.

Mohanty, Chandra Talpade (2003). ' "Under Western Eyes" Revisited: Feminist Solidarity through Anticapitalist Struggles.' *Feminism without Borders: Decolonizing Theory, Practicing Solidarity.* Durham, NC: Duke University Press, 222–251.

Mont Pèlerin Society (1947). Statement of Aims, www.montpelerin.org/statement-of-aims/.

Montaigne, Michel de (1958). *Essays.* Edited and translated by J. M. Cohen. Harmondsworth: Penguin.

Moore, Berrien III (2000). 'Sustaining Earth's Life Support Systems: The Challenge for the Next Decade and Beyond.' *International Geosphere-Biosphere Newsletter*, 41 (May), 1–2.

Morley, Iain (2006). 'Mousterian Musicanship? The Case of the Divje Babe I Bone'. *Oxford Journal of Archaeology*, 24(4), 317–433.

Morton, Timothy (2013). *Hyperobjects: Philosophy and Ecology after the End of the World*. Minneapolis: University of Minnesota Press.

Morsink, Johannes (1999). *Universal Declaration of Human Rights: Origins, Drafting and Intent*. Philadelphia: University of Pennsylvania Press.

Morsink, Johannes (2009). *Inherent Human Rights: Philosophical Roots of the Universal Declaration*. Philadelphia: University of Pennsylvania Press.

Mouffe, Chantal (2005). *On the Political*. London: Routledge.

Mulvey, Laura (2006). *Death 24x a Second: Stillness and the Moving Image*. London: Reaktion Books.

Murphy, Michelle (2017). 'Alterlife and Decolonial Chemical Relations'. *Cultural Anthropology*, 32(4), 494–503.

Nabhan, Gary Paul (2014). *Cumin, Camels, and Caravans: A Spice Odyssey*. Berkeley: University of California Press.

Nakamoto, Satoshi (2008). 'Bitcoin: A Peer-to-Peer Electronic Cash System'. 31 October, https://nakamotoinstitute.org/library/bitcoin/.

Nancy, Jean-Luc (1991). *The Inoperative Community*. Edited by Peter Connor. Translated by Peter Connor, Lisa Gardbus, Michael Holland and Simona Sawhney. Minneapolis: University of Minnesota Press.

Nancy, Jean-Luc (1998). *The Sense of the World*. Translated by Jeffrey S. Librett. Minneapolis: University of Minnesota Press.

Narayanan, C. S., M. M. Sree Kumar and B. Sankarikutt (2000). 'Industrial Processing and Products of Black Pepper'. *Black Pepper – Piper Nigrum*. Edited by P. N. Ravindran. Amsterdam: Harwood.

NASA (n.d.). 'The Golden Record'. Jet Propulsion Laboratory, https://voyager.jpl.nasa.gov/golden-record/.

Nijhuis, Michelle (2021). 'The Miracle of the Commons'. *Aeon*, https://aeon.co/essays/the-tragedy-of-the-commons-is-a-false-and-dangerous-myth.

Nixon, Rob (2012). 'Neoliberalism, Genre, and "The Tragedy of the Commons"'. *PMLA/Publications of the Modern Language Association of America*, 127(3), 593–599.

Nkrumah, Kwame (1965). *Neocolonialism: The Last Stage of Imperialism*. New York: International Publishers.

Nussbaum, Martha C. (1996). 'Patriotism and Cosmopolitanism'. *For Love of Country: Debating the Limits of Patriotism*. Edited by Joshua Clover. Boston, MA: Beacon, 3–17.

Osborne, Peter D. (2019). *Photography and the Contemporary Cultural Condition*. London: Routledge.

Ostrom, Elinor (2015). *Governing the Commons: The Evolution of Institutions for Collective Action*. Cambridge: Cambridge University Press.

Ovid (2022). *Metamorphoses by Ovid*. Translated by Stephanie McCarter. New York: Penguin.

Oxfam (2022). Inequality Kills. Oxfam Briefing Paper. Oxford: Oxfam International, https://oxfamilibrary.openrepository.com/bitstream/handle/10546/621341/bp-inequality-kills-170122-en.pdf.

Panayotakis, Costas (2021). *The Capitalist Mode of Destruction: Austerity, Ecological Crisis and the Hollowing Out of Democracy*. Manchester: Manchester University Press.

Papastergiadis, Nikos (2000). *The Turbulence of Migration: Globalization, Deterritorialization, and Hybridity*. Malden, MA: Polity Press.

Papastergiadis, Nikos (2012). *Cosmopolitanism and Culture*. Cambridge: Polity.

Papastergiadis, Nikos (2023). *The Cosmos in Cosmopolitanism*. Cambridge: Polity.

Parikka, Jussi (2015). *A Geology of Media*. Minneapolis: University of Minnesota Press.

Parisi, Luciana (2019). 'The Alien Subject of AI'. *Subjectivity*, 12(1), 27–48.

Pasquinelli, Matteo (2019). 'On the Origins of Marx's General Intellect'. *Radical Philosophy*, 2(6), 43–56.

Petropoulos, Georgios A. (2002). *Fenugreek – The Genus Trigonella*. London: Taylor and Francis.

Pettman, Dominic (2017). *Sonic Intimacies: Voice, Species, Technics (Or How to Listen to the World)*. Stanford, CA: Stanford University Press.

Plaga, Leonie Sara and Valentin Bertsch (2023). 'Methods for Assessing Climate Uncertainty in Energy System Models: A Systematic Literature Review'. *Applied Energy*, 331, 1–19.

Plato (1892 [380 BCE]). *Euthyphro*. Translated by Benjamin Jowett. *The Dialogues of Plato*, in 5 vols, 3rd edition revised and corrected. Oxford: Oxford University Press. Wikisource, https://en.wikisource.org/wiki/Euthyphro_(Jowett).

Plehwe, Dieter (2009). 'Introduction'. *The Road from Mont Pèlerin: The Making of the Neoliberal Thought Collective*. Edited by Philip Mirowski and Dieter Plehwe. Cambridge, MA: Harvard University Press, 1–42.

Pollock, Griselda (2022). *Killing Men and Dying Women: Imagining Difference in 1950s New York Painting*. Manchester: Manchester University Press.

Povinelli, Elizabeth A. (2006). *The Empire of Love: Toward a Theory of Intimacy, Genealogy, and Carnality*. Durham, NC: Duke University Press.

Protzman, Ferdinand (1999). 'The Photographer's Snap Judgment; When Hans Namuth Encountered the Superstars of Contemporary Art at Work, Something Clicked'. *The Washington Post*, 23 May, G06.

Pryke, Michael (2010). 'Money's Eyes: The Visual Preparation of Financial Markets'. *Economy and Society*, 39(4), 427–459.

Quijano, Aníbal and Immanuel Wallerstein (1992). 'Americanity as a Concept, or the Americas in the Modern World-System'. *International Journal of Social Sciences*, 134, 583–591.

Quijano, Aníbal (2007). 'Coloniality and Modernity/Rationality'. *Cultural Studies*, 21(2–3), 168–178.

Rabinbach, Anson (1990). *The Human Motor: Energy, Fatigue and the Origins of Modernity*. New York and Berkeley, CA: Basic Books and University of California Press.

Rancière, Jacques (1999). *Disagreement: Politics and Philosophy*. Translated by Julie Rose. Minneapolis: University of Minnesota Press.

Rancière, Jacques (2014). *The Intervals of Cinema*. Translated by John Howe. London: Verso.

Ravindran, P. N. (2000). *Black Pepper – Piper Nigrum*. Amsterdam: Harwood.

Ravindran, P. N. and K. J. Madhusoodanan (2002). *Cardamon – The Genus Elettaria*. London: Taylor and Francis.

Ravindran, P. N., K. Nirmal Babu and M. Shylaja (2004). *Cinnamon and Cassia – The Genus Cinnamomum*. London: CRC Press.

Ravindran, P. N. and K. Nirmal Babu (2005). *Ginger – The Genus Zingiber*. London: CRC Press.

Ravindran, P. N., K. Nirmal Babu and K. Sivaraman (2007). *Turmeric – The Genus Curcuma*. London: CRC Press.

Revill, David (1993). *The Roaring Silence: John Cage – A Life*. New York: Arcade.

Rizzi, Sofia (2021). 'Hear the World's Oldest Instrument, the 50,000-Year-Old Neanderthal Flute.' Classic FM, 21 October, www.classicfm.com/discover-music/instruments/flute/worlds-oldest-instrument-neanderthal-flute/.

Robbins, Bruce (1998). 'Introduction Part 1: Actually Existing Cosmopolitanism.' *Cosmopolitics: Thinking and Feeling Beyond the Nation*. Edited by Pheng Cheah and Bruce Robbins. Minneapolis: University of Minnesota Press, 1–19.

Robbins, Bruce and Paulo Lemos Horta (2017). 'Introduction.' *Cosmopolitanisms*. Edited by Bruce Robbins and Paulo Lemos Horta. Afterword by Kwame Anthony Appiah. New York: New York University Press, 1–17.

Roberts, John (2007). *The Intangibilities of Form: Skill and Deskilling in Art After the Readymade*. London: Verso.

Rorty, Richard (1993). 'The Priority of Democracy to Philosophy.' *Prospects for a Common Morality*. Edited by Gene Outka and John P. Reeder. Philadelphia: University of Pennsylvania Press, 254–278.

Rosenberg, Harold (1952). 'The American Action Painters.' *Art News*, 51(8), 22–23, 48–50.

Rosol, Christoph (2023) 1948. *Environing Media*. Edited by Adam Wickberg and Johan Gärdebo. London: Routledge, 75–92.

Rotman, Brian (1987). *Signifying Nothing: The Semiotics of Zero*. Stanford, CA: Stanford University Press.

Rubin, William (ed.) (1984). *Primitivism in 20th Century Art*, 2 volumes. New York: Museum of Modern Art.

Rudé, George (1980). *Ideology and Popular Protest.* London: Lawrence and Wishart.

Ruskin, John (1904 [1856]). *Modern Painters in Five Volumes, Volume Three.* London: J. M. Dent.

Russell, Catherine (2018). *Archiveology: Walter Benjamin and Archival Film Practices.* Durham, NC: Duke University Press.

Russolo, Luigi (1967 [1913]). *The Art of Noise.* New York: Great Bear Pamphlet/ Something Else Press.

Samuelson, Paul A. (1947). *Foundations of Economic Analysis.* Cambridge, MA: Harvard University Press.

Sartre, Jean-Paul (1971). *L'idiot de la famille: Gustave Flaubert de 1821 à 1857, Volume 2.* Paris: Gallimard (ebook 2017).

Sartre, Jean-Paul (2003 [1948]). *Being and Nothingness: An Essay on Phenomenological Ontology.* Translated by Hazel E. Barnes. London: Routledge.

Sartre, Jean-Paul (2004). *The Imaginary: A Phenomenological Psychology of the Imagination.* Translated by Jonathan Webber. Introduction by Arlette Elkaïm-Sartre and Jonathan Webber. London: Routledge.

Sassen, Saskia (2022). 'The Limits of Power and the Complexity of Powerlessness: The Case of Immigration.' *Routledge International Handbook of Contemporary Social and Political Theory.* Second edition. Edited by Gerard Delanty and Stephen P. Turner. London: Routledge, 456–465.

Schaeffer, Pierre (2017). *Treatise of Musical Objects: An Essay Across Disciplines.* Translated by Christine North and John Dack. Berkeley: University of California Press.

Schafer, R. Murray (1994). *The Soundscape: Our Sonic Environment and the Tuning of the World.* Rochester, VT: Destiny Books.

Sconce, Jeffrey (2000). *Haunted Media: Electronic Presence from Telegraphy to Television.* Durham, NC: Duke University Press.

Shahani, Chandru J., Michele H. Youket and Norman Weberg (2009). *Compact Disc Service Life: An Investigation of the Service Life of Prerecorded Compact Discs (CD-ROM).* Preservation Research and Testing Series No. 10. Prepared for the Library of Congress by William P. Murray. Washington, DC: Preservation Directorate, Library of Congress.

Shanken, Edward A. (2016). 'Contemporary Art and New Media: Digital Divide or Hybrid Discourse?' *A Companion to Digital Art*. Edited by Christiane Paul. New York: Wiley-Blackwell, 463–481.

Shannon, C. E. (1948). 'A Mathematical Theory of Communication'. *The Bell System Technical Journal*, 27 (July, October), 379–423, 623–656.

Shiva, Vandana (1988). 'Women in the Forest'. *Staying Alive: Women, Ecology and Survival in India*. New Delhi and London: Kali for Women and Zed Books, 53–91.

Smith, Terry (2009). *What Is Contemporary Art?* Chicago, IL: University of Chicago Press.

Smith, Ernie (2017). 'The Hidden Phenomenon That Could Ruin Your Old Discs'. Motherboard – Tech by Vice, 7 February, www.vice.com/en/article/mg9pdv/the-hidden-phenomenon-that-could-ruin-your-old-discs.

Smythe, Dallas (1977). 'Communications: Blindspot of Western Marxism'. *Canadian Journal of Political and Social Theory*, 1(3), 1–27. Reprinted in Dallas Smythe (1994), *Counterclockwise: Perspectives on Communication*. Edited by Thomas Guback. Boulder, CO: Westview Press, 266–291.

Sobchack, Vivian (2004). *Carnal Thoughts: Embodiment and Moving Image Culture*. Berkeley: University of California Press.

Sohn-Rethel, Alfred (1978). *Intellectual and Manual Labour: A Critique of Epistemology*. Translated by Martin Sohn-Rethel. Atlantic Highlands, NJ: Humanities Press.

Sontag, Susan (1977). *On Photography*. Harmondsworth: Penguin.

Southern Poverty Law Centre (n.d.). 'Garrett Hardin', www.splcenter.org/fighting-hate/extremist-files/individual/garrett-hardin.

Srinivasan, Rags and Agnieszka Zielinska (2019). *Data at the Edge: Managing and Activating Information in a Distributed World*. State of the Edge, spring, https://stateoftheedge.com/reports/data-at-the-edge-2019/.

Srnicek, Nick (2017). *Platform Capitalism*. Cambridge: Polity.

Steele, Beverley A. (2003). *Grenada: A History of Its People*. Oxford: Macmillan Caribbean.

References

Stiegler, Bernard (2003). 'Our Ailing Educational Institutions'. *Culture Machine*, 5, https://culturemachine.net/the-e-issue/our-ailing-educational-institutions/.

Storr, Robert (1999). 'A Piece of the Action'. *Jackson Pollock: New Approaches*. Edited by Kirk Varnedoe and Pepe Karmel. New York: Museum of Modern Art/Harry N. Abrahams, 33–70.

Suárez, Juan A. (2001). 'T. S. Eliot's "The Waste Land", the Gramophone, and the Modernist Discourse Network'. *New Literary History*, 32(3), 747–768.

Supran, Geoffrey and Naomi Oreskes (2021). 'Rhetoric and Frame Analysis of ExxonMobil's Climate Change Communications'. *One Earth*, 4 (May), 696–719.

Taçon, Paul S. C., Sally K. May, Ronald Lamilami, Fiona McKeague, Iain G. Johnston, Andrea Jalandoni, Daryl Wesley, Ines Domingo Sanz, Liam M. Brady, Duncan Wright and Joakim Goldhahn (2020). 'Maliwawa Figures: A Previously Undescribed Arnhem Land Rock Art Style'. *Australian Archaeology*, 86(3), 208–225.

Tadiar, Neferti X. M. (2022). *Remaindered Life*. Durham, NC: Duke University Press.

Tesco (2021). Our Code of Business Conduct. Welwyn Garden City: Tesco PLC, www.tescoplc.com/sustainability/documents/policies/our-code-of-business-conduct.

Thompson, E. P. (1991). *Time, Work-Discipline, and Industrial Capitalism. Customs in Common*. New York: New Press, 352–403.

Toscano, Alberto and Jeff Kinkle (2015). *Cartographies of the Absolute*. Alresford: Zero Books.

Tracy, Steven (2016). 'Beauty Is in the Ear of the Beholder: Eliot, Armstrong, and Ellison'. *The Edinburgh Companion to T.S. Eliot and the Arts*. Edited by Frances Dickey and John D. Morgenstern. Edinburgh: Edinburgh University Press, 161–170.

Tucker, Arthur O. and Thomas DeBaggio (2009). *The Encyclopedia of Herbs: A Comprehensive Reference to Herbs of Flavor and Fragrance*. Edited by Francesco DeBaggio. Portland, OR: Timber Press.

Turing, Alan M. (1950). 'Computing Machinery and Intelligence'. *Mind*, 59, 433–460.

UNHCHR (2024). *Protection of Civilians in Armed Conflict – June 2024 Update*. Geneva: United Nations High Commission for Human Rights.

UNHCR (n.d.). *The 1951 Refugee Convention and 1967 Protocol*. New York: United Nations High Commission for Refugees, www.unhcr.org/1951-refugee-convention.html.

United Nations (1948). *Universal Declaration of Human Rights*. New York: United Nations, www.un.org/en/about-us/universal-declaration-of-human-rights.

Usai, Paolo Cherchi (1994). *Burning Passions: An Introduction to the Study of Silent Cinema*. Translated by Emma Sansone Rittle. London: BFI.

Usai, Paolo Cherchi (2000). *Silent Cinema: An Introduction*. London: BFI.

Valéry, Paul (1933). 'Au sujet du Cimetière marin'. *La Nouvelle Revue Française*, 234 (March), 399–411.

Van den Bossche, Peter (2021). 'The Origins of the WTO'. *The Law and Policy of the World Trade Organization: Text, Cases, and Materials*. Peter Van den Bossche and Werner Zdouc. Fifth Edition. Cambridge: Cambridge University Press, 78–85.

van der Leeuw, Sander (2013). 'AIMES 2.0: Towards a Global Earth System Science'. *Global Change*, 81 (October), www.igbp.net/news/features/features/aimes20towardsaglobalearthsystemscience.5.30566fc6142425d6c911989.html.

van Dijk, José (2013). *Culture of Connectivity: A Critical History of Social Media*. Oxford: Oxford University Press.

van Doesburg, Theo (1968). *Grundbegriffe der Neuen Gestaltenden Kunst / Grondbeginselen der Nieuwe beeldende Kunst / Principles of Neo-Plastic Art (1918)*. Translated by Janet Seligman. Introduction by Hans M. Wingler. Postscript by H. L. C. Jaffé. London: Lund Humphries.

Vantage Market Research (2023). 'Global Pepper Market Size & Share to Surpass USD 5.3 Billion by 2030'. Pune and Washington, DC: Vantage Market Research, www.globenewswire.com/en/news-release/2023/03/16/2628401/0/en/Global-Pepper-Market-Size-Share-to-Surpass-USD-5-3-Billion-by-2030-Vantage-Market-Research.html.

Vasconcelos, José (1925). *La Raza Cósmica: Misión de la raza iberoamericana - Notas de viajes a la América del Sur.* Madrid: Agencia Mundial de Librería, www.filosofia.org/aut/001/razacos.htm.

Vercellone, Carlo (2007). 'From Formal Subsumption to General Intellect: Elements for a Marxist Reading of the Thesis of Cognitive Capitalism'. *Historical Materialism*, 15(1), 13–36.

Vidyashankar, Ganaganur Krishnappa (2014). 'Fenugreek: An Analysis from Trade and Commerce Perspective'. *American Journal of Social Issues and Humanities*, March–April, 162–170.

Virilio, Paul (1991). *The Aesthetics of Disappearance.* Translated by Philip Beitchman. New York: Semiotext(e).

Virno, Paolo (2007). 'General Intellect'. *Historical Materialism*, 15(3), 3–8.

Vizenor, Gerald (2009). *Native Liberty and Cultural Survivance.* Lincoln: University of Nebraska Press.

Vogl, Joseph (2015). *The Specter of Capital.* Translated by Joachim Redner and Robert Savage. Stanford, CA: Stanford University Press.

Vogl, Joseph (2023). *Capital and Ressentiment: A Short Theory of the Present.* Translated by Neil Solomon. London: Polity Press.

Vogt, William (1948 [2013]). *Road to Survival.* New York: Sloane Associates. Extract reprinted as chapter 12: 'History of Our Future'. *The Future of Nature: Documents of Global Change.* Edited by Libby Robin, Sverker Sörlin and Paul Warde. New Haven, CT: Yale University Press, 187–190.

von Neumann, John and Oskar Morgenstern (1944). *Theory of Games and Economic Behavior.* Princeton, NJ: Princeton University Press.

Wagner, Anne M. (1989). 'Lee Krasner as L.K.'. *Representations*, 25 (Winter), 42–57.

Wagner, Anne M. (1999). 'Pollock's Nature, Frankenthaler's Culture'. *Jackson Pollock: New Approaches.* Edited by Kirk Varnedoe and Pepe Karmel. New York: Museum of Modern Art/Harry N. Abrahams. 181–200.

Walcott, Derek (1990). *Omeros.* London: Faber.

Wallerstein, Immanuel (1974). *The Modern World System 1: Capitalist Agriculture and the Origins of the European World-Economy in the Sixteenth Century*. Berkeley: University of California Press.

Wallin, Nils L., Bjorn Merker and Steven Brown (eds) (2001). *The Origins of Music*. Cambridge, MA: The MIT Press.

Wang, Yan, Wei Song, Wei Tao, Antonio Liotta, Dawei Yang, Xinlei Li, Shuyong Gao, Yixuan Sun, Weifeng Ge, Wei Zhang and Wenqiang Zhang (2022). 'A Systematic Review on Affective Computing: Emotion Models, Databases, and Recent Advances'. *Information Fusion*, 83–84 (July), 19–52.

Wark, McKenzie (2017). 'Amy Wendling: Marx's Metaphysics and Meatphysics'. *General Intellects*. London: Verso (ebook).

Wark, McKenzie (2019). *Capital is Dead*. London: Verso.

Warrender, Keith (2022). *Forbidden Kinder: The 1932 Mass Trespass Re-Visited*. Altrincham: Willow Publishing.

Weart, Spencer R. (2008). *The Discovery of Global Warming*. Revised and expanded. Cambridge, MA: Harvard University Press.

Weintraub, E. Roy (2002). *How Economics Became a Mathematical Science*. Durham, NC: Duke University Press.

Wendling, Amy E. (2009). *Karl Marx on Technology and Alienation*. London: Palgrave.

Whitehead, Alfred North (1948). *Science and the Modern World: Lowell Lectures 1925*. New York: Macmillan.

Whyte, William H. (1956). *The Organization Man*. New York: Simon and Schuster.

Wiener, Norbert (1961 [1948]). *Cybernetics; or, Control and Communication in the Animal and the Machine*. Second edition. Cambridge, MA: The MIT Press.

Williams, Raymond (1989). *Resources of Hope: Culture, Democracy, Socialism*. Edited by Robin Gale. London: Verso.

Wolfe, Patrick (1999). *Settler Colonialism and the Transformation of Anthropology: The Politics and Poetics of an Ethnographic Event*. London: Cassell.

World Bank (2023). *World Development Report 2023: Migrants, Refugees, and Societies*. Washington, DC: World Bank, http://hdl.handle.net/10986/39696

World Social Forum (2005). 'Porto Alegre Manifesto in English'. Translated by Daniel Bloch. Open Democracy, 11 February, www.opendemocracy.net/en/porto-alegre-manifesto-in-english/.

Wraith, Matthew (2013). 'Throbbing Human Engines: Mechanical Vibration, Entropy and Death in Marinetti, Joyce, Ehrenburg and Eliot'. *Vibratory Modernism*. Edited by Anthony Enns and Shelley Trower. London: Palgrave.

Wright, Clifford A. (2007). 'The Medieval Spice Trade and the Diffusion of the Chile'. *Gastronomica*, 7(2), 35–43.

Young, James Webb (1994 [1940]). *A Technique for Producing Ideas*. Chicago, IL: NTC Business Books.

Zeiher, Cindy (2017). 'Struggle as Love *Par Excellence*: Zupancic *avec* Badiou'. *Can Philosophy Love? Reflections and Encounters*. Edited by Cindy Zeiher and Todd McGowan. London: Rowman and Littlefield, 297–310.

Zielinski, Siegfried (2006). *Deep Time of the Media: Toward an Archaeology of Hearing and Seeing by Technical Means*. Translated by Gloria Custance. Foreword by Timothy Druckrey. Cambridge, MA: The MIT Press.

Mediography

Anadol, Refik (2021). *Quantum Memories*, https://refikanadol.com/works/quantummemories/.

Anderson, Thom (2004). *Los Angeles Plays Itself*, 169 mins.

Beeple (2021). https://beeple-crap.com.

Brakhage, Stan (1959). *Window Water Baby Moving*, 12 mins.

Burton, Tim (1996). *Mars Attacks!* Tim Burton Productions, 106 mins.

Cukor, George (1938). *Holiday*, Columbia, 95 mins.

Dimkaroski, Ljuben (2017). 'Ljuben Dimkaroski plays the Divje Babe Bone Flute'. EMAProject European Music Archaeology Project, www.youtube.com/watch?v=AZCWFcyxUhQ.

Godard, Jean-Luc (1963). *Les Carabiniers*, Cocinor/Les films Marceau/Rome Paris Films/Laetitia Film, 75 mins.

Godard, Jean-Luc (1988–1998). *Histoire(s) du cinéma*, Canal+/Centre Nationale de la Cinématographie/France 3/Gaumont/La Sept/Télévision Suisse Romande/Vega Films, 266 mins.

Guggenheim, Davis (2006). *An Inconvenient Truth*, Lawrence Bender Productions/Participant Productions, 96 mins.

Hawks, Howard (1938). *Bringing Up Baby*, RKO, 102 mins.

Kwan, Daniel and Daniel Scheinert (2022). *Everything Everywhere All At Once*, IAC Films/Gozie AGBO/Year of the Rat/Ley Line Entertainment, 139 mins.

Lydia E. Pinkham's grandchildren (back), Boston Public Library, 1870–1900, www.flickr.com/photos/boston_public_library/8558306394/.

Martins, Edgar (2006). The Diminishing Present, https://edgarmartins.com/product/the-diminishing-present/.

McCarey, Leo (1937). *The Awful Truth*, Columbia, 91 mins.

Montgomery, Robert (1947). *The Lady in the Lake*, Metro-Goldwyn-Mayer, 105 mins.

Morrison, Bill (2004). *Light Is Calling*, 8 mins, https://youtu.be/yx0HzBiaVn4.

Namuth, Hans (1951). *Jackson Pollock '51*, produced by Hans Namuth and Paul Flakenberg, 9.30 mins, https://youtu.be/atu4uVT7bV8.

NGV (2020). *NGV Triennial 2020*. Melbourne: National Gallery of Victoria, www.ngv.vic.gov.au/exhibition/triennial-2020/.

Potter, H. C. (1948). *Mr Blandings Builds his Dream Home*, RKO, 93 mins.

Ray, Nicholas (1955). *Rebel Without a Cause*, Warner Bros., 111 mins.

REWIND Artists' Video (n.d.). https://rewind.ac.uk/.

Ritchie, Guy (1998). *Lock, Stock and Two Smoking Barrels*, Steve Tisch Company/Ska Films, 127 mins.

Robak, Tabor (2020). *Megafauna*. Melbourne: National Gallery of Victoria, www.ngv.vic.gov.au/virtual-tours/triennial-2020-tabor/.

References

Tan, Erika (2008). *The Syntactical Impossibility of Approaching with a Pure Heart*, https://ualresearchonline.arts.ac.uk/id/eprint/6396/.

Temple, Julian (1988). *Earth Girls Are Easy*, Kestrel Films, 100 mins.

Scott, Ridley (1982). *Blade Runner*, The Ladd Company, 112 mins.

Singer, Bryan (1995). *The Usual Suspects*, Spelling Film International/Blue Parrot/Bad Hat Harry, 102 mins.

Vadim, Roger (1968). *Barbarella*, Marianne Productions/Dino De Laurentiis/Cinematografica, 98 mins.

Wilcox, Fred McLeod (1956). *Forbidden Planet*, MGM, 99 mins.

Young, James (1926). *The Bells*, Chadwick Pictures, 73 mins.

Index

Adams, John Luther 50
Adorno, Theodor 12, 110–111, 124, 188
affect 7, 58, 76–82, 99–101, 127, 145, 185, 190
Agamben, Giorgio 87, 88
Ahmed, Sara 90, 97–98
AI *see* artificial intelligence (AI)
Althusser, Louis 173
Anadol, Refik 123–128
ancestors 6, 54, 56–58, 137, 169, 171, 178, 190–191, 200, 219–220, 232–236, 240–245
Angerer, Marie-Luise 56–57, 77, 184
Anzaldúa, Gloria 134, 152
Appadurai, Arjun 113
Appiah, Anthony 146
Archive of Australian Media Arts 222, 231
Arendt, Hannah 101
Aristotle 1, 6, 87
Arnhem Land rock art 195
Arrighi, Giovanni 140–141
artificial intelligence (AI) 160–171, 179–180, 184–186, 226, 234
Auden, W.H. 63, 95, 105
Australian Centre for the Moving Image 222
Ayache, Elie 113

Badiou, Alain 38–39, 82–86, 88, 97–98
Baier, Annette 141

Banda Islands 212
banking app 14
Barbarella (1968) 122
Barthes, Roland 63
Baudrillard, Jean 110
Beauty 9
Beeple 115–123, 126, 128, 166
Bells, The (1926) 196–197
Belmessous, Salina 237
Benjamin, Walter 43, 225, 238, 242
Berger, John 59
Berlant, Lauren 109–110, 243
Bertoia, Harry 53
Biggs, Simon 233
Big Rock Candy Mountain, The (1928) 239
Birkin, Jane 234
Bitcoin 40
Black—Scholes formula 112
Blade Runner (1982) 121
Blake, William 11, 32
Bloch, Ernst 9, 106–107, 111–112, 239
Braudel, Fernand 211
Bresson, Robert 13
Bringing Up Baby (1938) 66–86, 92, 94–99
British Petroleum 107, 192
Britton, Andrew 66–67, 86
Bryson, Norman 59

Cage, John 36, 50, 52, 175, 179
Campbell, Joseph 172

Camus, Albert 44
carbon footprint 107, 192
Castoriadis, Cornelis 149–150, 180, 188, 193–194, 196, 226
Castro, Fidel 219
Catullus 238
Cavell, Stanley 67, 72, 76, 96
Césaire, Aimé 154–155
Chaplin, Charlie 59–60, 127
charcoal 194–195, 217, 237
Chomsky, Noam 156
Chun, Wendy 102–103
Ciccia, Emanuele 208
Cicero 87–88, 240
cinephlia 67, 104
Clausewitz, Carl von 162
Clough, Patricia Ticineto 76–77
code 34–35, 158, 167–168, 173–174, 185
Coen, Deborah 202
Cohen, Tom 240–241, 242
Colebrook, Claire 240–241, 242
commons 41, 58, 180–181
communication 5–6
Connecticut 96
consumption, real subsumption of 35–36, 171–172, 173
COP Climate Change Conferences 4
Coulmas, Florian 148
Crutzen, Paul, and Eugene Stoermer 104, 201
Culpeper, Nicholas 213
Cusicanqui, Silvia Rivera 152

da Gama, Vasco 211
Davies, William 106
Dead Sea Scrolls 227

Deleuze, Gilles 13, 37, 40, 77, 188
Derrida, Jacques 87, 89, 224–228, 233
Descartes, René 136, 137, 156–157
Dioscorides 214
Divje Babe neanderthal flute 43, 45–48, 52, 54, 58, 61, 133–135, 200
Douglas, Mary 117–118
DuBois, W. E. B. 114
Duchamp, Marcel 117–118
DuPont 195–196
Dussel, Enrique 133, 136, 150–151, 152, 180, 187, 219
DVD disc rot 230–231

EaaSI *see* Emulation-as-a-Service (EaaSI)
Earth Girls are Easy (1988) 122
Earth-systems science 199, 201–207
Eco, Umberto 215
edge computing 174, 183–186, 235
Edwards, Paul N. 202–205
Ehrlich, Paul 15
Eliott, T. S. 48–54
Emulation-as-a-Service (EaaSI) 231, 233
Engels, Friedrich 29, 162, 187
Escobar, Arturo 131, 140
Everything Everywhere All At Once (2022) 38–39
Exxon 108

Fanon, Frantz 147
fantasy 122
Fellini, Federico 13
fenugreek 213–214
Ficino, Marsilio 216
Flusser, Vilém 42, 183

Forbidden Planet (1957) 121
Fossati, Giovanna 230
Foster, Hal 191
Foucault, Michel 37, 116, 215, 223, 229, 233, 234
fraternity 186–187
Frege, Gotlob 88–89, 93
Frick, Caroline 222–224
futures markets 111–112

Gabrys, Jennifer 206
Gadamer, Hans Georg 138, 158
Gaines, Jane 223
Galloway, Alex 168
General Agreement on Tariffs and Trade (GATT) 29–30
general cognition 8, 183–186, 188–189, 235
general imagination 9, 189, 193, 235
general intellect 41, 54, 127–128, 137, 167, 171, 179–180, 184, 187–188, 190, 234–235
Ghosh, Amitav 212
ginger 214
Glissant, Edouard 11, 100, 134, 150, 152, 154
Global Financial Crisis 2007–2008 113
gods 6, 190–191, 200, 206–207, 219–220, 235–236, 240–245
Golden Record 55–58, 60
Greenberg, Clement 178–179, 196
Grosfoguel, Ramón 142–143, 154
Guattari, Felix 133–134, 180

Habermas, Jürgen 39–40
Haraway, Donna 158
Hardin, Garrett 15–30, 41

Hayek, Friedrich 23–25
Hayles, N. Katherine 56–57, 77, 184
Hegel, Georg Wilhelm Friedrich 24–25, 29, 60, 92, 136, 149, 193
Helmholtz, Herman von 241
Hepburn, Katherine 68–77, 96
Hill, Geoffrey 237
Histoire(s) du cinéma (1989–1999) 226
Houghton, Sir John 206
Howe, James Wong 33–34, 79

Inconvenient Truth, An (2007) 108
impersons 166, 169, 170
International Institute for Sustainable Development 4
International Panel on Climate Change 203
Irigaray, Luce 93, 228

Jameson, Fredric 14, 76, 81

Kant, Immanuel 39, 132, 148–149
Kelly, Caleb 51
Kempadoo, Roshini 223
Kepler, Johannes 54
Kim, Christine Sun 51
Kincaid, Jamaica 155
Koons, Jeffrey 118

L'Herbier, Marcel 13
Lacan, Jacques 1, 34, 82, 86, 167
Lady in the Lake, The (1947) 90
language 41, 56, 84, 136–138, 148, 154–158, 185
large language models (LLMs) 158, 185
Larkin, Philip 103

Latour, Bruno 102–103
Leibniz, Gottfried Wilhelm 190
lemons 214–215
Les Carabiniers (1963) 159
Levi, Primo 114
Lévi-Strauss, Claude 47, 51, 125
Levinas, Emmanuel 83–87, 139, 143, 156–157
liar's paradox 63–66, 77
Liboiron, Max 44, 103–104, 132
Light is Calling (2004) 196–199, 208, 225
Limits to Growth, The 201
Llinnaeus, Carl 215
LLMs *see* large language models (LLMs)
Los Angeles Plays Itself (2004) 226
Lugones, María 101–102
Luhmann, Niklas 66
Lydia E. Pinkham's Vegetable Compound 214

Macintyre, Alasdair 21, 141–142, 148, 158–159
Macromedia Director 233, 234
Macy Conferences 190
Maldonado-Torres, Nelson 91, 147, 156
Manzoni, Piero 117–118
Marks, Laura U. 216
Mars Attacks! (1996) 122
Martins, Edgar 198
Marx, Karl 6, 41, 54, 106–107, 111, 128, 132, 137, 153
mass unconscious 8, 169–172, 180, 184, 188–189, 234–235, 239–242
Massumi, Brian 225

Mast, Gerald 67
Mauss, Marcel 47, 51
Mbembe, Achille 136, 147
McGrew, Tony 30
McLuhan, Marshall 173, 175–176
Mediation 5–6
Menckman, Rosa 125
Merton, Thomas 172
Midsummer Night's Dream, A 67, 79
Mignolo, Walter 142
migrants 108–109, 148, 154, 178, 243
military technology 161–163
Minsky, Hyman 31–32
Mirowski, Joseph 30–31
Mirowski, Philip 205
modelling 204–207
Mohanty, Chandra Talpade 151–152
Mont Pèlerin Society 22–30, 41, 187
Montaigne, Michel de 87–88, 91
Moore III, Berrien 202
Morrison, Bill 196–199, 208, 225
Morsink, Johannes 22
Morton, Timothy 95
Mouffe, Chantal 4–5, 235
Mr Blandings Builds His Dream Home (1947) 33–34, 37
Murphy, Michelle 44
music 36

Namuth, Hans 143, 195
Nancy, Jean-Luc 5, 176–177
Nawarla Gabarnmang 194–195, 198, 200
neo-fascism, fascism, neo-populism 78–80, 95, 105, 107, 187, 221–222, 234
nitrate film stock 197

Index

Nkrumah, Kwame 140
noise 35, 45, 49–50, 125, 127, 162–163, 164, 185–186
non-conscious 56-57, 58
non-identity 88–95
nostos 221
Nussbaum, Martha 146
nutmeg 212–213

Ogilvy & Mather 107
oikodicy 111–113
Osborne, Peter D. 198
overconsumption 110
Ovid 238
Oxfam 12

Papastergiadis, Nikos 146–148, 241, 242
Parisi, Luciana 128
Parton, Dolly 66
Pascal, Blaise 191
pathetic fallacy 49, 58
pepper 210–211, 213
phallic symbol 85–86
Picatrix (Ghayat al- Hakim) 216
Plato 6
Plehwe, Dieter 22
Pollock, Griselda 149–150
Pollock, Jackson 143–144, 149–150, 153, 165–166, 174–175, 178–179, 188–189, 195–196, 198–199
Povinelli, Elizabeth 66
pre-conscious 56

QR code 173
Quijano, Alberto 148

Rabinbach, Anson 242
Rancière, Jacques 4–5, 235
Rebel Without a Cause (1955) 43
repression 127
Rewind archive of video art 228–229
Riley, Terry 53–54
Robak, Tabor 120–123, 128
Robbins, Bruce 146–147
Roberts, John 116
Rorty, Richard 133
Rosenberg, Michael 188
Ruskin, John 58
Russell, Catherine 226

salt 215–216
Samuelson, Paul A. 19
Sartre, Jean-Paul 59, 60, 158, 201
Saturn, Saturnalia 238–239
Schaeffer, Pierre 50, 52, 57
Schafer, R. Murray 50, 51
Schönberg, Arnold 36, 49
Sconce, Jeffrey 48, 105
Second Viennese School (music) 36, 49
Shannon, Claude E. 18–20, 51, 162, 164, 178, 193
Silk Road 211
Simpson, Paul 167
Smythe, Dallas 63
Sobchack, Vivian 60
'Societies of Control' (Deleuze) 37
Sohn-Rethel, Alfred 17–18
Sontag, Susan 159
Speer, Albert 120
spices 208–217
Spiegl, Laurie 54
Stiegler, Bernard 232

Story of the Kelly Gang (1906) 230
survivance 44, 60–61, 119

Tadiar, Neferti X. M. 153–154
Taft-Hartley Act 20
Tan, Erica 125
Tesco 210
Time-to-live (TTL) 224
Tolstoy, Leo 13
Toscano, Alberto and Jeff Kinkle 14–15
Truax, Barry 50
Truth 9
TTL *see* Time-to-live (TTL)

Ulysses (James Joyce) 88
unconscious 34–35, 56, 167–168, 174
United Nations 186–187
United Nations Refugee Convention (1951) 133
Universal Declaration of Human Rights 12, 20–23, 132–141
Usai, Paolo Cherchi 227–229, 234

Valéry, Paul 13
van er Leeuw, Sander 205
Vizenor, Gérard 44

Vogl, Joseph 4, 106, 111–112
Vogt, William 201
von Neuman, John and Oscar Morgenstern 28–29
Voyager (satellites) 55–58

Walcott, Derek 183
Wallerstein, Immanuel 148, 159
Walsh, Catherine 142
Warhol, Andy 118
Waste Land, The (1922) 48–54
Weart, Spencer 205
Weintraub, E. Roy 28
Wendling, Amy 240–241, 242
West, Cornell 243
Westphalia 139–140
Whitehead, Alfred North 21, 167
Wiener, Norbert 37, 39
Window Water Baby Moving (Stan Brakhage) 91
Wolfe, Patrick 44
World Social Forum 219
World Trade Organization (WTO) 29–30

Zeiher, Cindy 99–100
Zola, Emile 13

MIT Press
Janet Rossi
255 Main Street, 9th floor
MA, 02142
US
MIT.edu
janett@mit.edu
617-253-2882

The authorized representative in the EU for product safety and compliance is

Easy Access System Europe Oü, 16879218
Mustamäe tee 50,
ECZ, 10621
EE
gpsr.requests@easproject.com
+372 56 968 939

ISBN: 9781915983305
Release ID: 152017994